D0850256

Revised Edition

TWO TESTAMENTS, ONE BIBLE

A Study of the Theological Relationship Between the Old & New Testaments

DAVID L. BAKER

INTERVARSITY PRESS
DOWNERS GROVE, ILLINOIS 60515

ISBN 0-8308-1765-4

Printed in the United States of America ∞

Library of Congress Cataloging-in-Publication Data
Baker, D. L.
   Two Testaments, one Bible: a study of the theological
  relationship between the Old and New Testaments/David L. Baker.
     p.   cm.
  Includes bibliographical references and indexes.
  ISBN 0-8308-1765-4
  1. Bible. N.T.—Relation to the Old Testament.   I. Title.
  BS2387.B33   1992
220.6—dc20   *91-31817*
                                                                CIP

15	14	13	12	11	10	9	8	7	6	5	4	3	2	1
04	03	02	01	00	99	98	97	96	95	94	93	92		

Contents

PART 2: FOUR MODERN SOLUTIONS

3. The New Testament as the essential Bible

PART 3: THREE KEY THEMES

Preface

This study was originally a PhD thesis, entitled 'The Theological Problem of the Relationship Between the Old Testament and the New Testament: A Study of Some Modern Solutions', which was accepted by the University of Sheffield in 1975. With only a few corrections and minor alterations it was published in 1976 by means of photo-reproduction directly from the typescript of the thesis. Chapter seven was also published in a slightly different form under the title 'Typology and the Christian Use of the Old Testament' in *SJT* 29.2 (1976). It is included here by kind permission of Professor T. F. Torrance, co-editor of the journal.

The second edition is different in many ways from the first edition. The material has been restructured and revised throughout. Some sections have been abridged or omitted, while others have been expanded and several completely new sections included. The purpose is to provide an introduction to the problem of the theological relationship between the Testaments, rather than an exhaustive survey. The number of scholars discussed has therefore been reduced compared with the first edition, so that the writings of just a few of the most important representatives of each major approach are analysed, criticized and compared. The detailed study of 'typology' in the first edition is now followed by studies of two other themes: 'promise and fulfilment' and 'continuity and discontinuity'. The conclusion is more substantial than in the first edition and includes a brief consideration of the implications of the study for Christian theology and the life of the church. Hopefully students and teachers, preachers and pastors, will find the book in its revised form useful as a statement and explanation of the theological relationship between the two Testaments of the Christian Bible.

Biblical quotations are taken from the RSV unless otherwise stated. Old Testament references are to the English Bible and differences in numbering in the Hebrew are not noted (those who use the Hebrew Bible will be aware of the differences).

The bibliographies are deliberately much smaller than in the first edition (in which they occupied 40% of the bulk of the work), though they have been brought up to date with some of the more important works published since 1975. Their aim is to be practical rather than comprehensive. Only works actually discussed or cited in the book and a few standard textbooks and surveys for further reading are included.

Citations in the text are in the briefest form possible, by means of the surname of the author and year of publication of the work in question (*e.g.* 'von Rad 1957'). If necessary, page numbers are added after a colon. Full details of a work may be found either in the bibliography at the end of the chapter in which it is cited or in the general bibliography at the end of the book. Quotes are generally from the most recent edition of a work, though the date used to identify the work is usually that of first publication to give a clearer sense of the historical development within scholarship.

The research for this book was carried out in the Department of Biblical Studies in the University of Sheffield (1971–73) and at Tyndale House, Cambridge (1973–75, 1989–90). I am grateful for the guidance of Professor David J. A. Clines, under whose supervision my thesis was written, and many other teachers, colleagues and friends in these two institutions who have supported and encouraged me along the way. Many libraries have made their facilities available to me, both directly and through the inter-library loan system. Financial support was provided at different stages by the Department of Education and Science, the Tyndale Fellowship for Biblical Research and the Overseas Missionary Fellowship, and without this I could never have undertaken the project. There are so many who have contributed directly or indirectly to the completion of this work that it would be impossible to thank them all specifically; however I must mention five who have given particular help and encouragement during the past year and a half as I have prepared the revised edition of the book: Bruce Winter, John Nolland, Malcolm Wylie, Stephen Ibbotson and – most of all – my wife Elizabeth. The final word of thanks goes to Inter-

Varsity Press for their willingness to publish both the first edition of this book, and now the second edition under the Apollos imprint.

I dedicate the book to my parents, who have supported and encouraged me unfailingly for over forty years.

David L. Baker

Abbreviations

Abbreviations are generally avoided in the text of the book, apart from those commonly used in English (such as *e.g.*). In parentheses and footnotes the names of *biblical books* are abbreviated as follows:

Gn., Ex., Lv., Nu., Dt., Jos., Jdg., Ru., 1, 2 Sa., 1, 2 Ki., 1, 2 Ch., Ezr., Ne., Est., Jb., Ps. (Pss.), Pr., Ec., Song, Is., Je., La., Ezk., Dn., Ho., Joel, Am., Ob., Jon., Mi., Na., Hab., Zp., Hg., Zc., Mal.

Mt., Mk., Lk., Jn., Acts, Rom., 1, 2 Cor., Gal., Eph., Phil., Col., 1, 2 Thes., 1, 2 Tim., Tit., Phm., Heb., Jas., 1, 2 Pet., 1, 2, 3 Jn., Jude, Rev.

Scholarly works are referred to by their author and date of publication and full details may be found in either the bibliography for the chapter in question or the general bibliography at the end of the book.

In the references and bibliographies the following abbreviations are also used:

ed. = edited by
ET = English translation
Fs = Festschrift
n. = footnote
n.d. = no date of publication given.

Part 1

The problem

1

Biblical foundations

1.1 Introduction

Christianity has the New Testament as the record and testimony of the life, death and resurrection of its founder, Jesus Christ, and of the formation of the Christian church. One of the most fundamental questions which has faced theology and the church in every age and still demands an answer today is whether or not Christianity also needs an *Old* Testament. Is the Old Testament to be thrown away as obsolete, or preserved as a relic from days of yore, or treasured as a classic and read by scholars, or used occasionally as a change from the New Testament, or kept in a box in case it should be needed some day? Or is the Old Testament an essential part of the Christian Bible, with continuing validity and authority alongside the New Testament?

The importance of this problem was forcibly expressed by Bernhard W. Anderson (1964: 1) in his introduction to a symposium on the significance of the Old Testament for the Christian faith:

> No problem more urgently needs to be brought to a focus than the one to which the following essays are addressed: the relation of the Old Testament to the New ... it is a question which confronts every Christian in the Church, whether he be a professional theologian, a pastor of a congregation, or a layman.

It is no exaggeration to say that on this question hangs the meaning of the Christian faith.

Twelve years later Juan Luis Segundo (1976: 487–488) reckoned that the problem still awaited a clear solution:

> What is the exact relationship between, for example, the revelation of Jesus in the New Testament and the revelation of God in the Old Testament? Though it may seem hard to believe, the fact is that this basic and important question has scarcely been given a clear answer over the past twenty centuries of Christian living. And that fact has conditioned the whole of theology.

The complexity of the problem is shown by the vast quantity of modern literature dealing with particular aspects of the relationship between the Testaments and the fact that there is still no comprehensive study and only a few detailed studies of the whole problem.[1]

There are several levels at which the problem of the relationship between the Old Testament and the New Testament[2] may be approached. One of the most obvious is the historical: it is indisputable that there is an historical relationship between the two Testaments, that the New Testament is historically later and to some extent derivative from the Old Testament.[3] It would be possible also to define linguistic, literary, sociological, psychological, ethical, philosophical and many other levels to the problem. The fact is that a comprehensive study of the problem of the relationship between the Testaments at all these levels has never been undertaken since it would be such a vast task. The present study concentrates on the theological level of the problem because, as has been increasingly recognized in modern biblical scholarship, the Old and New Testaments are first and

---

[1] *E.g.* Amsler (1960); Barr (1966); Bright (1967); Shih (1971); Gunneweg (1977). There are also two important symposia: *EOTI* and *OTCF*.

[2] Originally 'New Covenant' (*kainē diathēkē*) and 'Old Covenant' (*palaia diathēkē*). The terms are first found in Je. 31:31 and 2 Cor. 3:14 but were not used as designations for the two parts of a canon of Scripture until about AD 200, by Clement of Alexandria (Gunneweg 1977: 36). The word 'testament' comes from *testamentum*, the Latin translation of *diathēkē*.

[3] See, for example, Noth (1950) and Bruce (1969). *Cf.* below: ch. 9.1.a.

foremost theological works, and their linguistic, historical and ethical aspects are subordinate to this central concern. Moreover, since even the theological problem of the relationship between the Testaments is too complex to be dealt with in its entirety in a work of the present scope, this book will not enter into the detailed exegetical, historical or theological study of minor points but will concentrate on the major aspects of the problem, the major solutions proposed and the major issues involved. Sometimes this means that a question of considerable importance is dealt with only briefly, but references to more detailed discussions are provided in the footnotes and bibliographies.

The first part of the book delineates the problem of the theological relationship between the Testaments by means of a biblical and historical introduction. The second part is devoted to a study of four important modern solutions to the problem. In each case the work of the most important proponent of the solution is first analysed in detail and subjected to critique; then other works which fall in the same category are discussed more briefly in the final section of the chapter ('Comparison'). In the third part of the book three key themes that emerge from the consideration of the problem are investigated in greater detail. Finally, the results of the study are summarized in a conclusion which also considers some of their implications for theology and the church today.

1.2 Old Testament view of the New Testament

It might be thought that the earliest, and therefore definitive, approach to the problem of the relationship between the Testaments would be that of the New Testament. Yet important though this is, it is necessary to go further back into history: the Old Testament itself has not a little to say about its relationship to future faith. Indeed Bultmann, von Rad and others have taken the Old Testament's 'openness to the future' to be the controlling factor in its view of God, mankind and history.[4] This forward-looking aspect should not be over-emphasized: the Old

---

[4]See Bultmann (1949b: 183; *cf.* 15–56); von Rad (1960: 319–322, 332, 361–363, *etc.*); Zimmerli (1975: 238–240); *cf.* Brueggemann (1987).

Testament is also very concerned with past and present realities (*cf.* Vriezen 1966: 431–432). Nevertheless, a significant aspect of Old Testament faith and religion is its expectation of the future, as has been widely recognized in modern scholarship.

a. Development of future expectation

There can be little doubt that Israel had some kind of hope for the future from early times. This is apparent from such passages as Genesis 12:1–3; 49; Exodus 3:8; Numbers 24; Deuteronomy 33; 2 Samuel 7; 23:3–5; Amos 5:18 and Psalms 2; 45; 68; 110. Zimmerli (1968) has traced this hope of Old Testament man in great detail and points to seven examples of his future expectation in the primeval history alone (Gn. 1:26; 2:17; 3:14–20; 4:11–15; 6:5–8; 8:21–22; 11:4). Early Israel generally had an optimistic view of the future, expecting material and spiritual, political and family, blessing. This early salvation hope was mainly concerned with the continuation of the present order and – unlike that of the prophets – did not envisage a radical renewal, so the term 'eschatology' is an inappropriate description. All the same, there are elements in common with later eschatological ideas and the distinction should not be drawn too sharply.[5]

Eschatology may be defined broadly as 'ideas which envisage a radical change to be brought about by God in the future'. It is based on the conviction 'that history moves in a direction, that this direction is set by God, and that God acts within history to ensure this direction' (Davies 1980: 38). The narrower understanding of eschatology as a developed 'doctrine of the last things' is scarcely present in the Old Testament.[6]

Various attempts have been made to explain the origin and basis of Israel's eschatology. Smend (1893: 171–173, 218–222, 238–244) and Volz (1897) suggested its source to be nationalism. Gunkel (1895) and Gressmann (1905) pointed to mythical elements and argued for an origin in ancient Eastern mythological thought. Mowinckel (1922) found the basis of the Old Testament expectation in the enthronement festival and the disappointment which ensued when the kings of Israel proved to be far different from the ideal of kingship. There may well be

---

[5]*Cf.* Eichrodt (1933: 472–480); Jacob (1955a: 319–325); Preuss (1968).

[6]*Cf.* Vriezen (1953b: 200–203); Jenni (1962); Bright (1963); Clements (1965a: 103–106).

some truth in these observations, nevertheless such explanations are inadequate to account for Israel's distinctive expectation of the future (*e.g.* Eichrodt 1933: 494–499). More recent study has shown that Old Testament eschatology has both an historical and a theological basis. The presupposition of the Old Testament is its belief that God is active in the history of Israel. So the Old Testament's hopes for the future are based on the certainty that God is real though life may be hard (Vriezen 1953b: 228–229); on the tension between the immanence and hiddenness of God which leads to the hope that God's presence will be perfected in a future coming (Jacob 1955a: 317); on the perception of the radical sin and unbelief of the people which can only be overcome by God's grace (Bultmann 1933a: 27); and on the prophetic conviction that God will act in the future as he has acted in the past, though in an entirely new way (von Rad 1960: 116).

b. Prophetic eschatology

The classical period for the development of Israel's eschatology was that of the prophets.[7] Judgment and salvation are portrayed with unparalleled clarity in their message, as may be seen by looking at almost any page of their writings. The pre-exilic prophets attack the popular optimism of Israel and proclaim the radical judgment of God; the exilic prophets introduce optimism as they point to a new beginning, a new creation and a new salvation. At least four major features of the prophetic expectation of the future may be isolated: a time, a people, a place and a person.

Day of the Lord

From the beginning of the prophetic period there was a belief in a *time* ('day') when the Lord would intervene in the history of Israel (Am. 5:18–20). The expression 'day of the LORD' occurs only infrequently (see also Is. 13:6, 9; Ezk. 13:5; Joel 1:15; 2:1, 11, 31; 3:14; Ob. 15; Zp. 1:7, 14; Zc. 14:1) but related forms are common in the prophetic writings: for example, 'day of vengeance' (Is. 34:8; 61:2; Je. 46:10) and 'on that day' (Ezk. 29:21; Am. 3:14; *cf.* Is. 2:11–12; Je. 3:16–18).[8]

---

[7]See Vriezen (1953b); Clements (1965a: ch. 6); Zimmerli (1968: 86–137); Bright (1976); Hubbard (1983); Gowan (1986).

[8]On the 'day of the Lord', see Černý (1948); von Rad (1959); Gray (1974) and van Leeuwen (1974).

Spiritual renewal

The prophets look forward to a renewal of the *people* of God. After judgment there will be restoration (Je. 29:14; 30:3; Ezk. 16:53; Zp. 3:30). The nation will be exiled but a remnant will return (Is. 7:3; 10:20–22; Je. 23:3; Mi. 2:12; Zc. 8). They will take part in a new Exodus (Is. 4:5; 10:24–27; 35; 51:9–11; 52:12; Ho. 11:10–11; Zc. 10:8–11), a new covenant will be made (Je. 30 – 33; *cf.* Is. 55:3; Ezk. 16:60) and God will give them a new spirit (Ezk. 11:19; 36:26; 37:1–14; Joel 2:28; *cf.* Is. 11:2; Ezk. 18:31; Ho. 6:1–3).[9]

Materialistic hope

There was also a materialistic aspect to the eschatology of the prophets, particularly concerning the question of a *place*. This is often expressed by Utopian ideas of world renewal and has two main strands: the return of paradise is a theme which recurs in the prophetic writings (Is. 11:6–9; 25:8; 51:3; Mi. 4:3); and alongside this is the expectation of a renewed holy land (Is. 62:4; *cf.* 65:17; Je. 30:3; 32:6–15; Ezk. 20:40–42) and holy city (Is. 60 – 66; Ezk. 40 – 48; Mi. 4:1–2; Zc. 2).[10]

Messiah

Finally, when Israel's thoughts turned to the future they sometimes focused on a *person* whom God would send. That is hardly surprising in view of their belief in God's provision of individuals to meet the nation's political or spiritual need, in the form of prophets, judges, priests and kings. The concept of a Messiah, though hardly ever linked in the Old Testament with the Hebrew word from which it comes (*māšîaḥ*), may be perceived in various periods, especially in connection with the figures of the Son of David (2 Sa. 7; Is. 9; 11; *cf.* Pss. 89; 132) and the servant of the Lord (Is. 42; 49; 50; 53). Without doubt, the expectation of the Messiah is one of the most important ways in which the Old Testament looks forward to the New.[11]

---

[9]On the renewal of the people of God, see Hebert (1941: 58–65); Zimmerli (1960a); B. W. Anderson (1962; 1964); Ackroyd (1968); Buis (1968) and Hasel (1972).

[10]On materialistic hope, see Hebert (1941: 44–52); Gross (1956) and Porteous (1961).

[11]The classical studies of the Messiah are Klausner (1902–1950); Gressman (1929) and Mowinckel (1951). Among more recent works see Ellison (1953); Ringgren (1956); Coppens (1968; 1974); Rehm (1968); Becker (1977); Clements (1989) and Struppe (1989).

c. Apocalyptic eschatology

Towards the end of the Old Testament period apocalyptic began to take the place of prophecy. The beginning of this change may be seen in texts such as Isaiah 24 – 27 and 56 – 66, Daniel, Joel and Zechariah 9 – 14; and many apocalypses were written in the inter-testamental period. Von Rad (1960: 301–308; 1970: 263–282) argued that the origins of apocalyptic thought are to be found in the wisdom tradition, but the majority of scholars agree that apocalyptic is to be understood primarily as a development from prophecy, though not denying that there are also links with wisdom (see Bauckham 1978; P. D. Hanson 1983).

The initial impetus for this development may be seen in the disappointment experienced by those who returned from exile to the promised land with high hopes, but found themselves still under foreign rule and with little prospect of ever being an independent nation again. The Persian province of Judah was a mere shadow of the former kingdoms of Israel and could only with extraordinary stretching of the imagination be understood as the fulfilment of God's promises of glorious restoration. How could prophetic eschatology be reconciled with the harsh realities of life after the exile? The problem was resolved by visionaries who were able to look beyond national history to a new age of salvation which would be inaugurated by God. Thus there was a development towards transcendentalism (understanding the ultimate fulfilment of God's purpose to be beyond the history of this world) and dualism (contrasting the present age with the age to come).

Two of the most distinctive features of this apocalyptic eschatology are the figure of the 'son of man' (Dn. 7) and the picture of the resurrection of the dead (Is. 26:19; Dn. 12), both of which become very important in later Jewish and Christian thought.[12]

d. Expectations and tensions

One of the results of modern biblical study has therefore been to highlight the significance of the Old Testament's future expectation. The importance of this result should be appreciated, and

---

[12]On apocalyptic, see the symposia edited by Funk (1969); Mays (1971) and P. D. Hanson (1983). There are also many monographs on the subject, *e.g.* Russell (1964); Koch (1970); Morris (1973); P. D. Hanson (1975) and Rowland (1982). On the 'Son of man', see Borsch (1967); Ferch

though it is unnecessary to go to the extreme of interpreting the Old Testament solely with reference to the future, it is clear that the Old Testament in itself is incomplete and looks forward to completion by an act of God outside its limits. This act is to be performed by the same God in the context of the same history as acts described in the Old Testament, though in the apocalyptic literature there are hints that this divinely-directed history should be understood as something much more comprehensive than purely the national history of Israel or even the history of this world. It is expected that the new act will in many respects be analogous to earlier ones, yet at the same time be radically different and more comprehensive. Thus the Old Testament looks forward to the future; and according to Christian understanding looks forward to the New Testament.

However, the Old Testament closes not only with certain expectations of the future but also with inner tensions which remain unresolved. There is a tension between Jewish exclusivism and universal missionary concern, deriving ultimately from the belief in both the election of Israel and the world supremacy of the one God (Bright 1960: 442–446). There are also tensions in the roles of Israel's leaders: between prophet, priest and wise man (cf. Whitley 1963: ch. 4; McKane 1965; Clements 1965a: ch. 5; 1975: ch. 6), and between charismatic leader and dynastic monarch (cf. Eichrodt 1933: 441–442; von Rad 1957: 93–102). Above all, there is a tension in the Old Testament between divine sovereignty and human responsibility (cf. Seeligmann 1963): probably all the Old Testament authors are convinced of God's ultimate sovereignty over creation and history, but in practice it often seems that the divine purpose and will remain unfulfilled because of human sin and rebellion.

1.3 New Testament view of the Old Testament

Just as the Old Testament looks forward to the New, so the New Testament looks back to the Old. The writers of the New Testament were convinced that the Christ (Messiah) had been born, the long awaited Son of man had come. He had announced that

---

(1979) and Caragounis (1986); also most New Testament theologies. Translations and commentaries on many extra-biblical apocalypses may be found in Charlesworth (1983).

the day of the Lord had dawned, and the world and the people of God were about to be renewed.

a. Jesus and the Old Testament

According to R. T. France (1971), Jesus' use of the Old Testament had two main features: types and predictions. In persons, institutions and experiences of Old Testament Israel, Jesus saw 'types' of his own person and work which demonstrated the continuity between God's acts in past and present history. And in the messianic passages of the Old Testament, as well as more general eschatological hopes and passages about the work of God, Jesus found 'predictions' which he fulfilled in his life and future glory.

However Jesus' interest in the Old Testament was by no means limited to those passages which were specifically reflected or fulfilled in his life and work. As Jeremias (1971: 205) points out, 'Jesus lived in the Old Testament'. From the Old Testament he learnt about God and man, worship and ethics; and he frequently used Old Testament language in formulating his own teaching. Sometimes he followed contemporary methods of interpretation, but often Jesus' Old Testament interpretation was quite revolutionary (France 1971: 172–226). On the one hand he asserted firmly the absolute authority of the Old Testament (Mt. 5:17–20; 22:34–40), on the other he ventured to sharpen or suspend some of its provisions (Mt. 5:21–48; Mk. 7:14–23).[13]

b. The substructure of Christian theology

The early church developed a method of biblical study in which certain major passages of the Old Testament (especially from Isaiah, Psalms and the Minor Prophets) were interpreted as testimonies to Christ, according to C. H. Dodd (1952a). The principles of this interpretation are intelligible and consistent, and all the main New Testament writers agree on the selection of passages. Sentences from these passages are quoted not as independent testimonies but in order to point to the longer passage in which they have their context. These Old Testament passages and their New Testament interpretations contain the fundamental ideas about Christ which form the substructure of

---

[13]*Cf.* Jeremias (1971: 204–211); Goppelt (1975: 87–105). On Jesus' view of the Old Testament, see also J. W. Wenham (1972).

Christian theology. This distinctive way of using the Old Testament, Dodd argues, originates from Jesus himself (pp. 109–110; *cf.* above: ch. 1.3.a.).

The doctrinal significance of New Testament quotations of the Old has also been the focus of a detailed study by Barnabas Lindars (1961). His work is governed by two main presuppositions: the results of Dodd's research, referred to above; and the results of Qumran research, which have brought to light their distinctive *midrash pesher* method of biblical interpretation. In this method, significant events, more or less contemporary with the interpreter, were declared to be the realities to which Old Testament prophecies had looked forward. Stendahl (1954) and Ellis (1957) had previously shown the influence of this method on the biblical interpretation of Matthew and Paul respectively, and Lindars finds its influence throughout the New Testament (*cf.* Fitzmyer 1961; Longenecker 1970). In particular he uses form criticism to concentrate on two factors in the New Testament quotation of Old Testament passages: shift of application and modification of text. In this way he traces the apologetic of the early church from its core in the proclamation of Jesus' resurrection, through the presentation of his passion, earthly life and birth, to the conviction of his pre-existence.

c. New Testament interpretation of the Old

Almost all the New Testament writers quote frequently from the Old Testament, and such quotations inevitably involve interpretation of the significance of Old Testament texts. Samuel Amsler (1960a) has investigated Old Testament interpretation in Hebrews, 1 Peter, John, Paul, Acts and the Synoptic Gospels, deliberately starting with those in which the interpretation is most sophisticated and progressing to those where it is most simple. He concludes that the New Testament's interpretation is based on the *dei* ('it is necessary') of the passion and resurrection announcements in the Synoptic Gospels, which is summed up in Jesus' words recorded in the third Gospel: 'it is necessary that all that is written about me in the law of Moses, in the prophets and in the Psalms should be fulfilled' (Lk. 24:44). Amsler argues that, in spite of different emphases, there are several characteristics in their Old Testament interpretation which are common to all the New Testament authors:

● the New Testament authors have the same basic orientation to the Old Testament, recognizing that the significance of the gospel events is seen clearly

28

only in the light of the Old Testament;
● the New Testament authors recognize in the Old Testament a witness which corroborates their own;
● the New Testament authors claim the Old Testament to be an advance witness, a promise which shows the theological significance of events within the history of salvation prior to their occurrence; and
● the New Testament authors interpret the Old Testament as a witness to God's revelation and salvation in history.

This historical perspective is in contrast to the legal perspective characteristic of contemporary Judaism, and it is because of this perspective that the New Testament authors agree in their preference for citing certain parts of the Old Testament.

There has been a wealth of study of New Testament interpretation of the Old Testament in recent years and it is impossible to go into detail here.[14] For our present purpose it is sufficient to establish one main point, that the historical and theological basis for the writing of the New Testament was the Old Testament.

d. Fulfilment and resolution

Modern biblical study has clearly shown the extent and manner of the New Testament's dependence on the Old Testament. The New Testament proclaims the occurrence of a new and unprecedented act of God in the person of Jesus of Nazareth, yet a central aspect of this proclamation is that Jesus is the fulfilment of the hopes and expectations of the Old Testament. Moreover, in preaching, teaching, apologetics and ethics the Old Testament 'Scriptures' were the source and standard for the New Testament church.

---

[14]It is impossible here to summarize the results of much detailed research into the way different New Testament writers view the Old Testament. There are many works available for readers who wish to study this subject, *e.g.* Shires (1974); Longenecker (1975); A. T. Hanson (1980; 1983); Archer & Chirichigno (1983); Kaiser (1985); Ellis (1988); Juel (1988); Lindars Fs (1988). More detailed studies of the use of the Old Testament by particular New Testament authors include Stendahl (1954) and Gundry (1967) on Matthew; Suhl (1965) on Mark; Bock (1987) on Luke; Freed (1965) on John; Ellis (1957), A. T. Hanson (1974), N. T. Wright (1980) and Hays (1989) on Paul; and Schröger (1968) on Hebrews. For further bibliography, see Baker (1976: 34–40) and Lindars Fs (1988).

The material discussed in the preceding sections has been largely concerned with the explicit biblical relationship between the Testaments: in other words, the Old Testament's future expectation, the New Testament's dependence on the past and the relationship between the two. It would also be possible to analyse material concerned with the implicit relationship between the Testaments. Some of the tensions implicit in the Old Testament were mentioned above (ch. 1.2.d): it may be asked how far and in what way such tensions have been resolved in the coming of Jesus Christ. Have new tensions been created and what new understanding of the meaning of the Old Testament has now become possible? One of the key issues in the early church was the tension between Jew and Gentile, Israel and church; another was the interpretation of the Old Testament which was understood by Christians to affirm the messiahship of Jesus and by Jews to be reason for demanding that he be executed for blasphemy.

At this point we turn from the biblical material to consider how the theological problem of the relationship between the Testaments has been understood in the history of Christian interpretation of the Bible.

Bibliography (1)

Old Testament view of the New Testament (1.2)

Ackroyd, P. R. 1968: *Exile and Restoration: A Study of Hebrew Thought of the Sixth Century BC*, London.
Bauckham, R. J. 1978: 'The rise of apocalyptic', *Themelios* 3.2:10–23.
Becker, J. 1977: *Messianic Expectations in the Old Testament*, ET: Philadelphia, 1980 (German, 1977).
Borsch, F. H. 1967: *The Son of Man in Myth and History*, London.
Bright, J. 1963: 'Eschatology', *Dictionary of the Bible* (originally ed. J. Hastings, revised by F. C. Grant & H. H. Rowley), Edinburgh, [2]1963: 265–267.
—1976: *Covenant and Promise: The Prophetic Understanding of the Future in Pre-Exilic Israel*, Philadelphia.
Brueggemann, W. 1987: *Hope within History*, Atlanta.
Buis, P. 1968: 'La nouvelle alliance', *VT* 18:1–15.
Caragounis, C. C. 1986: *The Son of Man: Vision and Interpretation*, Tübingen (Wissenschaftliche Untersuchungen zum Neuen Testament 38).
Černý, L. 1948: *The Day of Yahweh and some relevant problems*, Prague.
Charlesworth, J. H. (ed.) 1983: *The Old Testament Pseudepigrapha, Volume 1: Apocalyptic Literature and Testaments*, Garden City, New York.
Clements, R. E. 1965a: *Prophecy and Covenant*, London.
—1989: 'The Messianic Hope in the Old Testament', *JSOT* 43:3–19.
Coppens, J. 1968: *Le Messianisme Royal*, Paris.

—1974: *Le Messianisme et sa Relève prophétique*, Gembloux (Bibliotheca Ephemeridum Theologicarum Lovaniensum 38).

Davies, P. R. 1980: 'Eschatology in the Book of Daniel', *JSOT* 17:33–53.

Ellison, H. L. 1953a: *The Centrality of the Messianic Idea for the Old Testament*, London (Tyndale Old Testament Lecture).

Ferch, A. J. 1979: *The Son of Man in Daniel Seven*, Berrien Springs, Michigan.

Funk, R. W. (ed.) 1969: 'Apocalypticism', *JTC* 6 (entire issue).

Gowan, D. E. 1986: *Eschatology in the Old Testament*, Philadelphia.

Gray, J. 1974: 'The Day of Yahweh in Cultic Experience and Eschatological Prospect', *Svensk Exegetisk Årsbok* 39:5–37.

Gressmann, H. 1905: *Der Ursprung der israelitisch-jüdischen Eschatologie*, Göttingen.

—1929: *Der Messias*, Göttingen (rewritten form of 1905).

Gross, H. 1956: *Die Idee des ewigen und allgemeinen Weltfriedens im alten Orient und im Alten Testament*, Trier (Trierer theologische Studien 7).

Gunkel, H. 1895: *Schöpfung und Chaos in Urzeit und Endzeit: Eine religionsgeschichtliche Untersuchung über Gen 1 und Ap Joh 12*, Göttingen.

Hanson, P. D. 1975: *The Dawn of Apocalyptic*, Philadelphia.

Hanson, P. D. (ed.) 1983: *Visionaries and their Apocalypses*, Philadelphia/ London (Issues in Religion and Theology 2; includes essays published 1971–83).

Hasel, G. F. 1972b: *The Remnant: The History and Theology of the Remnant Idea from Genesis to Isaiah*, Berrien Springs, Michigan.

Hubbard, D. A. 1983: 'Hope in the Old Testament', *TB* 34:33–59.

Jenni, E. 1962: 'Eschatology of the Old Testament', *IDB* 1:126–133 and 'Jewish Messiah', *IDB* 3:360–365.

Klausner, J. 1902–50: *The Messianic Idea in Israel: from Its Beginning to the Completion of the Mishnah*, ET: London, 1956 (German and Hebrew, 1902–21; Hebrew, [2]1927, [3]1950).

Leeuwen, C. van 1974: 'The Prophecy of the Yom YHWH in Amos v 18–20' in *Language and Meaning: Studies in Hebrew Language and Biblical Exegesis*, Leiden (OTS 19): 113–134.

Mays, J. L. (ed.) 1971: Various articles on apocalyptic, *Int* 25:419–501.

McKane, W. 1965: *Prophets and Wise Men*, London (SBT 44).

Morris, L. 1973: *Apocalyptic*, London.

Mowinckel, S. 1922: *Psalmenstudien II. Das Thronbesteigungsfest Jahwäs und der Ursprung der Eschatologie*, Christiana.

—1951: *He That Cometh*, ET: Oxford, 1956 (Norwegian, 1951).

Porteous, N. W. 1961: 'Jerusalem – Zion: the Growth of a Symbol', reprinted in *Living the Mystery*, Oxford, 1967: 93–111.

Preuss, H. D. 1968: *Jahweglaube und Zukunftserwartung*, Stuttgart (Beiträge zur Wissenschaft vom Alten und Neuen Testament 87).

Rad, G. von 1959: 'The Origin of the Concept of the Day of Yahweh', *Journal of Semitic Studies* 4:97–108. Much of this is also incorporated into von Rad (1960): 119–125.

—1970: *Wisdom in Israel*, ET: London, 1972 (German, 1970).

Rehm, M. 1968: *Der königliche Messias: im Licht der Immanuel-Weissagungen des Buches Jesaja*, Kevelaer, Rheinland.

Ringgren, H. 1956: *The Messiah in the Old Testament*, London (SBT 18).
Rowland, C. 1982: *The Open Heaven: A Study of Apocalyptic in Judaism and Early Christianity*, London.
Russell, D. S. 1964: *The Method and Message of Jewish Apocalyptic: 200 BC – AD 100*, London.
Seeligmann, I. L. 1963: 'Menschliches Heldentum und göttliche Hilfe: Die doppelte Kausalität im alttestamentlichen Geschichtsdenken', *ThZ* 19:385–411.
Smend, R. 1893: *Lehrbuch der alttestamentlichen Religionsgeschichte*, Freiburg/Leipzig ([2]1899).
Struppe, U. (ed.) 1989: *Studien zum Messiasbild im Alten Testament*, Stuttgart (Stuttgarter Biblische Aufsatzbände 6). Collection of essays originally published 1961–86, with introduction by U. Struppe.
Volz, P. 1897: *Die vorexilische Jahweprophetie und der Messias: in ihrem Verhältnis dargestellt*, Göttingen.
Vriezen, Th. C. 1953b: 'Prophecy and Eschatology' in *Congress Volume: Copenhagen 1953* (Supplements to *VT* 1): 199–229.
Whitley, C. F. 1963: *The Prophetic Achievement*, London.
Zimmerli, W. 1960a: 'Le nouvel "exode" dans le message des deux grands prophètes de l'exil' in Vischer Fs: 216–227.
—1968: *Man and His Hope in the Old Testament*, ET: London (German, 1968).

New Testament view of the Old Testament (1.3)

Archer, G. L. & Chirichigno, G. 1983: *Old Testament Quotations in the New Testament*, Chicago.
Bock, D. L. 1987: *Proclamation from Prophecy and Pattern: Lucan Old Testament Christology*, Sheffield (JSNT Supplement Series 12).
Ellis, E. E. 1957: *Paul's Use of the Old Testament*, Edinburgh.
—1988: 'Biblical Interpretation in the New Testament Church' in Mulder (1988): 691–725.
Fitzmyer, J. A. 1961: 'The use of explicit Old Testament quotations in Qumran literature and in the New Testament', *NTS* 7:297–333.
Freed, E. D. 1965: *Old Testament Quotations in the Gospel of John*, Leiden (SNovT 11).
Gundry, R. H. 1967: *The Use of the Old Testament in St. Matthew's Gospel: with special reference to the Messianic Hope*, Leiden (SNovT 18).
Hanson, A. T. 1974: *Studies in Paul's Technique and Theology*, London.
—1980: *The New Testament Interpretation of Scripture*, London.
—1983: *The Living Utterances of God: The New Testament Exegesis of the Old*, London.
Hays, R. B. 1989: *Echoes of Scripture in the Letters of Paul*, New Haven/London.
Juel, D. 1988: *Messianic Exegesis: Christological Interpretation of the Old Testament in Early Christianity*, Philadelphia.
Lindars, B. 1961: *New Testament Apologetic: The Doctrinal Significance of the Old Testament Quotations*, London.
Lindars Fs 1988: *It is Written: Scripture Citing Scripture: Essays in Honour*

of *Barnabas Lindars, SSF* (ed. D. A. Carson & H. G. M. Williamson), Cambridge.

Longenecker, R. N. 1970: 'Can we reproduce the Exegesis of the New Testament?', *TB* 21:3–38.

—1975: *Biblical Exegesis in the Apostolic Period*, Grand Rapids, Michigan.

Schröger, F. 1968: *Der Verfasser des Hebräerbriefes als Schriftausleger*, Regensburg.

Shires, H. M. 1974: *Finding the Old Testament in the New*, Philadelphia.

Stendahl, K. 1968: *The School of St. Matthew, and its Use of the Old Testament*, Philadelphia.

Suhl, A. 1965: *Die Funktion der alttestamentlichen Zitate und Anspielungen im Markusevangelium*, Gütersloh.

Wenham, J. W. 1972: *Christ and the Bible*, London.

Wright, N. T. 1980: 'The Messiah and the People of God: A Study in Pauline Theology with particular reference to the argument of the Epistle to the Romans', doctoral thesis, University of Oxford.

2

The two Testaments in the history of biblical interpretation

2.1 The early church

The writers of the New Testament were confronted with the problem of relating the events of the life, death and resurrection of Jesus with the words and events recorded in the Hebrew Bible. However it was only at a later date that the relationship between the New Testament itself and the Old Testament became a problem. Perhaps the most significant aspect of this was the change in role of the Old Testament. Jesus, Peter and Paul presupposed the Old Testament as the basis of their faith and their problem was to relate the *new* events in which they were involved to earlier ones. The post-New Testament church, on the other hand, adopted the New Testament as the basis of its faith and the *Old* Testament became the problem: how far was the Old Testament to be considered valid and relevant now the New Testament was complete, and in what way was the Old Testament related to the New?

a. The Apostolic Fathers

For the Apostolic Fathers the two Testaments formed one Bible. Both Old and New Testaments were accepted as Scripture, though the limits of the canon had not yet been finally defined. Texts from all parts of the Bible were cited in exhortation and argument, with literal and allegorical meanings each having their place.

b. Marcion

The simple acceptance of the Old and New Testaments as Scripture lasted only a few decades. In the middle of the second century Marcion of Sinope issued a challenge to the church's view of the relationship between the Testaments that has made him one of her most notorious heretics. Whether or not he should be considered a Gnostic, his thought was undoubtedly similar to Gnosticism in its dualistic emphasis. For Marcion there was a radical discontinuity between flesh and spirit, law and gospel, the god of Israel and the Father of Jesus, the Old Testament and the New Testament. Marcion followed his theory through to its logical conclusion and eliminated the Old Testament – together with parts of the New Testament which he considered inconsistent with the theory – from his Bible.

c. Reactions to Marcion

Like most heretics, Marcion gained a certain following but failed to convince the majority of the church. Nevertheless his challenge was a serious one and several of the early church's greatest theologians devoted much energy to countering his arguments. Justin Martyr (c.100–165), a leading apologist, rejected dualism and argued for the unity of God's revelation: the Old Testament itself looks forward to the Messiah and the new covenant. Irenaeus (c.130–c.200) considered Christ to be the link between the Testaments: for him the Old Testament, while subordinate in the scheme of progressive revelation, was nevertheless of real value for a complete understanding of God's activity in history. Tertullian (c.160–c.225) systematically refuted Marcion's dualism, showing that even Marcion's own version of the Bible presented a Christ who was the fulfilment of the law and the prophets. Finally Origen (c.185–c.254), perhaps the greatest biblical scholar of the early church, and Clement of Alexandria (c.150–c.215) added their voices to the defence of the Old Testament against Marcion, dealing with many of its difficult texts by means of allegorical or spiritual interpretation.

d. Theodore and Augustine

Orthodoxy prevailed over Marcion and the Old Testament was preserved as part of the church's Bible. Two of the most significant interpreters of the Bible in the succeeding years were Theodore of Mopsuestia (c.350–428) and Augustine of Hippo (354–430).

Theodore was an outstanding commentator of the Antioch school of interpretation, which emphasized the importance of the literal meaning of the text in contrast to the Alexandrian school (*e.g.* Origen) which emphasized the allegorical meaning. He understood the relationship between the Testaments primarily in terms of historical development, although he also saw Old Testament events as types of New Testament ones.

Augustine did not follow any one school but drew upon any kind of interpretation which served to illuminate the Bible, though he clearly had a liking for allegory. In a sense his work was the transition from the early church to the Middle Ages: it was the culmination of several centuries of Christian thought and became the foundation of theology in the West for the following centuries. He expressed his view of the relationship between the Testaments in words that have become classical:

> To the Old Testament belongs more fear,
> just as to the New Testament more delight;
> nevertheless in the Old Testament the New lies hid,
> and in the New Testament the Old is exposed.[1]

2.2 Middle Ages

In the Middle Ages biblical interpreters generally followed closely the methods of the Fathers and like them understood the Bible as a unity which witnesses to Christ. Those of particular interest include Bernard of Clairvaux (1090–1153), Hugh of St Victor (*c*.1096–1142), Thomas Aquinas (*c*.1225–74) and Nicholas of Lyra (*c*.1270–*c*.1340). A fourfold interpretation – literal, allegorical, moral and anagogical – was employed, but increasingly there was a tendency to stress the literal meaning (influenced partly by contemporary Jewish scholarship, *e.g.* Rashi). The New Testament was considered to be continuous with the Old Testament, though superior to it: the theological meaning of the Old Testament is seen clearly only after the coming of the New Testament (Hugh); the Old Testament is imperfect and the New Testament perfect, like a seed compared to a tree (Aquinas).

---

[1]'Multum et solide significatur, ad Vetus Testamentum timorem potius pertinere, sicut ad Novum dilectionem: quanquam et in Vetere Novum lateat, et in Novo Vetus pateat' (*Quaestiones in Exodum* 73).

2.3 Reformation

The central issue of the Reformation was the Bible. Alongside the primary concern with its authority and role in the church, there was also a renewed interest in the interpretation of the Bible. A major proportion of the works of both Luther and Calvin were commentaries and expositions of biblical books. They emphasized literal interpretation rather than allegory and were convinced that the whole Bible is Christocentric. However, these two aspects were not always easy to reconcile and the problem of the relationship between the Testaments became a very real one.

a. Luther

Martin Luther (1483–1546) recognized both the unity and the diversity of the Bible. For him the unity was in God who revealed himself in Christ and the diversity in the contrast between law and gospel. It was the contrast, however, which was the dominant factor, as is shown by the summary of his position in his 'Preface to the Old Testament' (1523):

> The ground and proof of the New Testament is surely not to be despised, and therefore the Old Testament is to be highly regarded. And what is the New Testament but a public preaching and proclamation of Christ, set forth through the sayings of the Old Testament and fulfilled through Christ? (paragraph 2).

> The Old Testament is a book of laws, which teaches what men are to do and not to do . . . just as the New Testament is gospel or book of grace, and teaches where one is to get the power to fulfil the law. Now in the New Testament there are also given . . . many other teachings that are laws and commandments . . . Similarly in the Old Testament too there are . . . certain promises and words of grace . . . Nevertheless just as the chief teaching of the New Testament is really the proclamation of grace and peace through the forgiveness of sins in Christ, so the chief teaching of the Old Testament is really the teaching of laws, the showing up of sin, and the demeaning of good (paragraph 4).

b. Calvin

John Calvin (1509–64) also recognized both the similarities and the differences between the two Testaments, but in contrast to Luther he stressed the similarities. In his *Institutes of the Christian Religion* (1536–59) he devoted 23 sections to the similarities compared with only 14 to the differences. Both law and gospel were understood as aspects of one covenant:

> Christ, although he was known to the Jews under the law, was at length clearly revealed only in the Gospel (II.ix, title).

> The covenant made with all the patriarchs is so much like ours in substance and reality that the two are actually one and the same . . . First, we hold that carnal prosperity and happiness did not constitute the goal set before the Jews to which they were to aspire. Rather, they were adopted into the hope of immortality . . . Secondly, the covenant by which they were bound to the Lord was supported, not by their own merits, but solely by the mercy of the God who called them. Thirdly, they had and knew Christ as Mediator, through whom they were joined to God and were to share in his promises (II.x.2).

> I freely admit the differences in Scripture . . . but in such a way as not to detract from its established unity . . . all these pertain to the manner of dispensation rather than to the substance (II.xi.1).

c. The Anabaptists

One of the most significant groups among those in the sixteenth century who proposed a more radical reformation than the main-line reformers was the Anabaptists. They agreed fervently with the principle of *sola scriptura* but in its application they tended to concentrate on the New Testament and to distinguish it from the Old. The Old Testament was understood to be preparatory for the final revelation of the New and to have authority for the Christian only insofar as it witnesses to Christ, agrees with the New Testament and is relevant to Christian living. It was therefore the New Testament that the Anabaptists considered normative for Christians, though they did not completely reject the Old Testament and often interpreted it allegorically or spiritually in order to find Christian teaching in it.

d. Council of Trent

The feature of the Roman Catholic Counter-Reformation that was most significant for interpretation of the Bible was the Council of Trent.[2] In its fourth session (8 April 1546) the Council decreed that the purity of the gospel be preserved in the church, and described that gospel in the following words:

> This Gospel was promised of old through the prophets in the Sacred Scriptures; Our Lord Jesus Christ, Son of God, first promulgated it from His own lips; He in turn ordered that it be preached through the apostles to all creatures as the source of all saving truth and rule of conduct.

No doubt the Reformers would have agreed with that; but the Council differed decisively from the Reformers on two issues: the relationship of Scripture and tradition, and the restriction of biblical interpretation to the church. The decree continues:

> This truth and rule are contained in the written books and unwritten traditions . . . [the Synod] receives and venerates with the same sense of loyalty and reverence all the books of the Old and New Testaments . . . together with all the traditions.

Then in a second decree from the same session it was decreed that:

> no one, relying on his own prudence, twist Holy Scripture . . . contrary to the meaning that holy mother the Church has held and – since it belongs to her to judge the true meaning and interpretation of Holy Scripture – that no one dare to interpret the Scripture in a way contrary to the unanimous consensus of the Fathers.

The implications for the understanding of the relationship between the Testaments were that the unity of the Bible was recognized, with a relationship of promise and fulfilment between the two Testaments, but there was little room for

---

[2]The text of 'The Canons and Dogmatic Decrees of the Council of Trent' may be found in Schaff (1877: 79–83).

further investigation since acceptance of the traditional interpretation was mandatory. There was little change in this outlook until the twentieth century.

2.4 Seventeenth to nineteenth centuries

The Reformation brought a new concern for serious study of the Bible, but the correct way of understanding the relationship between the Testaments was far from settled. During the next three centuries there was a polarization between the upholders of orthodoxy and more progressive thinkers. The period may conveniently be bisected for study, with the figure of Schleiermacher standing at the juncture of the two halves.

a. Orthodoxy

The predominant characteristic of biblical study in the years immediately following the Reformation was orthodoxy. Several important creeds and confessions were formulated to define the orthodox faith more precisely; and a systematic kind of study developed which was not unlike that of the Middle Ages and is often termed 'Protestant Scholasticism'. Calvin's view of the relationship between the Testaments was widely followed and the Old Testament highly regarded.

b. Reaction to orthodoxy

Orthodoxy was not to survive long without a reaction. In the seventeenth and eighteenth centuries an increasing number of theologians became dissatisfied with traditional ways of interpreting the Bible. The influence of grammatical-historical biblical scholarship, federal theology (developed by Cocceius, 1603–69) and rationalism (exemplified by Hobbes, 1588–1679, and Spinoza, 1632–77) brought about a more humanistic approach to the Bible and consequently a greater readiness to reject parts which were considered less acceptable, particularly in the Old Testament. This trend was continued in the eighteenth century by the works of Lessing (1729–81) and Kant (1724–1804) although there were also many who combined traditional piety with scholarly biblical study (*e.g.* Bengel, 1687–1752, and Wesley, 1703–91).

c. Schleiermacher

The nearest significant approach to Christian rejection of the Old Testament since Marcion, though less audacious than that of the second-century heretic, was made by Friedrich Schleiermacher (1768–1834). With a background of Pietism, Rationalism and Romanticism, he wrote voluminously and widely. In his dogmatic theology (1821: section 12) he virtually denied any theological relationship between the Old Testament and the New Testament, not disparaging the former as Marcion had done but placing it on the same level as heathenism (Greek and Roman thought). His discussion of the doctrine of Holy Scripture dealt with the Old Testament only in a postscript:

> The Old Testament Scriptures owe their place in our Bible partly to the appeals the New Testament Scriptures make to them, partly to the historical connexion of Christian worship with the Jewish Synagogue; but the Old Testament Scriptures do not on that account share the normative dignity or the inspiration of the New (section 132).

Schleiermacher's suggestion therefore was not the elimination of the Old Testament from the Bible but the transposition of the two Testaments to show the priority of the New Testament. Thus the Bible would consist primarily of the New Testament but the Old Testament would be retained as an appendix.

d. Historical criticism

In spite of the influence of his thought, few took seriously Schleiermacher's view of the Old Testament until a century later (as he himself had predicted, 1821: section 132). The dominant influence in nineteenth-century biblical interpretation was historical criticism, leading to an understanding of the relationship between the Testaments primarily in historical rather than theological terms: the Old Testament contains the history of the theocracy, the New Testament records the coming of Jesus Christ as the final stage of this history.

e. Conservative reaction

The increasing acceptance of historical criticism in the nineteenth century did not prevent a number of conservative scholars from defending and developing more traditional approaches to the Bible. Their reassertion of the orthodox belief in the inspiration of the Bible was however combined with a readiness to consider new ideas and they made a lasting contribution to biblical interpretation. J. C. K. von Hofmann (1841–44) developed the idea of 'salvation history', which has influenced much later theology based on this concept (*cf.* below: ch. 6); while Hengstenberg's *Christology* and Franz Delitzsch's commentaries on the Old Testament are still in print a century later.

2.5 The developmental approach

At the beginning of the twentieth century the most widely accepted way of understanding the relationship between the Old Testament and the New Testament was a developmental approach which was based on the evolutionary idea of history and the results of historical criticism of the Bible. The essence of this approach may be characterized by the concept of 'progressive revelation'. This understanding was the primary background upon which the modern solutions examined in the present work were formulated and so it will be examined in some detail now. The work of two significant British writers will first be considered and then others will be mentioned more briefly.

a. A. F. Kirkpatrick

Kirkpatrick (1891: 112–116) pointed out that the New Testament affirms the permanent value of the Old Testament by explicit statements (*e.g.* Mt. 5:17; Rom. 15:4; 1 Cor. 10:11; 2 Tim. 3:14–17) and also by continually using it in expounding Christ and his work. The simplicity of Old Testament moral demands and the depth of its praise and devotion are of continuing value in the Christian era and so the church should recognize its permanent value as teaching about national, social and personal life (pp. 130–133). However, the greatest value of the Old Testament is in relation to the New Testament.

First, the Old Testament is the essential historical basis of the New Testament and Christianity, without which they cannot be properly understood (pp. 123–126). The coming of Christ was the consummation of a long history of God at work in human affairs.

Secondly, study of the language, concepts and theology of the Old Testament is essential for proper understanding of the New Testament (pp. 126–127). The New Testament is written in the

Hebraic Greek of the Septuagint and many fundamental New Testament ideas such as righteousness, holiness, sacrifice and sin come from the Old Testament and can be understood only with reference to it.

Thirdly, every Christian can find encouragement in the Old Testament by looking at God's outworking of his plan in spite of human weakness and failure (pp. 127–130). Reading the Old Testament will clarify the close link between prophecy and fulfilment and strengthen the Christian hope that God will bring victory for Christ's kingdom, even though there may be much discouragement in the interim.

Kirkpatrick concluded with a warning not to confuse the two Testaments: the Old Testament has its value for the Christian but it is clearly different in this respect from the New Testament (pp. 133–139). It must not be used as a court of appeal for Christian doctrine although support for that may well be found in it, nor may it be used to justify anything contrary to the mind of Christ. He argued that the Old Testament is valid for the church only in so far as it is fulfilled in Christ and this demands recognition of the completion, realization, development and universalization in Christ of what was before incomplete and limited. Christ has given a deeper insight into God and his purpose for humanity, thereby enabling a new perception of his working in the Old Testament.

b. R. L. Ottley

In the last of his 1897 Bampton Lectures (*Aspects of the Old Testament*), Ottley discussed use of the Old Testament in the New Testament and in the contemporary church.

First, according to Ottley, the New Testament understands the Old Testament revelation as fragmentary, varied and rudimentary (1897: 337–400). The Old Testament is the record of a developing religion and revelation, and is therefore to be interpreted historically; every part, whether type or prophecy, sign or promise, is incomplete and looks forward to God's perfect plan for the future. Moreover the New Testament recognizes that much in the Old is imperfect and must be assessed by the standard of the gospel. New Testament exegesis of the Old is notable for its breadth and freedom, its concern with morals and human duty, and its messianic nature. It represents the Old Testament as an 'organic whole, to which the Messiah and His Kingdom are the key ... a shadow of good things to come' (p. 396).

Secondly, Ottley was convinced of the importance of the Old

Testament in the life of the church (pp. 401–436). He suggested six ways in which the Old Testament may be used. The first three concern the intrinsic value of the Old Testament:

- for education in morals;
- in the spiritual life; and
- in social righteousness.

The other three concern understanding of the Old Testament in the context of the whole Bible:

- the main purpose of the Old Testament, as of the New, is to reveal the mind, character and will of God (it also shows God's preparation for the coming of the Messiah and introduces the concept of suffering, the chosen tool for accomplishment of God's purpose, the perfection of man);
- the Old Testament witnesses to Christ (the theology of the Old Testament presupposes its unity as a history of redemption, to which the coming of a redeemer is a natural climax; a prefiguration of Christ may be seen in law, history, prophecy, song and wisdom; moreover the idealistic nature of much of the Old Testament is sufficient to describe it as messianic); and
- the Old Testament serves as an aid to interpretation of the New (many of the most fundamental concepts of the New Testament are taken from the Old: for example, the concepts of Christ, kingdom of God and Son of God would be virtually unintelligible without the Old Testament).

c. Other writers

According to B. F. Westcott (1889: 480–482), the writer to the Hebrews represents the whole Bible as a revelation of God's way of salvation, initially 'in many and various ways' and finally 'by a Son'. It is presupposed that the Old Testament has a spiritual meaning and significance, though its historical truth is also taken seriously. The Old Testament points forward to Christ and in him alone it finds true fulfilment. Thus it is used in Hebrews to explain and illustrate the correspondences between different stages in the fulfilment of God's purpose:

The object of the writer is not to show that Jesus fulfils the idea of the Christ, and that the Christian Church

44

fulfils the idea of Israel, but, taking this for granted, to mark the relation in which the Gospel stands to the Mosaic system, as part of one divine whole (p. 481).

W. H. Bennett (1893: 39–40) asserted that the Old Testament 'not only prepares a way for the New, but also contains special and characteristic truths stated once and for all'. Two decades later (1914) he discussed the problem of the relationship between the Testaments in more detail, using the concept of 'progressive revelation'. The Old Testament is a record of a divine revelation in two forms: history [of God and his people] and teaching [about religion and morals] (p. 7). Its greatest value, according to Bennett, is in relation to Christ, witnessing to him and explaining his significance, though much in it is not surpassed by the New Testament but of continuing value in itself. The Christian should not only follow Christ's example in using the Old Testament as a guide for everyday life and religion, but should recognize in its developing revelation and religion a preparation for Christ and the New Testament (pp. 25–44). There is a two-way relationship between the Testaments: the New Testament cannot be properly understood without the Old, so also the Old Testament can be truly appreciated only when studied in the light of the New (pp. 48–49).

George Adam Smith (1899: 145–176) approached the problem by means of the idea of 'the Spirit of Christ in the Old Testament'. He deliberately avoided the traditional approaches of typology and messianic prophecy, considering that in practice they are too vaguely defined and indiscriminately used so that they result in artificial or arbitrary interpretation. Besides this, he argued that these approaches are inadequate because they fail to interpret in the light of Christ many parts of the Old Testament which unquestionably 'breathe His Spirit' (p. 147). The Spirit of Christ may be perceived in the Old Testament both in its human ideals – and their enactments in Israel's heroes – and in its divine revelation.

A. B. Davidson (1904: 1–12) considered Old Testament theology to be a development, so that the two Testaments must neither be separated (which would remove all authority from the Old Testament) nor equated (which would imply that the Old Testament is as advanced as the New). The Old Testament describes God's activity in establishing his kingdom, which was completed only in Christ, but it does not follow that the former events and institutions are nothing more than foreshadowings of the future. Indeed most Israelites never saw beyond the

immediate significance of those events and institutions. Davidson argued that it was only a few of the more perceptive thinkers
(*e.g.* the prophets) who saw the imperfection of the events and
institutions, looked deeper to the fundamental idea they
embodied and expressed 'their longing and certainty that the
idea would yet be realised' (p. 9).

C. F. Kent (1906) treated the Old Testament as the record of a
varied, extended and yet incomplete revelation. It looks for the
coming of One who will crystallize and perfect its teachings, and
exemplify them in his own life, a coming which is recorded in
the New Testament. In spite of some obvious differences, the
New Testament has many important similarities to the Old
Testament. 'Each Testament is but a different chapter in the
history of the same divine revelation. The one is the foundation
on which the other is built' (p. 61). So the Old Testament tells of
preparation and expectation, the New Testament of a fulfilment
much greater than the highest expectations.

d. Analysis

There were many works during the period around the turn of
the century on the Old Testament and its relationship to the
New, only a few of which have been mentioned above. Many of
these works were produced primarily to present, explain and
justify historical criticism to ministers and lay people, and to
show its positive contribution to the understanding of the Bible.
All the authors mentioned accepted the historical-critical
method, at least in principle, and assumed the Bible to be a
document which is both human and divine, an account of
human history and a revelation from God.

They agreed that the Old Testament is indispensable for the
modern church and has two major uses. In itself, the Old Testament 'enshrines truths of permanent and universal validity'
(Driver 1905: 20) and may be used for instruction in social
relationships, national life, and personal morality and devotion.
And in relationship to the New Testament, the Old Testament is
to be used in three main ways: first, the Old Testament is the
most important historical basis of the New; secondly, an understanding of the language, concepts and theology of the Old
Testament is essential for interpretation of the New; and finally,
the Old Testament is in some sense a witness to Christ (though
the meaning of this is not always defined very closely).

In these works a balance was generally maintained between
the obvious differences of the Old Testament from the New and
the belief that the two are essentially a unity. On the one hand,

the Old Testament was considered to be incomplete and imperfect, presenting early stages in a development or progression, and must be judged by the standard of the final and perfect revelation in Christ. Moreover the Old Testament is concerned with a nation, the New with a supranational people of God. On the other hand, in both Testaments it is one God who speaks and one plan of redemption which is presented. The two extremes of separating and identifying the two Testaments were therefore rejected.

The fundamental concept underlying all the works discussed is that of 'progressive revelation' (*cf.* Moltmann 1964: 69–71, 74–76). The Old Testament was considered to have permanent value both as preparatory revelation and also in looking beyond itself to the perfect revelation in Christ. Today the term 'progressive revelation' is outmoded, along with the optimistic evolutionary idea of history which it presupposed. Nevertheless, this was the view of the Bible which formed the basis of twentieth-century biblical interpretation and many of the key ideas of modern biblical theology are to be found in these works. The Bible was understood to be a history of redemption and the Old Testament in particular was considered to be oriented to the future. The way in which 'prophecy and fulfilment' was interpreted was not unlike modern interpretations of 'promise and fulfilment', and typology was conceived – at least by Westcott – in a similar way as by many modern scholars.

Westcott's statement that 'each promise fulfilled brings the sense of a larger promise' (1889: 482) could almost have been taken from Moltmann's *Theology of Hope* (1964). The assertion that the Old Testament 'does not merely contain prophecies; it is from first to last a prophecy' (quoted by Kirkpatrick 1891: 124) might have found a place in Vriezen's Old Testament theology (1966). Ottley (1897) took the Bible to be the history of redemption, considered the Old Testament to point toward the future, perceived reinterpretation of texts within the Bible and mentioned typology: in fact most of the major themes of von Rad's Old Testament theology (1957–60) were in his lecture! Even Bultmann's radical view of the Old Testament was foreshadowed in McFadyen's assertion that the Old Testament did not bring the redemptive purpose of God to fulfilment but 'by its repeated failures pointed men to something more strong and saving than itself' (1903: 347).

e. Conservatism

It is clear that the prevailing solution to the problem of the relationship between the Testaments at the beginning of the twentieth century was that of the developmental approach, characterized by the concept of 'progressive revelation'. Even the more conservative sections of the church, Protestant Fundamentalism and Roman Catholicism, adopted this solution.

One section of Protestant thought, sometimes called 'Fundamentalism' after a series of tracts entitled *The Fundamentals* issued in the early part of the twentieth century, rejected many of the presuppositions, methods and results of historical criticism. On the problem of the relationship between the Testaments, however, its view was not greatly different from the consensus of contemporary scholarship. James Orr (1906), for example, considered divine guidance rather than natural evolution to be the principle of development, but nevertheless accepted in general terms the concept of progressive revelation as a description of the relationship between the Testaments (*cf.* Pierson 1906; Patton 1926).

Within the Roman Church at the beginning of the century there was a stronger reaction to historical criticism than that in Protestantism, since it was supported by the official maintenance of orthodox teaching about the Bible. As with Fundamentalism, however, its concern was mainly to defend those areas of Christian faith threatened by historical criticism and the question of the relationship between the Testaments was not one of them. Until the present day the Old Testament is commonly seen in Roman Catholic theology as the historical and theological preparation for the New Testament.[3] This differs from the developmental approach in that it stresses divine ordering and overruling in history whereas the latter tends to be more concerned with human evolutionary development, but the resultant views of the relationship between the Testaments are very similar.

2.6 Neo-Marcionism

One result of the developmental approach to the problem of the relationship between the Testaments was a devaluation of the Old Testament. It was indeed natural that what was considered to be imperfect and preparatory should be less highly regarded

---

[3]Heinisch (1949–50: 3); Grelot (1962a: 21–22, 196–209, 275–286); J. L. McKenzie (1967).

than a later superior stage of revelation. In the 1920s two well-known German scholars took this devaluation to its logical but extreme conclusion and resurrected the proposal of Marcion, only temporarily revived by Schleiermacher, that the Old Testament should be excluded from the Christian Bible. Friedrich Delitzsch's view of the Old Testament was summed up in the title of his two-volume work: *The Great Deception* (1920–21). And Adolf von Harnack concluded his standard work on Marcion (1921) with the oft-quoted thesis:

> To reject the Old Testament in the second century was a mistake which the Church rightly rejected; to keep it in the sixteenth century was a fate which the Reformation could not yet avoid; but to retain it after the nineteenth century as a canonical document in Protestantism results from paralysis of religion and the Church.[4]

a. The Nazi Bible

Though their intention was explicitly theological rather than political, the works of Friedrich Delitzsch and von Harnack were published about the time that anti-Semitic thought began to develop in Germany after the First World War and they no doubt aided its growth and penetration into biblical studies. In the years between the two wars an increasingly fierce debate raged over the Old Testament: the Nazis and theologians sympathetic to their cause attacked it vehemently, while those who were brave enough defended it with equal vehemence. The Nazis and 'German Christians' (*Deutsche Christen*) aimed to eliminate every trace of Judaism from Christianity. This involved rejection of the Old Testament and its god, and its replacement by Nordic and Aryan literature. In this they invoked the support of Luther, who they claimed would have done the same had he lived in the twentieth century (*cf.* Wiener 1945; Rupp 1945). Some (*e.g.* Rosenberg) despised the Old Testament completely, others (*e.g.* Leffler) recognized its historical and religious value but advocated that serious Germans should forget the Old Testament and study their own history and piety. It was at least consistent that those who hated and fought Jews should do the same to Jewish literature. It was also consistent that they should

---

[4]These views were naturally not received without question: see *e.g.* Sellin (1921); *cf.* Kraeling (1955: ch. 10); Bright (1967: 64–67).

try to purge the New Testament of Jewish elements, as Marcion had done eighteen centuries before. The Nazi 'Bible' was indeed a very select collection of extracts from the Christian Scriptures and it is not surprising that the Nazi 'Christ' was very different from the usual referent of the word. Tanner (1942) comments: 'the crucifixion was only the first in a long series of devices by which the Western world has attempted to be rid of Jesus . . . the most subtle of these devices has been reinterpretation' (p. 52).

b. Defence of the Old Testament

Naturally such attacks on the Old Testament provoked a reaction among biblical scholars, many of whom sided with the Confessing Church (*Bekennende Kirche*) in the German Church Struggle (*Kirchenkampf*). Some openly condemned the anti-Semitism of National Socialism and its adherents, but most simply reaffirmed in different ways the value of the Old Testament for the Christian faith. Wilhelm Vischer, Karl Barth, Hans Hellbardt and Otto Procksch claimed the Old Testament for the church by interpreting it as a witness to Christ, thus diverting attention from its relevance to the Jews (see further below: ch. 4). Emil Brunner, another Dialectic theologian, argued that 'the understanding of the Old Testament is the criterion and the basis for understanding the New' (1930: 264). This was because of the characteristic Old Testament ideas which are presupposed but not explicitly defined in the New: the idea of a personal creator God, eschatological realism and the people of God. We cannot therefore replace the Old Testament with our own national history and piety.[5]

c. Implicit Marcionism

The Third Reich fell, and with it the most extreme forms of neo-Marcionism disappeared. Open attack on the Old Testament lost its political motivation and would have been likely to bring its proponent into disrepute. However there are other

---

[5]Dietrich Bonhoeffer also wrote and spoke much about this question (see Kuske 1967; Andersen 1975). In spite of the Third Reich, many Old Testament studies were published in Germany during the 1930s. Gerhard von Rad, for instance, published 28 books and articles during the years 1933–39 and another ten during the war (see bibliography in von Rad Fs 1971). Eichrodt's famous *Theology of the Old Testament* was also published in this period.

more subtle ways to dispose of the Old Testament. We can, for example, be 'generous' and give it to the Jews. This was done in effect by Isaac G. Matthews (1947) in his presentation of Israel's religious history. Though he traces the history up to AD 135, he virtually never refers to Christ or Christianity, assuming that Judaism is the natural continuation of Old Testament religion. He concludes:

> Judaism, the religion of the book, and of a people scattered to the four corners of the earth but united in allegiance to the one God, was well equipped to succeed in the struggle of existence. By losing its life as a nation, it saved itself as a religion. Happy was the man whose delight was in the law of the Lord, in whose law he meditated day and night (p. 268).

A similar tendency is found in the approach to mission which substitutes other national religions and literatures for the Old Testament as the basis for preaching Christianity (*cf.* Filson 1951: 136). Pandipeddi Chenchiah considered the Old Testament to be inferior to the New and unnecessary for non-Jewish Christians, arguing that the Hindu scriptures were a better preparation for the gospel (*praeparatio evangelii*) for the people of India.[6] Moreover the same thing often happens in Western churches when modern thought and culture are used as a 'lead-in' to presentation of the Christian message and 'modern' studies such as the social sciences are introduced to theological curricula at the expense of biblical (especially Old Testament) studies.

On an even more basic level, there is in the church a habit of simply ignoring the Old Testament. It is thought to be difficult to understand or irrelevant to modern life and therefore it is rarely read and expounded (or it is read in terms of the New Testament; *cf.* Michalson 1964: 62). In many churches, relatively few sermons are preached on the Old Testament[7] and

---

[6]See Boyd (1975: 158–159; *cf.* 137–138); also Phillips (1942: 14–21). The religious traditions of Africa have also been seen as preparation for the Gospel, and thus to be analogous to the Old Testament, but this has not led to implicit Marcionism. On the contrary, the Old Testament is highly valued by African Christians (Phillips 1942: 6–13; Shorter 1978: 22; Mbiti 1986: 36, 50, 156). See also Sovik (1982).

[7]In a survey a few years ago of lectionaries used in North Sumatra, it was found that in all churches surveyed there were more sermons on

Bible study groups spend relatively little time on Old Testament passages.

It is clear therefore that the modern church, in spite of its official rejection of Marcionism and neo-Marcionism, has often allowed implicit Marcionism in practice.

2.7 The problem today

The implication of Marcionism was separation of the two Testaments. In other words, the Old and New Testaments were considered to belong to two different religions, so that there is no theological relationship between them. If Marcion had been right the present study would be a pointless exercise; but among serious biblical theologians, in spite of the implicit Marcionism which often affects the church in practice, there is virtually unanimous agreement that Marcion was not right. There are today many different evaluations of the Old Testament and interpretations of its relationship to the New, but it can at least be said that one assured result of modern scholarship has been the recognition of the existence of a theological relationship between the two Testaments of the Christian Bible.

The task which remains to be undertaken is the definition of this relationship. Many of the most significant modern studies of the relationship between the Testaments were published during two decades of the twentieth century – the thirties and the fifties. They may be classified into four main approaches and these are discussed in detail in the second part of the present work. In the seventies a number of new approaches to biblical interpretation also had their relevance for the problem and they are discussed at various points in the book.

a. The nineteen-thirties

The twentieth-century church gradually digested the results of nineteenth-century scholarship, following in general the developmental approach to the relationship between the Testaments (*e.g.* Burney 1921; Welch 1933; Elmslie 1948; Higgins 1949). Meanwhile a number of scholars were reconsidering the conclusions of their nineteenth-century predecessors and expressed a deep dissatisfaction with them. In particular the

---

the New Testament than on the Old, and in one church there was only one sermon on the Old Testament in a whole year.

anti-Semitic attacks on the Old Testament in the 1930s high-lighted the problem of the relationship between the Testaments and gave a new impetus to finding a more satisfactory solution. Two of the most important modern solutions to the problem of the relationship between the Testaments stem from the troubled years of the thirties: in 1933, the year of the rise of National Socialism, Rudolf Bultmann published an important essay on 'The Significance of the Old Testament for the Christian Faith' in which he emphasized the radical difference between the Old Testament and the New Testament; then in the following year, Wilhelm Vischer's major work, *The Witness of the Old Testament to Christ*, appeared. Friedrich Baumgärtel and Gerhard von Rad, although their major works were published two decades later, were also concerned in the early part of their careers with the issues raised by the German Church Struggle; and probably every modern study which takes serious account of German theology has been influenced in some way by the debates of the 1930s.

b. The nineteen-fifties

The next major contribution to the theological understanding of the Old Testament in relation to the New was made by the collaborators of the *Biblischer Kommentar Altes Testament*, an Old Testament commentary project launched in 1952 with a series of programmatic essays.[8] These essays dealt with aspects of the theological interpretation of the Old Testament such as typology, re-presentation, actualization, promise and fulfilment, salvation history and tradition. The commentaries themselves

---

[8]The essays which first set out the principles for the *Biblischer Kommentar* (BK) were written by von Rad, Noth, Zimmerli, Kraus and Wolff and published in *EvTh* 12 (July/August 1952). ETs of three of the essays were published in *Int* (1961) and again in *EOTI*. The essays provoked a heated debate about the interpretation of the Old Testament and two scholars in particular wrote major responses to the programme: Friedrich Baumgärtel (1952: 106–127; *cf.* below: ch. 3.3.b) and Arnold A. van Ruler (1955; *cf.* below: ch. 5). Several of the collaborators of the BK replied to their critics and elaborated their programme further in five essays published in *EvTh* 16 (August/September 1959), three of which are translated in *EOTI*. In the same year BK commenced publication with a slim volume on Lamentations by Kraus. Many volumes in the series have now appeared, including a number of outstanding commentaries such as those of Kraus on Psalms, Zimmerli on Ezekiel, Wolff on the minor prophets, and Westermann on Genesis.

follow an original pattern for the systematic interpretation in five stages of each biblical passage (*cf.* Wolff 1952):

● *Text* (translation and textual criticism);
● *Form* (literary analysis);
● *Ort* (setting);
● *Wort* (exegesis); and
● *Ziel* (aim).

The most interesting and important stage for the question of the relationship between the Testaments is the final one, in which the theological significance of the passage is considered in the context of the whole Bible, including the New Testament. Several of the programmatic essays and other writings by members of the '*Biblischer Kommentar* group' are discussed in this book, in particular the works of Gerhard von Rad, Walther Zimmerli, Hans Walter Wolff and Claus Westermann.

However the German-speaking church and its theological scholarship were not the only source of new theological ideas in the post-war period. Significant approaches to the problem were also attempted in Dutch (*e.g.* Arnold van Ruler, Kornelis Miskotte), French (*e.g.* Edmond Jacob, Samuel Amsler) and English-speaking scholarship (*e.g.* H. H. Rowley, George Knight). A selection of articles from the nineteen-fifties was collected by Westermann and published under the title *Essays on Old Testament Interpretation* (*EOTI*).

c. The nineteen-seventies

During the nineteen-sixties a good deal was written about the relationship between the Old and New Testaments, mostly interacting with and building on the ideas put forward in the thirties and fifties. Bernhard Anderson, for example, took Bultmann's essay of 1933 as the basis for an international symposium on *The Old Testament and Christian Faith* (*OTCF*, 1964).

It was during the following decade that some major new approaches to biblical interpretation became apparent, some of which had implications for the relationship between the Testaments. Interestingly the main source of new ideas during this period was no longer Europe but the Americas. Four particularly important new approaches have emphasized the significance of the canon of Scripture, the use of literary and social-scientific methods in biblical interpretation, and the role of 'praxis' as the starting-point of theology.

The canonical approach

In 1970 Brevard Childs started a major debate with his thesis that biblical theology and exegesis should be done in the context of the Christian canon of Scripture, a thesis which he developed with great fervour and impressive scholarship in many works published during the following years. Childs' proposal provoked many reactions, both positive and negative, but perhaps its greatest significance for biblical interpretation in general lies in his insistence on the importance of studying the biblical text in its final form (*cf.* Barton 1984b: 25–28). The intentions of the original authors and the processes by which their writings were edited and transmitted are of interest to him only insofar as they enable us to understand better the meaning of the canonical form of the text. However the relevance of his work to the problem of the relationship between the Testaments lies primarily in his interpretation of the Old Testament as Christian Scripture and this will be discussed in greater detail in chapter four below.

Literary approaches

The text in its final form is also the focus of interest in most modern literary approaches to the Bible. Older methods of literary study (such as source, form, tradition and redaction criticism) tended to dissect texts in the attempt to discover their origins and growth, whereas newer methods (such as rhetorical criticism, structuralism and narrative analysis) are more interested in texts as texts, which are considered to have an objective value in themselves. The aesthetic dimension of the Bible as literature has been re-emphasized, as the concern of scholars has shifted from the history of the text to its present shape, from obtaining knowledge of the past to understanding the impact of the text on its readers in the present.

Recently 'reader-response criticism' has begun to develop literary theory still further, suggesting that the text is not in fact an objective reality that exists apart from its readers; rather there may be several different but equally valid 'readings' of the same text. In this sort of approach the emphasis shifts again from the text itself to its audience/readership.[9]

The main point at which literary approaches to the Bible

---

[9]On modern literary study of the Bible, see Alter (1981); Clines (1982); Barton (1984a); Sternberg (1985); Gunn (1987); Long (1988); Morgan & Barton (1988: 203–268).

touch on the problem of the relationship between the Testaments is in their understanding of 'story' and its relationship to biblical 'history', and this will be discussed in chapter six below.

A pragmatic approach

Liberation theology originated in the Roman Catholic Church of Latin America in the nineteen-sixties, as an expression of Christian faith from the perspective of the poor and oppressed. During the nineteen-seventies it spread into many other churches and parts of the world, taking many new forms, for example the Minjung theology of South Korea (CTC-CCA 1983) and the Kairos theology of South Africa (Kairos 1985). It has affinities with European theologies of revolution and of hope, with black theology and feminist theology, though it is by no means derivative from them. On the contrary it has been described as 'the first non-imitative theology to have sprung from the Third World nations; indeed, the first creative theological thought to have arisen outside of Europe or North America since the earliest years of the Church' (Kirk 1979: 204; *cf.* Hanks 1983: 61–69).

In reaction to theologies which have emphasized dogma, liberation theology has emphasized 'praxis' (*i.e.* historical practice or reality). Theology is understood as 'critical reflection on praxis' (Gutiérrez 1971: 6–15) and the key to this new approach is the praxis of liberation, which involves an intimate bond between theoretical theology and the practical life of faith (Boff 1986: 15–18). Some liberation theologians have emphasized the relevance of the Old Testament to current political struggles, seeing the Exodus in particular as a paradigm of liberation from oppression; while others have preferred New Testament themes such as the coming of the kingdom of God and the person of Jesus as one who identified himself with the poor. Concerning the relationship between the two Testaments, liberation theologians have not produced a distinctive solution, though a number of their works touch on the problem and will be referred to at various points below. Their approach to biblical interpretation is essentially pragmatic, being concerned to address the needs and reflect on the faith of the people of God in their everyday lives, in their suffering and hope.

Social scientific approaches

The methods of the social sciences have long been used in the study of Christianity, particularly in the form of psychology and sociology of religion. More recently sociological methods have been used for the study of the biblical text itself, for instance in

Gerd Theissen's analyses of the sociology of early Christianity (1974–77) and in Norman Gottwald's reinterpretation of the origin of Israel as a revolutionary class-struggle by peasants against the Canaanite feudal system (1979). There have also been psychological, anthropological and socio-economic studies of specific phenomena (*e.g.* prophecy, apocalyptic, wealth and poverty) and exegeses of biblical texts which have made use of social scientific methods.[10]

Sociological studies of the Bible have an obvious relevance to the concerns of liberation theology (see previous section) and the two approaches have been brought together in a wide-ranging collection of essays edited by Gottwald under the title *The Bible and Liberation: Political and Social Hermeneutics* (1983). However they have little to contribute to an understanding of the *theological* relationship between the Testaments.

Bibliography (2)

The history of biblical interpretation

Blackman, E. C. 1957: *Biblical Interpretation: The Old Difficulties and the New Opportunity*, London.

CHB 1963–70: *The Cambridge History of the Bible*, Cambridge (volume 1: ed. P. R. Ackroyd & C. F. Evans, 1970; volume 2: ed. G. W. H. Lampe, 1969; volume 3: ed. S. L. Greenslade, 1963).

Dugmore, C. W. (ed.) 1944: *The Interpretation of the Bible: Edward Alleyn Lectures 1943*, London.

Harnack, A. von 1921: *Marcion: Das Evangelium vom fremden Gott*, Leipzig [2]1924 (reprinted Darmstadt 1960; [1]1921).

Kraus, H. -J. 1956a: *Geschichte der historisch-kritischen Erforschung des Alten Testaments*, Neukirchen [3]1982 ([1]1956).

Megivern, J. J. (ed.) 1978: *Bible Interpretation: Official Catholic Teachings*, Wilmington. Collection of documents from AD 170–1976.

Morgan, R. & Barton, J. 1988: *Biblical Interpretation*, Oxford.

Nineham, D. E. (ed.) 1963: *The Church's Use of the Bible: Past and Present*, London.

Preus, J. S. 1969: *From Shadow to Promise: Old Testament Interpretation from Augustine to the Young Luther*, Cambridge, Massachusetts.

Wood, J. D. 1958: *The Interpretation of the Bible: A Historical Introduction*, London.

See also several works in the general bibliography, especially Kraeling

---

[10]For further discussion and bibliography on the use of the social sciences in biblical interpretation, see Morgan & Barton (1988: 138–166).

(1955), Grant (1963/84), Kraus (1970), Harrington (1973) and Rogerson (1988).

The early church (2.1)

Blackman, E. C. 1948: *Marcion and His Influence*, London.
Daniélou, J. 1948a: *Origen*, ET: New York 1955 (French 1948).
—1964/73: *A History of Early Christian Doctrine*, ET: London 1964 (volume 1), 1973 (volume 2; French n.d.).
Evans, E. (ed.) 1972: *Tertullian: Adversus Marcionem*, Oxford.
Froehlich, K. 1984: *Biblical Interpretation in the Early Church*, Philadelphia. Translations of patristic texts.
Grant, R. M. 1957: *The Letter and the Spirit*, London.
Greer, R. A. 1961: *Theodore of Mopsuestia: Exegete and Theologian*, London.
Hagner, D. A. 1973: *The Use of the Old and New Testaments in Clement of Rome*, Leiden (SNovT 34).
Hanson, R. P. C. 1959: *Allegory and Event: A Study of the Sources and Significance of Origen's Interpretation of Scripture*, London.
Hay, D. M. 1973: *Glory at the Right Hand: Psalm 110 in Early Christianity*, Nashville/New York (SBL Monograph Series 18).
Horbury, W. 1988: 'Old Testament Interpretation in the Writings of the Church Fathers' in Mulder (1988): 727–787.
Kelly, J. N. D. 1958: *Early Christian Doctrines*, London: ch. 3.
Kerrigan, A. 1952: *St. Cyril of Alexandria, Interpreter of the Old Testament*, Rome (Analecta Biblica 2).
Kugel, J. L. & Greer, R. A. 1986: *Early Biblical Interpretation*, Philadelphia.
Lawson, J. 1948: *The Biblical Theology of Saint Irenaeus*.
O'Malley, T. P. 1967: *Tertullian and the Bible: Language – Imagery – Exegesis* (Latinitas Christianorum Primaeva 21).
Polman, A. D. R. 1955: *The Word of God according to St. Augustine*, ET: London 1961 (Dutch 1955).
Shotwell, W. A. 1965: *The Biblical Exegesis of Justin Martyr*, London.
Sundberg, A. C. 1964: *The Old Testament of the Early Church*, Cambridge, Massachusetts/London (Harvard Theological Studies 20).
See also von Campenhausen (1968) in the general bibliography.

Middle Ages (2.2)

Gribomont, J. 1946: 'Le lien des deux Testaments, selon la théologie de saint Thomas: Notes sur le sens spirituel et implicite des Saintes Écritures', *ETL* 22:70–89.
McNally, R. E. 1959: *The Bible in the Early Middle Ages*, Westminster, Maryland (Woodstock Papers 4; Scholars Press reprint 1986).
Smalley, B. 1952: *The Study of the Bible in the Middle Ages*, Oxford.
Torrance, T. F. 1962: 'Scientific Hermeneutics According to St. Thomas Aquinas', *The Journal of Theological Studies* 13: 259–289.

Reformation (2.3)

Althaus, P. 1963: *The Theology of Martin Luther*, ET: Philadelphia, 1966 (German, ²1963): chs 9 & 19.

Bornkamm, H. 1948: *Luther and the Old Testament*, ET: Philadelphia, 1969 (German, 1948).

Calvin, J. 1536–59: *Institutes of the Christian Religion*, ET: Philadelphia, 1960 (originally published in six Latin/French editions, 1536–59).

Carter, C. S. 1928: *The Reformers and Holy Scripture: A Historical Investigation*, London.

Estep, W. R. 1975: *The Anabaptist Story*, Grand Rapids, Michigan (¹1963, ²1975): 140–145.

Forde, G. O. 1983: 'Law and Gospel in Luther's Hermeneutic', *Int* 37: 240–252.

Forstman, H. J. 1962: *Word and Spirit: Calvin's Doctrine of Biblical Authority*, Stanford, California.

Grin, E. 1961: 'L'unité des deux Testaments selon Calvin', *ThZ* 17: 175–186.

Heintze, G. 1958: *Luthers Predigt von Gesetz und Evangelium*, Munich (Forschung zur Geschichte und Lehre des Protestantismus 10.11).

Hesselink, I. J. 1967: 'Calvin and Heilsgeschichte' in Cullman Fs: 163–170.

Keeney, W. E. 1968: *The Development of Dutch Anabaptist Thought and Practice from 1539–1564*, Nieuwkoop: 31–43.

Kidd, B. J. 1933: *The Counter-Reformation 1550–1600*, London.

Kraus, H. -J. 1968: 'Calvin's Exegetical Principles', ET in *Int* 31 (1977): 8–18 (German, 1968).

Leith, J. H. 1971: 'John Calvin – Theologian of the Bible', *Int* 25: 329–344.

Luther, M. 1523–34: 'Prefaces to the Old Testament', ET in *Luther's Works* (American Edition) 35, Philadelphia, 1960: 233–333.

—1525: 'How Christians Should Regard Moses', ET in *Luther's Works* (American Edition) Vol. 35, Philadelphia, 1960: 155–174 (originally a sermon preached on 27 August 1525).

Parker, T. H. L. 1986: *Calvin's Old Testament Commentaries*, Edinburgh.

Pelikan, J. 1959: *Luther the Expositor: Introduction to the Reformer's Exegetical Writings*, St Louis (companion volume to *Luther's Works*).

Russell, S. H. 1968: 'Calvin and the Messianic Interpretation of the Psalms', *SJT* 21: 37–47.

Sick, H. 1959: *Melanchthon als Ausleger des Alten Testaments*, Tübingen (BGBH 2).

Sider, R. J. 1974: *Andreas Bodenstein von Karlstadt: The Development of his Thought 1517–1525*, Leiden: 105–122.

Wenger, J. C. 1957: 'The Biblicism of the Anabaptists' in *The Recovery of the Anabaptist Vision* (Harold S. Bender Fs; ed. G. F. Hershberger), Scottdale, Pennsylvania: 167–179.

Williams, G. H. 1962: *The Radical Reformation*, Philadelphia.

Wolf, H. H. 1958: *Die Einheit des Bundes: Das Verhältnis von Altem und Neuem Testament bei Calvin*, Neukirchen (Beiträge zur Geschichte und Lehre der Reformierten Kirche 10).

Wood, A. S. 1960: *Luther's Principles of Biblical Interpretation*, London (Tyndale Historical Theology Lecture 1959).

Seventeenth to nineteenth centuries (2.4)

Carpenter, J. E. 1903: *The Bible in the Nineteenth Century*, London.

Delitzsch, Franz 1881: *Old Testament History of Redemption*, Edinburgh.

Frei, H. W. 1974: *The Eclipse of Biblical Narrative: A Study in Eighteenth and Nineteenth Century Hermeneutics*, New Haven/London.

Fritsch, C. T. 1951: 'The Interpreter at Work: V. Bengel, the Student of Scripture', *Int* 5: 203–215.

Glover, W. B. 1954: *Evangelical Nonconformists and Higher Criticism in the Nineteenth Century*, London.

Hengstenberg, E. W. 1829–35: *Christology of the Old Testament and a commentary on the Messianic predictions of the Prophets*, ET: Edinburgh, ^{2}1854–58 (German, 1829–35, ^{2}1854–57).

Johnston, O. R. 1951: 'The Puritan Use of the Old Testament', *EQ* 23: 183–209.

Krentz, E. 1975: *The Historical-Critical Method*, London.

Maier, G. 1974: *The End of the Historical-Critical Method*, ET: St Louis, 1977 (German, 1974).

Preuss, C. 1950: 'The Contemporary Relevance of Von Hofmann's Hermeneutical Principles', *Int* 4:311–321.

Rogerson, J. 1984: *Old Testament Criticism in the Nineteenth Century: England and Germany*, London.

Schleiermacher, F. 1821: *The Christian Faith*, ET: Edinburgh, 1928 (German, 1821, ^{2}1830).

Schütte, H. -W. 1970: 'Christlicher Glaube und Altes Testament bei Friedrich Schleiermacher' in *Fides et communicatio: Festschrift für Martin Doerne zum 70.Geburtstag* (ed. D. Rössler *et al.*), Göttingen: 291–310.

Smith, T. L. 1985: 'John Wesley and the Wholeness of Scripture', *Int* 39:246–262.

Smith, W. R. 1881: *The Old Testament in the Jewish Church: A Course of Lectures on Biblical Criticism*, London, ^{2}1892 (^{1}1881).

Stuhlmacher, P. 1975: *Historical Criticism and Theological Interpretation of Scripture*, ET: Philadelphia, 1977 (German, 1975).

Willi, T. 1971: *Herders Beitrag zum Verstehen des Alten Testaments* (BGBH 8), Tübingen.

See also Hayes & Prussner (1985): 1–142.

The developmental approach (2.5)

Bennett, W. H. 1893: 'Old Testament' in *Faith and Criticism* (Essays by Congregationalists), London: 1–47.

—1914: *The Value of the Old Testament for the Religion of Today*, London.

Davidson, A. B. 1904: *The Theology of the Old Testament*, Edinburgh.

Driver, S. R. 1905: 'The Permanent Religious Value of the Old Testament', *The Interpreter* 1: 10–21 (reprinted in *The Higher Criticism*: 71–88).

Grelot, P. 1962a: *Sens chrétien de l'Ancien Testament: Esquisse d'un traité dogmatique*, Tournai.

Heinisch, P. 1949–50: *History of the Old Testament*, ET: Collegeville, Minnesota, 1952 (German, 1949–50).

Kent, C. F. 1906: *The Origin and Permanent Value of the Old Testament*, London.

McKenzie, J. 1967: 'The Values of the Old Testament', *Concilium* 3.10:4–17.

Orr, J. 1906: *The Problem of the Old Testament, Considered with Reference to Recent Criticism*, London.

Ottley, R. L. 1897: *Aspects of the Old Testament*, London (Bampton Lectures, 1897).

Patton, F. L. 1926: *Fundamental Christianity*, New York.

Pierson, A. T. 1906: *The Bible and Spiritual Criticism*, London.

Robinson, H. W. 1913: *The Religious Ideas of the Old Testament*, London (²1956, revised by L. H. Brockington, has only minor changes).

Smith, G. A. 1899: *Modern Criticism and the Preaching of the Old Testament*, London, n.d. (lectures at Yale, 1899).

Vidler, A. 1934: *The Modernist Movement in the Roman Church: Its Origins and Outcome*, Cambridge.

Neo-Marcionism (2.6)

Andersen, F. I. 1975: 'Dietrich Bonhoeffer and the Old Testament', *RefTR* 34: 33–44.

Chandler, A. R. 1945: *Rosenberg's Nazi Myth*, New York.

Delitzsch, Friedrich 1920–21: *Die grosse Täuschung*, Stuttgart/Berlin, two volumes (I: 1920; II: 1921).

Kuske, M. 1967: *Das Alte Testament als Buch von Christus: Dietrich Bonhoeffers Wertung und Auslegung des Alten Testaments*, Göttingen n.d. (dissertation, 1967).

Leffler, S. 1935: *Christus im Dritten Reich der Deutschen: Wesen, Weg und Ziel der Kirchenbewegung "Deutsche Christen"*, Weimar, Thür.

Matthews, I. G. 1947: *The Religious Pilgrimage of Israel*, New York/London.

Mbiti, J. S. 1986: *Bible and Theology in African Christianity*, Nairobi.

Nicolaisen, C. 1966: *Die Auseinandersetzung um das Alte Testament im Kirchenkampf 1933–1945*, Hamburg (dissertation).

—1971: 'Die Stellung der "Deutschen Christen" zum Alten Testament' in *Zur Geschichte des Kirchenkampfes: Gesammelte Aufsätze II* (ed. H. Brunotte, Arbeiten zur Geschichte des Kirchenkampfes 26), Göttingen: 197–220.

Niemöller, W. 1956: *Die Evangelische Kirche im Dritten Reich: Handbuch des Kirchenkampfes*, Bielefeld.

Phillips, G. E. 1942: *The Old Testament in the World Church: With Special Reference to the Younger Churches*, London/Redhill (Lutterworth Library, 13).

Rosenberg, A. 1930: *Der Mythus des 20.Jahrhunderts: Eine Wertung der seelischgeistigen Gestaltkämpfe unserer Zeit*, Munich, [30]1934 ([1]1930).

Rupp, G. 1945: *Martin Luther: Hitler's Cause – or Cure?*, London/Redhill.

Sellin, E. 1921: *Das Alte Testament und die evangelische Kirche der Gegenwart*, Leipzig-Erlangen.

Shorter, A. (ed. and introduction) 1978: *African Christian Spirituality*, London.

Sovik, A. 1982: 'The Old Testament and Other "Old Testaments"' in *The Significance of Judaism for the Life and Mission of the Church: Report of a Consultation, August 1982*, Geneva 1983 (Lutheran World Federation): 55–61.

Tanner, E. S. 1942: *The Nazi Christ*, Tulsa, Oklahoma.

Wiener, P. F. 1945: *Martin Luther: Hitler's Spiritual Ancestor*, London.

The problem today (2.7)

Alter, R. 1981: *The Art of Biblical Narrative*, New York.

Barton, J. 1984b: 'Classifying Biblical Criticism', *JSOT* 29:19–35.

Burney, C. F. 1921: *The Gospel in the Old Testament*, Edinburgh.

Clines, D. J. A. *et al.* (ed.) 1982: *Art and Meaning: Rhetoric in Biblical Literature*, Sheffield (JSOT Supplement Series, 19).

CTC–CCA 1983: *Minjung Theology: People as the Subjects of History*, Maryknoll, New York (revised edition; [1]1981).

Elmslie, W. A. L. 1948: *How Came Our Faith: A Study of the Religion of Israel and its Significance for the Modern World*, Cambridge.

Fuliga, J. B. 1986: 'A Critique of Latin American Liberation Theology', *EAJT* 4.2:52–61.

Gottwald, N. K. 1979: *The Tribes of Yahweh: A Sociology of the Religion of Liberated Israel, 1250–1050 B.C.E.*, Maryknoll, New York.

Gunn, D. M. 1987: 'New Directions in the Study of Biblical Hebrew Narrative', *JSOT* 39:65–75.

Higgins, A. J. B. 1949: *The Christian Significance of the Old Testament*, London.

Kairos Theologians, The 1985: *The Kairos Document: Challenge to the Church*, Braamfontein.

Kraus, H. -J. 1956d: *Klagelieder (Threni)*, Neukirchen [2]1960 ([1]1956, BK 20).

—1960/78: *Psalmen*, Neukirchen, [5]1978 (completely revised, [1]1960, BK 15).

Long, B. O. 1988: 'A Figure at the Gate: Readers, Reading, and Biblical Theologians' in Childs Fs: 166–186.

Sternberg, M. 1985: *The Poetics of Biblical Narrative: Ideological Literature and the Drama of Reading*, Bloomington, Indiana.

Theissen, G. 1974–75: *The Social Setting of Pauline Christianity: Essays on Corinth*, ET: Philadelphia, 1982 (German, 1974–75).

—1977: *Sociology of Early Palestinian Christianity*, ET: Philadelphia, 1978 (German, 1977).

Welch, A. C. 1933: *The Preparation for Christ in the Old Testament*, Edinburgh.

Westermann, C. 1974–82: *Genesis*, ET: London/Minneapolis 1984–86

(German, 1974–82, three volumes, BK 1).

Wolff, H. W. 1961–: *Dodekapropheton*, Neukirchen (five volumes published so far, four of them in ET, BK 14).

Zimmerli, W. 1969: *Ezekiel*, ET: Philadelphia, 1979–83 (German, 1969, two volumes, BK 13).

On liberation theology see also works by Boff, Gutiérrez, Hanks & Kirk in the general bibliography.

Part 2

Four modern solutions

3

The New Testament as the essential Bible

3.1 Rudolf Bultmann

The first solution to the problem of the relationship between the Testaments that we shall investigate is that of Rudolf Bultmann, a noted German New Testament scholar in the middle of the twentieth century. At the time of the German Church Struggle he contributed to the debate about the Old Testament by an article entitled 'The Significance of the Old Testament for the Christian Faith' (1933a). In this article he affirmed the Old Testament to be part of the 'history out of which we come', so that it would be senseless to retain Christianity and reject the Old Testament: 'it is either-or: keep either both or neither' (pp. 20–21). He formulated the theological problem of the relationship between the Testaments by asking whether and to what extent the Old Testament can be revelation for the Christian faith and concluded that this is possible in an indirect way.

It is commonly thought that Bultmann rejected the Old Testament. Part of a sentence in his article, 'to the Christian faith the Old Testament is no longer revelation' (p. 31), has been quoted as his view of its relationship to the New, ignoring the next few words which read: 'as it has been, and still is, for the Jews'. But in fact, in spite of certain provocative and frequently misunderstood statements, Bultmann did not revive Marcion's notorious separation of the Testaments, nor did he yield to the pressure of National Socialist antipathy to the Old Testament. The Old Testament, though not a Christian book, was for Bultmann the

67

presupposition of the New Testament and Christianity.

Our first task is to understand clearly Bultmann's essay mentioned above and also his later essay on 'Prophecy and Fulfillment' (1949a). This will be followed in the following section (ch. 3.2) by a critique of his proposal.[1]

a. The significance of the Old Testament for the Christian faith

The developmental approach

Bultmann points out that the developmental approach (*cf.* above: ch. 2.5) treats the Bible as a source for understanding the historical development of religion, specifically the religions of Israel and the early church (1933a: 8–13). Moreover, it regards the Old Testament as the source of Christianity, in that the 'ethical monotheism' which was perfected in Jesus originated and developed in Israel. The cultic and nationalistic elements of the Old Testament were eventually subordinated to this spiritual faith in the preaching of the prophets, and Jesus simply continued – albeit in a distinctive and unsurpassed way – their message. It follows that the relationship between the Testaments is straightforward: the only difference between the two is progression. On this view the more sophisticated teaching in the New Testament – concerning Christology, eschatology, soteriology, *etc.* – is not merely unnecessary, but obscures the basic message of Jesus and therefore must be rejected as mythology.

The problem with this approach, according to Bultmann, is that it does not fit the New Testament. Elimination of sophisticated ideas as being mythology involves loss of the distinctively Christian element of the New Testament, its affirmation that God and man can meet only in the person of Jesus Christ. Moreover, the basic message of Jesus cannot be used as a critical standard for eliminating mythology, because it is not simply ethical teaching about the Fatherhood of God and love for others but an eschatological message which points to the dawn of a new age. Jesus' message itself, which is intimately connected in the New Testament with the Christian proclamation of Jesus' person, must therefore be regarded as mythological. It follows that the result

---

[1]Other writings of Bultmann concerning the relationship between the Testaments include those of 1940; 1948a; 1949b; 1950c and 1957a.

of the developmental approach is to remove the Christian element from Christianity, making it nothing more than a refined Judaism.

Bultmann refrains from forming a judgment on the developmental approach in general, however, arguing that its concern is with the historical relationship between the religions of the two Testaments and therefore irrelevant to the theological problem of their relationship. A truly theological approach to the problem will ask 'whether the Old Testament still has a meaning for the faith which perceives in Jesus Christ the revelation of God' (p. 12). In contrast to the objective developmental approach which does no more than analyse the relationship between historical phenomena, a subjective approach is required which will consider what is the significance of the Old Testament for the Christian faith.

An existential approach

Bultmann asks 'what basic possibility [the Old Testament] presents for an understanding of human existence (*Daseinsverständnis*)' (p. 13). This he claims is a 'genuinely historical' (*echt geschichtlich*) approach to the problem of the relationship between the Testaments because its concern is not simply to place events in the context of world history, but to discover their relevance to us as human beings (pp. 13–21).

Such a 'genuinely historical' approach to the Old Testament leads to expression of the relationship between the Testaments in terms of law and gospel. The Old Testament is the presupposition (*Voraussetzung*) of the New, not in the sense of religious evolution but in the sense that it is necessary first to be under the law before it is possible to comprehend Christ as the end of the law. Moreover, even when one is no longer under the law but under grace, faith is 'a reality only by constantly overcoming the old existence under the Law' (p. 15). So the law does not cease to exist for the Christian who is freed from it; but it ceases to be a means of justification.

When the Old Testament acts in this way as the presupposition of the New it loses its specifically Old Testament character. The cultic and ritual demands are now obsolete and the moral demands – though still valid – are not unique to the Old Testament since all know the law in this general sense (Rom. 1:32).

Further, since what is vital is that the law – rather than the Old Testament – be understood, it is not essential that the law be the Old Testament itself. Human beings may come to a realization of their nothingness simply through their own relationships with other people or through contemplation of some other history.

The reason for using the Old Testament is expedience: its expression of God's demand is exceptionally direct and clear.

Nevertheless, although as law it is addressed to 'a particular people who stand in a particular ethnic history which is not ours' (p. 17), the Old Testament confronts us with an understanding of existence that is relevant to us. This understanding of existence shows mankind to be subject to the unconditional moral demand of God, which is neither idealistic nor utilitarian but existential. We are creatures living in history who are called not to a timeless ideal but to temporal and historical behaviour in obedience to God.

This Old Testament understanding of existence is also that of the New Testament and Christianity, in contrast to the humanistic or idealistic understanding of existence which characterizes Greek thought. Modern history has both Greek and biblical roots, and so the Old Testament is an important part of that history and a proper understanding of human existence today depends on serious interaction with the Old Testament. In particular, the Old Testament is essential to understand the contemporary significance of Christianity. Thus Bultmann concludes that it would be senseless to hold onto Christianity and at the same time discard the Old Testament: the two must be accepted or rejected together.

The Old Testament as revelation

On an existential interpretation alone there would be no difference between the Testaments, since both have the same understanding of existence. A further question must therefore be considered (pp. 21–35): in what sense, if at all, is it right to treat the Old Testament as revelation for the Christian faith? To hear the Old Testament as Word of God is quite a different matter from the recognition that it is existentially part of Christian history.

In order to answer this question it is necessary first to define more precisely the relationship between law and gospel in the Old Testament. Existence under the law in the Old Testament is in the first place existence under grace, since it is by grace (in election and covenant) that God called his people into being and by grace (in forgiveness and faithfulness) that God keeps sinful and unfaithful Israel as his people. If 'gospel' is understood as 'the proclamation of God's grace for the sinner' it is certainly known in the Old Testament, even if not always in an equally radical way (Pss. 51; 90:7–8; 130; cf. 103:14–16). And God in the Old Testament requires first of all not moral behaviour but trust in his grace, that is, faith (Ps. 147:10–11;

Je. 9:23–24; Is. 45:23–25; 30:15; 7:9; 28:16).

It follows that Israel's sin is unbelief, the radical nature of which is perceived by the prophets: the people deserve nothing but judgment from God. Yet in this situation eschatological hope is born, as sin and judgment release the possibility of forgiveness and salvation by God's grace (Ezk. 36:22–27; 37:1–14; Je. 31:33–34). 'So far as Israel conceived the idea of God radically by grasping the ideas of sin and grace radically, the faith of the Old Testament is hope' (p. 28). In other words, although they are aware of its radical nature, the prophets experience the gospel of grace only partially: its fulfilment is yet to come. That fulfilment is in fact the distinctive element of the New Testament as compared with the Old.

Thus the difference between the Testaments becomes clear: in Jesus Christ God has inaugurated the new age. What God has done in Jesus is not an historical event in the same sense as the events which constituted Israel as a people and benefit succeeding generations of that people. God's eschatological act in Christ has shifted the locus of his revelation from ethnic history to personal existence. So Christians do not look for God's grace in past history but meet it existentially in the Word proclaimed to them. In contrast to Israel, whose existence depends on its history, the church is a community bound together by the message which it exists to proclaim.

The answer to the question of whether the Old Testament may be considered revelation for the Christian faith now begins to emerge. According to Bultmann, Israel and the church are fundamentally different entities and therefore Old Testament history is not Christian history. Grace in the Old Testament is specifically directed to Israel, whereas the law is an expression of God's universal moral demand on mankind. Therefore the Old Testament, although in itself both gospel and law, is for the Christian only law. It follows the Old Testament history is not revelation for Christians in the same way as for Jews.

This does not necessarily mean that the Old Testament itself, apart from its history, cannot be revelation for the Christian faith. The possibility remains open that Christians may claim the Old Testament as God's Word to them, as an expression of what is made fully clear only in Christ. This is the approach of the New Testament and the early church, by whom the Old Testament is interpreted eschatologically, as written for Christians and in Christ receiving its true meaning. However Bultmann considers such 'scriptural proof' to be inconsistent with the original meaning of the Old Testament and unable to convince and produce genuine faith. Moreover, this approach results in finding once more what is already known in Christ and thus effectively denies that the Old Testament is God's Word in the true sense.

So the Old Testament is not revelation for Christians in the historical sense as it is for the Jews, nor in the direct eschatological sense as it is treated in the New Testament. The question still remains, however, whether there is any legitimate sense in which the Old Testament may be understood as Word of God by those who have read the New Testament. Bultmann assumes that Jesus Christ is God's Word to mankind and argues that any other words which elucidate this Word are therefore God's Word indirectly (*in vermittelter Weise*). The Old Testament contains an understanding of human existence which is normative for Christian life, *i.e.* human creatureliness and sin as revealed by the law and God's grace as expressed in the gospel. Faith takes hold of the Old Testament, sees in it an image of its own existence, and claims it as God's Word. In this indirect sense the Old Testament may be considered revelation for the Christian faith. If this is done, two conditions apply: the Old Testament must be used literally (though without its original reference to Israel) and only to the extent that it really prepares for the Christian understanding of existence.

b. Prophecy and fulfilment

Prediction

Bultmann begins his second essay with the claim that the early church understood prophecy as prediction, the foretelling of future events, and fulfilment as the occurrence of what was foretold (1949a: 50–55). He distinguishes two aspects of this understanding of prophecy. First, the Old Testament contains messianic prophecies, which are concerned with the *eschaton* (final event) that has become present for the church. Secondly, the Old Testament as a whole is understood to be a book of prophecy whose words point to Christ. Thus the early church's use of the Old Testament combines Jewish eschatological tradition with the allegorical tradition of Hellenistic culture.

Such a view of prophecy and fulfilment, Bultmann argues, is impossible today. The New Testament approach may be followed when it treats Old Testament prophecies as eschatological promises of salvation, but not when it ignores the original meaning of the biblical text. Often the New Testament writers read a Christian meaning into Old Testament texts so that prophecy is only recognized retrospectively, after the fulfilment has occurred. No doubt this method was valuable in the apologetic of the early church, but it has several shortcomings. It is theologically untenable, because difficult doctrines such as that of the crucifixion are not overcome by pointing out that they were prophesied in the Old Testament but by understanding their real significance. It is arbitrary, since the interpretation is not exegesis but eisegesis (reading meanings into the text). It is unnecessary, since the texts are made to affirm Christian truths which are known already. Moreover, in spite of its superficial value in defending the Christian faith, this method really has the effect of concealing the true stumbling-block of faith and the proper way to deal with it.

History

In the nineteenth century von Hofmann advanced a view of prophecy as history: the history of Israel is prophetic history which finds its fulfilment in Christ and the church (Bultmann 1949a: 55–58). Thus prophecy is not the foretelling of future historical events but the movement of history towards a goal. Each word and event of the Old Testament is to be understood in its plain historical meaning and has prophetic significance only by virtue of its place in the prophetic history. The goal of history is Christ and so history is a prophecy of Christ.

Von Hofmann's view, according to Bultmann, is a theologically irrelevant philosophy of history. It cannot prove Christ, since Christ must be recognized as the goal of history before this view becomes possible, and in any case the real significance of Christ cannot be confirmed by a philosophical view but only by faith. The attempt to understand prophecy as history is a move in the right direction but 'according to the New Testament, Christ is the end of salvation history . . . not in the sense that he signifies the goal of historical development, but because he is its eschatological end' (p. 58).

Covenant, kingdom and people of God

Dissatisfied with the ideas of prediction and history, Bultmann works out an understanding of prophecy on the basis of the New Testament conviction that Christ is the eschatological end of salvation history. His method is to examine three Old Testament concepts which are eschatologically reinterpreted in the New Testament (pp. 59–72).

First, God's *covenant* with his people is based on mutual loyalty, originated by God's election and maintained by the people's obedience. Bultmann argues that in popular thought this obedience is conceived primarily as sacrificial worship, a condition which can realistically be fulfilled by a people as such. If it was conceived in moral terms, obedience could only be expected of the individual within the people, and the covenant would no longer be a relationship between God and the people as an entity. The natural consequence of this popular belief is to root the security of an individual not in his own moral behaviour but in being a member of the chosen people.

It became clear to the Old Testament prophets, as to John the Baptist and Jesus, that there was a problem. They objected to assumptions that God was linked to the land and that the covenant was unbreakable. They were convinced of the necessity for a moral aspect to the covenant, though this meant that it could no longer be the relationship between God and an empirical people. 'God's covenant with a people whose individuals suffice for the moral demands of God as members of the people is an eschatological concept, because such a people is not a real empirical and historical, but an eschatological, dimension' (p. 61). So the New Testament reinterprets eschatologically the Old Testament idea of covenant, affirming that the promises of Jeremiah (31:31–34) and Ezekiel (37:26–28) have been fulfilled in the church. Thus Bultmann argues that the church is not an empirical and historical people: although it is inaugurated by the death of Christ and membership is linked with the sacraments, these do not have the same historical significance as the Sinai event and the worship of the Old Testament had for Israel. The New Testament counterpart to the Old Testament covenant institutions is not to be found in any material observance but in the spiritual institution of salvation. 'The new covenant is a radically eschatological dimension, that is, a dimension outside the world, and to belong to it takes its members out of the world' (p. 63).

Secondly, Bultmann points out that it was common among Semitic peoples to represent their gods as kings and Israel was no exception. The *kingdom of God*, a tenet of Israelite faith from pre-exilic times, was celebrated every New Year in an enthronement festival. Its implications were that God expected obedience from his people, acted as their judge and helped them in war.

The end of the monarchy and God's abandonment of his people to Babylon was naturally a crisis for the belief in the kingdom of God. In the event, however, the belief was not discarded but was re-formed into an eschatological concept. Both during and after the Exile it was obvious that God's kingdom had not yet been established in the world, and so prophets projected their hopes further into the future while apocalyptists looked beyond the present age to a supernatural age of salvation. Jesus took up this eschatological view of the kingdom of God, 'no longer understood in the sense of Old Testament theocracy, as the dominion of the divine king in the liberated land . . . but as the wonder of a new era for the world breaking in from heaven' (p. 66). For Jesus and Paul the kingdom of God was a present reality, the new age was realized in the formation of the church:

> The rule of God and so of Christ is therefore something completely different from what Old Testament prophecy had expected. It is eschatological and supramundane in its entirety; and the man who has a part in it is, as it were, already taken out of the world, so that he lives no longer 'according to the flesh,' however much he still lives 'in the flesh' (2 Cor. 10:3) (p. 67).

Thirdly, Bultmann argues that in the Old Testament the concept of the *people of God* is shown to be in conflict with that of a national state. Gideon recognized the impossibility of serving more than one ruler (Jdg. 8:23), and the monarchy was subject to continual prophetic criticism for neglecting its responsibility to God as the true monarch. So theocracy was an ideal rather than a reality during much of the Old Testament period. After the Exile Israel might perhaps be described as a theocracy, but by this time it had forefeited its existence as a state and become a religious community. Such a community, limited to Jews and bound together by its exclusive worship, was scarcely the realization of the people of God.

A new conception of the people of God was introduced by the New Testament claim that in Christ the new age has arrived. Now the church has become the people of God, the true Israel, not an 'empirical historical entity' but an 'eschatological unit'. Membership of the people is no longer through birth but through individual calling and setting apart by God. So the idea of the people of God, like the ideas of the covenant and the kingdom of God, becomes in the New Testament an eschatological idea which is realized in Christ and his church.

Miscarriage and promise

In the light of his study of these three concepts Bultmann develops a view of prophecy as miscarriage and promise (pp. 72–75). He argues that Old Testament Jewish history 'is fulfilled in its inner contradiction, its miscarriage (*Scheitern*). An inner contradiction pervades the self-consciousness and the hope of

Israel and its prophets' (p. 72). The miscarriage of history shows the impossibility of realizing the covenant, kingdom of God and people of God within the historical community of Israel. In so doing, however, the miscarriage becomes a promise since God's grace is available only to those who recognize the complete impossibility of their situation. Thus the fulfilment is not the result of historical development (which is miscarriage) but the result of encounter with the grace of God (which is an eschatological new creation).

Such an interpretation of Old Testament history, Bultmann claims, follows from Paul's view of the law as a false way of salvation, which must however be known in order to understand faith as the true way (*cf.* Gal. 3:22–24; Rom. 10:4; 11:32). He concludes:

> Faith requires the backward glance into Old Testament history as a history of failure, and so of promise, in order to know that the situation of the justified man arises only on the basis of this miscarriage (p. 75).

3.2 Critique

Bultmann's solution to the problem of the relationship between the Testaments raises many important issues. We shall look in particular at his existential methodology, the nature of history, the antithesis between law and gospel, his idea of the miscarriage of history and his understanding of the people of God.[2]

a. Existence

G. Ernest Wright (1969) categorizes Bultmann's approach to the relationship between the Testaments as 'existentialist Christomonism'. Thus for Bultmann the concept of existence is 'the

---

[2]The most important work on Bultmann's view of the relationship between the Testaments is a symposium edited by B. W. Anderson entitled *The Old Testament and Christian Faith* (*OTCF*, 1964), which includes a translation of his 1933 essay and responses by Anderson, Cullmann, Dillenberger, J. L. McKenzie, Michalson, A. Richardson, J. M. Robinson, Vischer, Voegelin, Westermann, and G. E. Wright. Other studies include Westermann (1955); Barr (1965) and N. J. Young (1966).

methodological starting point of theology' (1930: 92), and the central distinctive characteristic of the New Testament is the idea that 'man's relation to God is bound to the person of Jesus' (1933a: 11). Existential theology is undoubtedly one of the most basic influences on Bultmann's theology (cf. Macquarrie 1955), so it is not surprising that he formulates the problem of the relationship between the Testaments in terms of the possibilities for human existence which they express.

There is, of course, no inherent objection to an existential investigation of the problem and Bultmann's investigation is not without profit. He shows effectively, for example, something of the historical value of the Old Testament for modern Christendom (1933a: 20–21; cf. 1950c). Also, by means of the concept of 'presupposition', he illuminates the way in which the Old Testament embodies God's moral demand and thus functions as preparation for the New (1933a: 15–17).

A fundamental limitation of the existential method, however, is its own self-limiting nature. By definition its concern is with human existence and therefore only indirectly with God. Bultmann's existential interpretation of Pauline theology, for instance, is concerned 'with God not as He is in Himself but only with God as He is significant for man', so that 'Paul's theology can best be treated as his doctrine of man' (1948a: 191). It follows that existential interpretation of the Bible, however illuminating, will be inadequate because the Bible is concerned not only with mankind and its experience of God but with God, who in the beginning created the universe (Gn. 1:1) and in the end will be all in all (1 Cor. 15:28). Moreover, if the Christ-event is relevant only to the existence of the individual, as Bultmann claims, it is not the fulfilment of the promise of the Old Testament which embraced not only individuals but the people of God and the world (Westermann 1964).

In any case, as Bultmann (1933a: 20) himself recognizes, the result of an existential investigation of the problem of the relationship between the Testaments is merely to show that both have the same understanding of human existence. To determine the difference between the two it is necessary to formulate the problem in a specifically theological way: 'what is meant by saying that the Old Testament is revelation, and to what extent, if any, can the Christian proclamation really be related to the Old Testament understood as God's revelation?' (1933a: 21).

b. History

The nature and significance of history is one of the most funda-mental issues raised by Bultmann's work.[3] It is unnecessary to go into this in detail here, but two points must be mentioned. First, Bultmann recognizes that there is a historical (*historisch*) relation-ship between the Testaments (1949b: 15–56; *cf.* 1933a: 8; 1948a: 108–121): the Old Testament is a historical document which in many ways has influenced the formation of the New Testament. Secondly, Bultmann argues that it is more profitable to consider the relationship between the Testaments in a 'gen-uinely historical' (*echt geschichtlich*) way (1933a: 13–15), by which he means that one should try to reactualize the understanding of human existence expressed in the Old Testament in order to gain an understanding of one's own existence:

> Thus the Old Testament is the presupposition of the New. Not in the sense of a *historical* (*historisch*) view, as though the historical phenomenon of the Christian religion had become possible only on the basis of the evolving history of religion attested by the Old Testa-ment; but rather in the *material* (*sachlich*) sense that man must stand under the Old Testament if he wants to understand the New.

The problem with this view is that Bultmann, while emphasizing the existential significance of the past, fails to grasp adequately another aim of serious historical study, namely to find out what actually happened at a particular point in time and space (*cf.* Wright 1964). The implications of this method are rejection of the world and history, features which characterize Gnosticism (Voegelin 1964). The fault in Bultmann's approach is not in what he says, which is generally unexceptionable, but in the omission from his system of the question of reality. An important factor in both Old and New Testaments is that God acts in real history to bring about salvation (*cf.* Richardson 1964a; see further below: ch. 6.2.e).

---

[3]See also 1957a; *cf.* A. Richardson (1964); Rottenberg (1964); N. J. Young (1969); Thiselton (1980); Nash (1984). A bibliography of nearly one thousand works concerning theology and history is given by R. North (1973).

c. Law and gospel

One of the classic expressions of the relationship between the Testaments is Luther's antithesis between law and gospel (*cf.* above: ch. 2.3.a). Bultmann gives his provisional approval to this, attributing its truth to the fact that the Reformation period still had 'a genuinely historical relation to the Old Testament' (1933a: 14). He argues that on this basis existence under the law is the presupposition of existence under grace. Thus the Old Testament is the presupposition of the New Testament, since the gospel can be understood only by one who is under the divine law, which is expressed with incomparable clarity in the Old Testament (*cf.* 1957b; Michalson 1964). The message of the gospel is that Christ, the end of the law, gives freedom from the law and opens up a new way to holiness by means of grace (Bultmann 1940).

At this point Bultmann's argument is to be rejected. Paul does of course contrast law and gospel as false and true ways of salvation (Gal. 3 – 4 *etc.*) but that does not mean that there is anything wrong with the law in itself, so long as it is used according to its original intention (which was not to bring about salvation). Siegwalt (1971) and Braulik (1984) have shown that both Testaments essentially consider the law to be the consequence rather than the presupposition of the covenant (*cf.* Zimmerli 1975). Those who had been saved by God's grace were expected to respond in obedience to God's law (*cf.* Hals 1980). It is therefore more appropriate to treat 'gospel and law' as complementary than 'law and gospel' as antithetical (*cf.* Barth 1935; Dodd 1951a).

Bultmann is aware of this objection to his thesis and attempts to forestall it by showing that the Old Testament contains the idea of grace as well as that of law, so that from its own point of view the Old Testament may be considered to be both law and gospel (1933a: 22–31). Moreover, he appears to admit the priority of grace over law in the Old Testament when he writes: 'the people are not constituted as a people by first obeying the Law but, rather, God's grace precedes, so that obedience is always to occur through faith in God's prevenient and electing grace' (1933a: 23). This however does not affect his acceptance of the law/gospel antithesis, since he goes on to argue that grace in the Old Testament is different from grace in the New Testament. In the Old Testament grace is bound to the history of Israel whereas in the New it is eschatological, God's act in Jesus Christ having ended his gracious activity in the people of Israel. Thus Bultmann concludes that from the Christian point of view the Old Testament is no longer gospel but only law (1933a: 29–31).[4]

d. Miscarriage and promise

Probably the most original, important and controversial aspect of Bultmann's solution to the problem of the relationship between the Testaments is his interpretation of prophecy as miscarriage and promise (1949a: 72–75). He argues that Old Testament history contains an inner contradiction between the ideal of the people of God and the reality of the empirical community; and that the failure to resolve this contradiction resulted in the miscarriage of history. Paradoxically, however, this miscarriage amounts to a promise, since it proves the impossibility of human ways and directs humanity to the grace of God, which alone can deal with the situation.

This idea is in fact not entirely original. Attention may be drawn to the remark of McFadyen (1903: 347) that the Old Testament 'by its repeated failures pointed men to something more strong and saving than itself'. More recently Phythian-Adams (1934) has argued that Christianity is 'the triumphant sequel' of Judaism, in which 'the tragedy of the Old Covenant is transfigured in the glory of the New' (p. 5). Nevertheless Bultmann's proposal is distinctive in its radical assertion of contradiction and miscarriage in Old Testament history and demands a serious response. Such a response is provided by Miskotte (1963: 167):

> The consequences of this conception are enormous and disastrous. For this means that not only is the meaning of the Old Testament history found solely in profound meaninglessness, but also that no meaningful history can be ascribed to the New Testament community; the new beginning, inaugurated by Christ, is in no sense the beginning of a real historical development ... The inevitable result of this is a failure to appreciate the Law, a withdrawal from history, a depreciation of the world, a negation of

---

[4]On law and gospel, see also Hirsch (*cf.* below: ch. 3.3.a); Thielicke (1948); Knight (1962); Sanders (1975); Fuller (1980) and Chiu (1984); *cf.* Barclay (1986).

creation, a deafness to the typical Old Testament affirmation of god-given life.

In short, Bultmann's existential method involves depreciation of history and because of this it cannot deal adequately with the Old Testament, which is essentially a historical document. The conclusion must be drawn that Bultmann's proposal, perceptive and illuminating as it is, does not fit the Bible (*cf.* Zimmerli 1952: 117–120; Marquardt 1968: 636).

e. People of God

Another element of Bultmann's proposal which must be questioned is his view of the people of God. In the Old Testament, on the one hand, he says that 'God's forgiveness is inextricably tied up with the destiny of the people' and 'so far as man belongs to this people, he can take comfort in the grace of God' (1933a: 29; *cf.* 1957a: 21–22). In the New Testament, on the other hand, 'the message of the forgiving grace of God in Jesus Christ is not a historical account about a past event, but . . . addresses each person immediately as God's Word' (1933a: 30; *cf.* 1957a: 31–32). The Church is therefore 'not a sociological entity, an ethnic or cultural community bound together by the continuity of history; but is constituted by the proclaimed Word of God's forgiveness in Christ and is the community of this proclamation' (1933a: 30–31). So Bultmann concludes that the church has no history as ethnic, national and cultural communities have their history.[5]

This view is at variance with biblical teaching. In the Old Testament salvation was not automatic through membership of the people: it was this very presumption that was one of Israel's greatest failings. On the contrary, salvation was given to Israelites only on the condition of obedience (Dt. 30:15–20) and the possibility of finding God and salvation was open also to non-Israelites (Ruth; Is. 56:3–8). In the New Testament, moreover, salvation is tied to the church in the sense that it is offered to those who identify themselves with Christ in this particular

---

[5]1933a: 31; *cf.* 1949a: 62. His view is rather similar to that of the Jewish scholar Martin Buber (1951), who contrasts two types of faith: in early Israel faith (*'emûnâ*) is trust in someone and is an attribute of a nation; in early Christianity faith (*pistis*) is acknowledgment of the truth of something and is an attribute of individuals. For a criticism of this simplistic view, see Vriezen (1966: 123n.).

way, though again it is not automatic but dependent on a personal relationship with God (Acts 2:37–47; Eph. 2:11–22). The church is indeed brought together by its message and exists to proclaim it, but it is not thereby prevented from being a historical and cultural community, a 'sociological entity'. There is, of course, a contrast between the Old Testament people of God as a nation based on political and military power and the New Testament people of God as an international religious community without any political power (Westermann 1978: 218–221). But although history does not have the same significance in a spiritual community as in an ethnic one, the church nevertheless has a history and believes God to be at work in that history.

Bultmann (1949a) also claims that the covenant, kingdom of God and people of God are ideals that were shown to be unrealizable in Israel as a historical entity. However, although it is true that the reality fell far short of the ideal, it does not necessarily follow that the ideal was unrealizable. On the contrary, the people who entered into covenant with God at Sinai were given perfectly realistic moral and ceremonial obligations to keep as an expression of their loyalty. They broke the covenant not because they *could* not keep these obligations – in which case they would scarcely have been considered guilty – but because they *would* not keep them. So also the kingdom of God was not an unrealizable ideal: the problem was not that Israel could not be a theocracy but that she refused to be one and demanded a human king to rule her like the other nations.

One consequence of Bultmann's contrast between Old Testament Israel and the New Testament church is his first condition for Christian reading of the Old Testament as God's Word, *i.e.* 'that the Old Testament is used in its original sense, although without its original reference to the Israelite people and their history' (1933a: 34). In this Bultmann reveals an inner contradiction in his approach: he insists on historical-critical principles of interpretation, so that the Old Testament is understood in 'its original sense'; and yet in order to fit his theory of a radical contrast between Israel and the church he has to exclude the most fundamental aspect of that original sense, the Old Testament's reference to Israel and its history.[6]

---

[6]On the 'people of God', see Dahl (1956); Cazelles (1966); Ottaviani Fs (1966); Bruce (1968: 51–67); Ehrhardt (1968) and Goldingay (1987: 59–96). On the relationship between Israel and the church, see below: ch. 9.3.

f. A relationship of contrast

The central idea which may be drawn from Bultmann's solution to the problem of the relationship between the Testaments is that the New Testament is the essential Bible and the Old Testament its non-Christian presupposition. Other important aspects include the antithesis between law and gospel, the view of Old Testament history as miscarriage (and thereby promise) and the contrast between Israel and the church. The dominant characteristic of Bultmann's solution is therefore 'contrast': he assumes that the New Testament is the real Bible and categorizes the Old Testament as theologically secondary, obsolete and non-Christian.

It would be foolish to dismiss the work of so important a theologian as Bultmann too quickly. He has been accused of Marcionism (*e.g.* Surburg 1974) but in fact, in spite of certain similarities between his approach and that classic heresy, Bultmann does not follow Marcion's separation of the god of the Old Testament from the God of the New. Moreover, unlike Marcion, Bultmann is happy to retain the Old Testament in the church as a historical document and even with certain qualifications as the indirect Word of God (*cf.* Marlé 1956: 482; Michalson 1964). The perceptiveness with which Bultmann has analysed certain aspects of the problem is not to be doubted and his work contains valuable insights into biblical theology. Nevertheless a number of fundamental objections to his solution have been indicated, in particular that he bases it on an understanding of existence which involves depreciation of Old Testament history, and that he misunderstands the Bible in his conceptions of law and gospel, the miscarriage of history and the people of God.

3.3 Comparison: other 'New Testament' solutions

It has been shown in the previous section that Bultmann assesses the Old Testament negatively – or at least not very positively – as the non-Christian presupposition of the New Testament, which records a history of miscarriage and is to be contrasted with the New Testament by means of the law/gospel antithesis.

Now we shall look at and evaluate the proposals of four other scholars who offer 'New Testament' solutions to the problem of the relationship between the Testaments, *i.e.* solutions which consider the New Testament to be the essential Bible and the Old Testament in some way inferior or less important.

a. Emanuel Hirsch

Hirsch was a New Testament scholar who supported the 'German Christian' movement in the 1930s (see above: ch. 2.6). He took the New Testament to be the essential Bible, and emphasized the contrast between the Testaments. However, for Hirsch the Old Testament was not the presupposition of the New but its antithesis. It has no direct relevance to the Christian, although it serves to illuminate the distinctive nature of Christianity as gospel by presenting its opposite: legalistic Judaism. The characteristic theme of Hirsch's approach is 'law and gospel' (*cf.* above: ch. 3.2.c; von Rad 1937) and he interprets it in the most radical way possible so that the two are irreconcilably contrasted. This view was particularly attractive in Nazi Germany and lent weight to contemporary anti-Semitic rejection of the Old Testament, although Hirsch himself did not advocate this. He recognized that the Old Testament has a limited value for Christian preaching (1936a) and asserted that in the history of Christianity it has been blessed with God's authority as a preacher of the law (1935:8). Hirsch's solution to the problem of the relationship between the Testaments is even more extreme than that of Bultmann: its implication is virtual dissolution of the relationship.

b. Friedrich Baumgärtel

Baumgärtel's solution has certain similarities to that of Bultmann, especially in its assumptions that the Old Testament is to be understood through the spectacles of the New and that there is a contrast between the two, but there are also important differences between his view and Bultmann's.

His major work is entitled *Promise* (*Verheissung*) and was written about twenty years after Bultmann's essay. He propounds a threefold thesis (1952: 7).[7] First, the Christian faith is founded

---

[7]Many of Baumgärtel's other works also concern the relationship between the Testaments, *e.g.* those of 1925; 1938; 1954a; 1954b & 1967. There have been many critiques of Baumgärtel's work, *e.g.* Köhler (1953: 248–251); von Rad (1953b); Westermann (1955: 128–133) and L. Schmidt (1975).

on God's 'promise in Christ' (Eph. 3:6), which Baumgärtel defines by means of a creed: Jesus Christ, my Lord, has saved me, a lost and condemned man, from every sin; so that I may be his, live under him in his kingdom, and serve him in eternal righteousness, innocence and bliss. Secondly, God has authenticated his promise by the passion and resurrection of Jesus Christ. Thirdly, the Christian participates in the promise through the Gospel. This threefold basis of faith is developed and used by Baumgärtel to determine the nature of promise in the Bible and thus to establish how the Old Testament is to be understood from the point of view of the Gospel.

Promise in Christ

The New Testament, according to Baumgärtel (1952: 7–27), conceives 'promise' as an absolutely valid pledge made by God. Its characteristic aspects are:

- facticity (in the promise God is presently active);
- existence (the promise establishes and supports existence);
- judgment (realization of the promise is also judgment on sin);
- grace (the promise is given by God's grace);
- universality (the promise is valid for all believers, Jews and Gentiles); and
- futurity (the Old Testament promise of the future is understood by the New Testament to express a present gift, since it has come true in Christ).

This concept of promise has a double relationship to the Old Testament promise: the promise in Christ includes the promise of the Old Testament, though the promise in Christ itself cannot be found in the Old Testament.

There are many individual promises in the Old Testament, but beneath all these stands one basic promise, the statement of grace: 'I am the Lord your God'. The preaching of the Old Testament interprets this characteristically in terms of law and nation, so that in practice it is quite different from the promise in Christ. However it is this basic promise – from which every promise of the Old Testament derives its essence – which is relevant for Christian faith.

The promise in Christ offers salvation which is to be appropriated in faith; and faith, according to the New Testament, is simply to hold on to the promise (1952: 37–39; cf. 1954a: 151). Thus Baumgärtel defines the basis of Christian experience and he then elaborates its implications. The Christian, he argues, experiences the revelation of the existence of the transcendent God together with awareness of his or her own worldliness. Christians also experience a sense that this divine revelation is intended for them and yet it frightens them; that God opens the way to blessing and also judges their sin.

The Old Testament as promise
The Old Testament is theologically understood in faith if by faith its message is conceived as promise, according to Baumgärtel (1952: 39–64). Thus the experience of Old Testament people under the basic promise corresponds to that of the Christian, although the two are not identical. In the Old Testament God is revealed as the living Lord and man as a mortal creature; this divine revelation confronts mankind under the law with the demand of God's will; and God reveals his will in the law and prophets to judge sin and grant blessing. So Baumgärtel, like Bultmann (see above: ch. 3.2.a), recognizes an essential congruity between the conceptions of human existence in the Old and New Testaments. There are indeed important differences, in particular that the Old Testament does not know the New Testament concept of eternal life, nor does it conceive an individual to be in relationship with God other than as a member of the people of Israel. Nevertheless, he considers that Israel under God's basic promise fundamentally experiences God as the revealed Lord just as Christians under the promise in Christ experience him as their Lord, although the distinctively Old Testament character of the Old Testament experience must not be ignored.

Baumgärtel has argued earlier that the promise in Christ includes the promise of the Old Testament. It follows that the Old Testament is in fact old and therefore abolished. Christ is the confirmation of God's basic promise but not of the way in which the Old Testament conceives the realization of the promise and the blessing which accompanies it. By faith Christians have living communion with God, something for which Old Testament believers can only wait. Such waiting is abolished for Christians, whose life under the promise in Christ is based on faith in the certainty of present salvation.

It is questionable, however, whether it is valid to draw such a strong contrast between Old and New Testament man. Baumgärtel admits that there is a sense in which the Old Testament is not abolished for Christians. Those within the new covenant are fellow-travellers with those of the old covenant, experiencing under the divine promise a history which – like that of Israel – is salvation (and disaster) history. To the Christian, as to Israel, God has revealed himself and opened the way of faith; the Holy Spirit calls, illumines and sanctifies in order to incorporate into the one Christian church; and the cross of Christ judges so that freedom may be achieved.

The Christian understanding of the Old Testament

The implication of Baumgärtel's argument for Christian understanding of the Old Testament is twofold (1952: 64–71).

First, the Old Testament is the present word of God to Christians, to those who stand under the promise in Christ. Christians understand the Old Testament as a witness to God's basic promise, which has become a reality for them through Christ, and thus the Old Testament speaks to them of Jesus Christ. It does not only judge and humble but also raises up and imparts power, thus becoming gospel to the Christian.

Secondly, according to Baumgärtel, the Old Testament is relevant for the Christian faith only when understood as promise. Many understand it in terms of prediction (*cf.* below: ch. 8.1.b) but such an understanding is irrelevant to faith since Christian existence cannot be based on human insight but only on trust in God's grace in Christ, the realization of the promise. Christological interpretation is also inappropriate because the Old Testament does not develop a Christology by making statements about the person, office and work of Jesus Christ. Thus Baumgärtel concludes that the Old Testament is related to Jesus Christ not primarily by prediction or Christology but in its basic promise – 'I am the Lord your God' – which the Christian faith affirms to have come true in Jesus Christ.

Several consequences for theology and preaching follow from Baumgärtel's argument (1952: 128–159). The Old Testament message is characterized as promise, a concept derived not from Old Testament promises but from the New Testament understanding of promise. Old Testament interpretation cannot be based on prediction and fulfilment, nor on typology, but only on the New Testament's own principle of interpretation: promise in Christ. Preaching of the promise from the Old Testament is simple on the theological level but difficult on the practical level, since the 'holy simplicity' of the basic promise has to be communicated in a meaningful way to the ordinary person in the street.

A relationship of contrast

Like Bultmann, Baumgärtel considers the relationship between the Testaments to be a relationship of contrast. He claims that the Old Testament idea of promise is closely linked to the law and the people of Israel, in contrast to the New Testament idea which is characterized by grace and universality (1952: 7–27). Moreover the Old Testament does not know the New Testament ideas of eternal life and personal relationship with God in the present (1952: 40, 49–53; cf. 1954a: 146–147). Baumgärtel's clearest expression of this contrast, however, is to be found in an article published two years later than his book: 'the Old Testament is the witness of faith from a strange religion' (1954a: 147). He argues that from the perspective of the history of religions it is indisputable that Israelite religion is different from Christian religion (1954a: 138); and in practical terms Christians find they cannot understand the Old Testament because it belongs to a radically different situation in the history of piety (1954a: 147–149). Thus for Baumgärtel the Old Testament can be understood only as *Old* Testament (1952: 49–53; 1954a: 150).

A relationship of witness

Another important aspect of Baumgärtel's view of the relationship between the Testaments is the idea of 'witness', that is, he understands the Old Testament as a witness to the promise in Christ. This is possible in two ways: the Old Testament is the witness of God's realization through Christ of his basic promise; and the Christian affirms that Christ has realized the basic promise of the Old Testament (1952: 64–71). In itself, to be sure, the Old Testament would not be understood in this way; but Christians can recognize the Old Testament to be a witness of God's promise in Jesus Christ, as they interpret it on the basis of the prior understanding given by the New Testament (1954a: 134–139; cf. 1954b: 298–303). Thus it is clear that for Baumgärtel the New Testament is the essential Bible, though the Old Testament is also of continuing value if it is understood in the light of the New.

c. Franz Hesse

Hesse (1960a) states clearly his view of the superiority of the New Testament over the Old. He argues that the New Testament is more directly related to Christians than the Old is and therefore has a higher position. Yet his judgment on the Old Testament is not entirely negative and he recognizes that it does have authority for the Christian (1959: 293).

Perhaps the two most important concepts in Hesse's view of the relationship between the Testaments are those of 'promise' and 'salvation history'. In a similar way to Baumgärtel, although he does not explicitly base his argument on Baumgärtel's work, Hesse develops the concept of 'promise' as the key to Old Testament interpretation (1966: ch. 4). He understands the concept to have three aspects – pledge, factic gift and eschatological blessing – and affirms that beyond the form of Old Testament promises as human predictions there is a basic promise which is determinative for the message of the whole Old Testament. He asserts moreover that in the Old Testament God's salvation history is seen 'as the history of promise, promise subsequently redeemed in Christ' (1959: 294). Or, to put it another way, since this promise is expressed in words, 'in, with, and under the Old Testament Word, witness is borne to the redemptive activity of God which finds its *telos* [end] in Jesus Christ'.

At this point Hesse draws attention to a problem which has concerned many scholars, namely that the biblical picture of salvation history is different in some respects from that reconstructed by historical criticism (1959: 295–299). He writes:

> The Old Testament does indeed set out to describe the redemptive activity of God which happens in, with, and under the history of Israel; but the Old Testament witnesses have a conception of the course of this history which does not agree with the actual course (1959: 295).

Because he accepts the results of historical criticism, Hesse considers the Old Testament presentation of history to be defective. In the New Testament, on the other hand, history is crucially important and there are only secondary differences between what the New Testament says and what actually happened.

Thus there is a difference between the function of history in the two Testaments, according to Hesse. The New Testament is superior to the Old because its witness is based on real historical events and so constitutive for Christian faith; whereas the witness of the Old Testament often contradicts the real basis of salvation history and so is not constitutive for Christian faith, though it 'smooths the way' for it and deepens our understanding of it.

Hesse claims not only that the Old Testament gives an incomplete picture of salvation history, but also that it records human response to God's words and activity which does not always witness to salvation history but can even go directly against it (1959: 299–304). Human listening can misunderstand or disobey God's voice: indeed, every response to God's word in the Old Testament is inadequate and often also misconceived or even perverted. Hesse explains that this happens because the faithful people of the Old Testament live in a situation where God's revelation has not yet been clearly received. From the viewpoint of the history of religions, it could be said: 'the Old Testament religion is something qualitatively different from the faith of the New Testament' (p. 300). Yet even in the error and disobedience of the Old Testament, God is present, since it was he who ordered history in such a way that salvation history includes a history of condemnation. Therefore Hesse concludes that all of the Old Testament may be understood as a witness of the Word of God, which addresses Christians insofar as they are still on the way to salvation and thus Old Testament people (1959: 304–313).

Hesse's view of the relationship between the Testaments clearly emphasizes the value of the New Testament and depreciates the Old. Although he does not reject the Old Testament completely or deny it a place in the Christian Bible, Hesse considers that it is the New Testament which is constitutive for Christian faith and that the Old Testament has only indirect authority.

d. Antonius H. J. Gunneweg

Two facts provide the starting point for Gunneweg's *Understanding the Old Testament* (1977): the fact that the Old Testament is a collection of Israelite and Jewish writings and the fact that it is also part of the Christian canon of Scripture. Can these two facts be reconciled, or do we have to choose one and ignore the other as was done in the early church by the allegorical approach on the one hand and Marcion on the other? Gunneweg's work consists mainly of a survey of German scholarship relating to the problem and he also indicates some of his own views, though they are not developed into a systematic proposal (*cf.* Mays 1979). He discusses both allegorical interpretation (pp. 31–35, 40–42, 48, 106, 143–147) and Marcionism in its various forms (pp. 39, 115–120, 142–172), concluding that:

> The only attempt which was thought to have appropriated the *whole* of the Old Testament for Christianity, namely the allegorical approach practised in the early church, proved to be a pseudo-solution; it no longer allowed the Old Testament to have a message of its own, but attributed to it a different, Christian sense (p. 219).

Moreover

> For the most part the New Testament speaks the language of the Old and therefore presupposes its

validity as a testimony to one and the same God. Thus the rejection of the Old Testament would not only make the message of the New Testament incomprehensible, but curtail its content. That is why Marcionitism – in its ancient and more recent forms – is always an attack on the very substance of Christianity (p. 236).

The Old Testament therefore has continuing validity in the Christian church, according to Gunneweg, but only insofar as it is validated by the New Testament. In other words, the New Testament is the criterion for the canonicity of the Old and this leads him to a differentiated approach which means in effect that *parts* of the Old Testament are valid for Christians (pp. 48–51, 170–172, 218–223, 227). In particular, the Old Testament understanding of human existence and the world and its monotheistic conception of God are presuppositions for the Christian proclamation of Jesus Christ (pp. 223–232). The Old Testament provided the early Christians with a language by means of which witness to Christ was formulated, though Gunneweg argues that Christian proclamation and faith are not necessarily bound to that Old Testament language for always: it is only the testimony of the New Testament which is binding for Christianity (pp. 16, 38, 232–236). Thus for Gunneweg, like Bultmann, the New Testament is the essential Bible and the Old Testament is its non-Christian presupposition.

Bibliography (3)

Barclay, J. M. G. 1986: 'Paul and the law: observations on some recent debates', *Themelios* 12:5–15.

Barr, J. 1965: 'Taking the Cue from Bultmann', *Int* 19:217–220.

Baumgärtel, F. 1925: *Die Bedeutung des Alten Testaments für den Christen*, Schwerin i. Mecklb.

—1938: 'Zur Frage der theologischen Deutung des Alten Testaments', *Zeitschrift für systematische Theologie* 15:136–162.

—1967: 'Das Offenbarungszeugnis des Alten Testaments im Lichte der religionsgeschichtlich-vergleichenden Forschung', *ZTK* 64:393–422.

Braulik, G. 1984: 'Law as Gospel: Justification and Pardon According to the Deuteronomic Torah', *Int* 38:5–14.

Buber, M. 1951: *Two Types of Faith*, London.

Bultmann, R. 1917–60: *Glauben und Verstehen* (Bultmann's collected essays):
   I: 1933, ET as *Faith and Understanding*, London, 1969;
   II: 1952, ET as *Essays: Philosophical and Theological*, London, 1955;
   III: 1960, ET of some of the essays in *Existence and Faith: Shorter Writings of Rudolf Bultmann*, London, 1961.

—1930: 'The Historicity of Man and Faith', ET in *Existence and Faith*: 92–110 (German, 1930).

—1940: 'Christ the End of the Law', ET in *Essays*: 36–66 (German, 1940).

—1950: 'The Significance of the Jewish Old Testament Tradition for the Christian West', ET in *Essays*: 262–272 (German, 1950).

—1957a: *History and Eschatology: The Gifford Lectures 1955*, Edinburgh.

—1957b: 'Is Exegesis without Presuppositions Possible?', ET in *Existence and Faith*: 289–296 (German, 1957).

Cazelles, H. 1966: 'The Unity of the Bible and the People of God', *Scripture* 18:1–10.

Chiu, A. 1984: 'The Dialectic between Law and Gospel: Christian Responsibility for the World', *EAJT* 2.1:1–10.

Dahl, N. A. 1956: 'The People of God', *Ecumenical Review* 9:154–161.

Dillenberger, J. 1964: 'Revelational Discernment and the Problem of the Two Testaments' in *OTCF*: 159–175.

Ehrhardt, A. 1968: 'A Biblical View of the People of God', *The American Ecclesiastical Review* 159:126–138.

Fuller, D. P. 1980: *Gospel and Law: Contrast or Continuum?*, Grand Rapids, Michigan.

Hals, R. M. 1980: *Grace and Faith in the Old Testament*, Minneapolis.

Hesse, F. 1959: 'The Evaluation and Authority of Old Testament Texts', ET in *EOTI*: 285–313 (German, 1959).

—1966: *Das Alte Testament als Buch der Kirch*, Gütersloh.

Hirsch, E. 1935: 'Gottes Offenbarung in Gesetz und Evangelium: 20 Thesen' in *Die Bekenntnisse und grundsätzlichen Äusserungen zur Kirchenfrage, III: Das Jahr 1935* (ed. K. D. Schmidt), Göttingen: 37–40.

—1936: *Das Alte Testament und die Predigt des Evangeliums*, Tübingen.

Kegley, C. W. (ed.) 1966: *The Theology of Rudolf Bultmann*, London. Includes comprehensive bibliography of Bultmann's writings to 1965.

Macquarrie, J. 1955: *An Existentialist Theology: A Comparison of Heidegger and Bultmann*, London (republished Harmondsworth, 1973).

Marlé, R. 1956: 'Bultmann et l'Ancien Testament', *NRT* 78:473–486 (ET in *Rudolf Bultmann in Catholic Thought*, ed. T. O'Meara & D. Weisser, New York/London, 1968: 110–124).

Marquardt, F.-W. 1968: 'Christentum und Zionismus', *EvTh* 28:629–660.

Mays, J. L. 1979: 'The Old Testament as Christian Canon' (review of Gunneweg 1977), *Int* 33:406–410.

Nash, R. H. 1984: *Christian Faith and Historical Understanding*, Grand Rapids, Michigan.

North, R. 1973: 'Bibliography of Works in Theology and History', *History and Theory* 12:55–140.

Ottaviani Fs 1966: *Populus Dei: Studi in onore del Card. Alfredo Ottaviani*, Rome.

Phythian-Adams, W. J. 1934: *The Call of Israel: An Introduction to the Study of Divine Election*, Oxford.

Richardson, A. 1964a: 'Is the Old Testament the Propaedeutic to Christian Faith?' in *OTCF*: 36–48.

Sanders, J. A. 1975: 'Torah and Christ', *Int* 29:372–390.
Siegwalt, G. 1971: *La Loi, chemin du Salut: Étude sur la signification de la loi de l'Ancien Testament*, Neuchâtel.
Surburg, R. F. 1974: 'The New Hermeneutic Versus the Old Hermeneutics in New Testament Interpretation', *The Springfielder* 38:13–21 (not available to me, abstract in *New Testament Abstracts* 19.27).
Voegelin, E. 1964: 'History and Gnosis' in *OTCF*: 64–89.
Young, N. J. 1966: 'Bultmann's View of the Old Testament', *SJT* 19:269–279.
—1969: *History and Existential Theology: The Role of History in the Thought of Rudolf Bultmann*, London.
See also works by Bultmann, Baumgärtel, Hesse and Gunneweg in the general bibliography.

4

The Old and New Testaments as equally Christian Scripture

4.1 Wilhelm Vischer

The most important of Wilhelm Vischer's many writings is his programmatic work, *The Witness of The Old Testament to Christ* (1934). He wrote against the background of the conventional view in the early part of the century which saw the Bible as part of the general history of religion, in which the relationship between the Testaments was interpreted in terms of 'progressive revelation' (see above: ch. 2.5), and the revival of Marcion's proposal to throw the Old Testament out of the window (ch. 2.6). These solutions did not completely satisfy either the church or biblical scholarship and the political situation in Europe in the thirties made the need for an answer all the more pressing.

Just as Barth's commentary on Romans (1918/21) heralded the end of liberal theology and the beginning of a new era in biblical interpretation, so Vischer's study of the Old Testament witness to Christ (1934, 1942) signified a turning-point in the history of Old Testament interpretation. Although Vischer had written on the subject in the late twenties and early thirties, and Barth's work was pointing in a similar direction (see below: ch. 4.3.a), it was the first volume of Vischer's major work which started a debate in the thirties that continued into the sixties. Today there is still a wide diversity of solutions to the problem of the Old Testament – which is the justification for the present work – and few would follow all that Vischer said, but there is fairly general agreement that a solution to the problem must be at least theological, if not necessarily Christian.

We shall begin our analysis of Vischer's work with his major book. In the first section the argument of the introductory essay in that book will be summarized, showing the theoretical basis of his thesis. Then his interpretation of the Old Testament will be considered, with reference to the rest of his major book and to certain other exegetical writings. The final section of the analysis will be given to another theoretical essay which Vischer published more recently as a response to Rudolf Bultmann.

a. The witness of the Old Testament to Christ

In the introductory essay to his major work (1934), Vischer makes ten points.

'Jesus is the Christ' (pp. 7–8). This is the statement of faith of the Bible and the Christian church. The Old Testament defines the word 'Christ' and the New Testament supplies the name 'Jesus', thus identifying Jesus as the Christ. So the Old Testament points forward to the New and the New Testament points back to the Old.

The Christ has come and he is Jesus of Nazareth (pp. 8–11). This close relationship between the Testaments is clear in the way Luke, for example, presents the good news. The angels who speak to Zechariah, Mary and the shepherds each announce that God is about to fulfil the promises made in the Old Testament. At his dedication in the Temple Jesus is recognized by Simeon as the Christ; and when he is twelve he visits the Temple again and reveals his own awareness that he is the Son of God. After baptism and temptation he commences his ministry in Galilee with the astounding claim that through his presence Scripture is being fulfilled. Jesus' claim to be the Christ inevitably means a short ministry and an early death, and it might be thought that such a death disproves his claim. But the testimony of the New Testament is that this happened according to Scripture, that in his life and death Jesus was the Christ promised in the Old Testament. In their encounter with the risen Lord and in receiving the promised Holy Spirit, the disciples are given the knowledge and power to witness that Jesus is indeed the Christ.

Jesus is the Christ of the Old Testament (pp. 11–14). The intention of the apostles in their witness to Jesus as the Christ is not to give a Christian interpretation to the 'historical Jesus', but simply to proclaim that Jesus is the Christ of the Old Testament. Jesus Christ is a historical event which is the source and goal of all history, yet he is a real man whose historicity is proved by his birth and above all by his death.

The Bible is a witness to Jesus Christ (pp. 14–17). Consistent with the historicity of Jesus Christ are the historical documents which support it. The Bible is not Holy Scripture because it fell from heaven but because it tells about Jesus Christ, the Son of God made flesh. It contains words of men and women rooted in history. To some this may be a stumbling-block to belief that it is also the Word of God, but it is no more a stumbling-block than the incarnation of the Word of God. Thus historical and linguistic study are essential to understand the Old Testament, though without the operation of the Holy Spirit the writings are dead. So there is a logical circle: God reveals himself in Jesus Christ, Jesus Christ is attested by the Bible and the Bible is made effective by the Holy Spirit of God.

Jesus Christ is the decisive event of history (pp. 18–19). According to the Bible, Jesus Christ is not merely one of many historical facts but the origin and destination of history, who lived in history and died to take away the sin of the world.

Jesus Christ has united the Old and New Testaments (pp. 19–21). The death of Christ has made the two Testaments one and it is only if they are a unity that Jesus is really the Christ. It follows that believers before and after Christ share the same salvation through the same mediator, thus belonging to one church of Christ. This is possible because Jesus Christ was not only a specific event in history but is eternally present (Heb. 13:8) and therefore contemporary with every Christian.

Jesus Christ has fulfilled the Old Testament promises (pp. 22–24). The essence of the unity of the Testaments, according to the New Testament, is that Jesus the Christ has fulfilled what was promised by the law and the prophets. This does not mean however that the Old Testament is now unnecessary. The promises, though fulfilled, are not dissolved: on the contrary, they are clarified and completed and the expectation becomes even more vigorous. 'To the witness of the old covenant Jesus is near as the Coming One; to those of the new covenant as the Returning One.'

The Old Testament belongs to the Christian canon (pp. 25–27). It is often asked whether the church was right to bring together both Old and New Testaments into one Bible. No doubt there could be piety on the basis of the New Testament alone, but Christianity demands both Testaments as a basis since it claims that Jesus is the Christ, in the sense that the Old Testament defines 'Christ'. It was natural and essential therefore that Christians should appropriate Israel's Bible as their own.

Is Jesus the Christ? (pp. 27–33). The unity of the Testaments is the basis of the Christian church, since without the Old

96

Testament the church cannot be *Christ*ian. At this point, however, the question arises whether the New Testament interpretation of the Old as a witness to Jesus the Christ is correct. It is not merely a question of faith: the Bible consists of human words and these words must be examined intellectually to see if they really point to Jesus Christ. True scholarly study will read the Old Testament naïvely, not assuming that it already knows its content but discovering in it the meaning of 'Christ'. The ultimate decision whether or not Jesus is the Christ, although a matter of faith, is a decision based on the testimony of Scripture and intelligent study will show that it has a sound basis.

The Old Testament is a witness to Christ (pp. 33–34). Vischer concludes his introduction by quoting J. G. Hamann's citation of Augustine: 'Read the prophetic books without reference to Christ – what couldst thou find more tasteless and insipid? Find therein Christ, and what thou readest will not only prove agreeable, but will intoxicate thee.'

b. Old Testament interpretation

A few examples of Vischer's Old Testament interpretation are now selected for special study, not because of their unusual features – which would give an unbalanced impression of his method – but almost at random, in order to understand his view of the relationship between the Testaments in a wider context.[1] The examples are presented in chronological order of Vischer's writing, which happens to coincide with their order in the Hebrew Bible.

Genesis 14 (1934: 128–133)

Abraham is unaffected by the campaign of the kings but in loyalty to Lot he leads his 318 'devoted servants' into battle. On his return in triumph he is met by the priestly king of Salem (Jerusalem), the city where God's rule and presence are revealed from David to Jesus and the end of all things. The letter to the Hebrews compares the priesthood of Melchizedek with that of Christ: neither belongs to a priestly family but both are accredited directly by God. Thus before God makes the covenant with Abraham, Melchizedek reveals 'the office of the Son, who is

---

[1]Vischer has written widely on the Old Testament and only a few examples of his interpretation are discussed here. For other examples see his works of 1944; 1954c; 1958 and 1961b.

eternal and perfect' (Heb. 7:28), agreeing with Jesus' declaration that Christianity is older than Judaism (Jn. 8:58).

Exodus 3:13–14 (1934: 169–170)

Moses asks God his name and is given the name *YHWH*, not a conventional divine name but 'an utterance in the first person in which the subject does not become an object but remains subject'. It is a revelation not of a new God but of the God of the fathers, known formerly as El Shaddai [God Almighty].

1 Samuel 17 (1942: 203–209)

In the absence of any other volunteers David responds to Goliath's challenge to Israel, implicitly a challenge to the God of Israel. His only visible weapon is a staff and sling but he has the invisible armour of the panoply of God (Eph. 6:13). In the name of the Lord, David defeats the giant and delivers Israel, and in his faith in that same name he is appointed king of Israel and founder of the messianic dynasty. Thus the shepherd becomes the princely witness to the promised true Shepherd, through whom God delivers and rules his people (Jn. 10; *cf*. Ezk. 34).

Jeremiah 1:4–10 (1955)

The most significant aspect of Jeremiah's call is that he is appointed as prophet to the nations. Yet unlike Paul the apostle to the nations (Gal. 1:15–16; *cf*. Je. 1:5), who travels the world to fulfil his ministry, Jeremiah stays at home and addresses most of his prophecies to Jerusalem and Judah. God speaks to the nations through Israel, and so Jeremiah's mission to superintend the destruction and rehabilitation of Israel is indirectly a mission to the world. Both Jeremiah and Paul concur in their message that not only Israel but every nation of the world is subject to God's justice and dependent on his grace.

Amos 5 (1959)

The message of Amos is as relevant to present-day Christians as to the Israelites, though both groups are inclined to ignore it on the assumption that they have a special relationship with God. Amos does not deny this special relationship, but shows that it is the very uniqueness of God's people which makes them especially liable to God's justice (Am. 3:2; *cf*. Lk. 12:48). In Jesus Christ God has given Christians even more than he gave Israel, and therefore his demand on them will be correspondingly greater and their unfaithfulness will be all the more serious. Like Israel the church is condemned to death for its sin and empty religion; like Israel it is given a last chance of life if it will 'seek the Lord' (Am. 5:1–6; *cf.* Jn 5:39–40). If his people do this 'it may be that the LORD, the God of hosts, will be gracious to the remnant of Joseph' (Am. 5:15).

Job (1961)

God's truth is Jesus Christ, mankind's lie is to make Jesus Christ into Christianity. The book of Job exposes this lie and points to this truth. It tells the story of a man who was upright and trusted God fully with no ulterior motives. He rejected his friends' attempts to explain life theologically and accepted only God's own solution, 'God's free, joyous goodness which is the meaning and ground of the world' (p. 144). No doubt Job feared God for nought, but more important is the fact that God loves mankind for nought. The truth of this book is not proved by Job but by Jesus Christ, in whom God has taken the part of Job. Jesus was humiliated and tempted and he placed his life in God's hands on the Cross, who answered him by raising him from the dead.

Nehemiah (1971)

As the king's minister with special responsibilities and governor of Jerusalem, Nehemiah supervises the fortification of the holy city. He is neither priest nor prophet but a politician who realizes that there is a political aspect to the kingdom of God. The Jews have only a high priest at the head of their renewed state but, although the Persian regime would scarcely have tolerated its open expression, they nurture a hope for a king which is not satisfied until Jesus declares with authority that God's kingdom is at hand and is acclaimed by the crowd on his entry into Jerusalem.

c. Everywhere the Scripture is about Christ alone

The essence of Vischer's approach to the relationship between the Testaments is clear in his major work. A more recent theoretical essay, 'Everywhere the Scripture Is about Christ Alone' (1964), will now be mentioned briefly, showing that after thirty years his position is still fundamentally the same.[2]

Vischer's starting-point is Bultmann's radical claim that the Old Testament is not genuinely God's Word for Christians (see above: ch. 3) and he examines this in some detail (pp. 90–97).

---

[2]He has also written several other theoretical essays on the subject (*e.g.* 1938; 1960).

He takes issue in particular with Bultmann's distinction between the Old Testament (in which revelation is bound to the history of Israel) and the New Testament (in which revelation confronts the individual in the proclaimed Word). Concerning the Old Testament, Vischer admits that God's revelation is bound to the history of his people, but he argues that membership of that people is not enough: faith and obedience are required to experience the grace of God. Concerning the New Testament, Vischer acknowledges that the particularity of revelation is broken and consequently God's act in Jesus Christ is understood differently from his acts in the Old Testament, nevertheless, 'the New Testament asserts that *God's deed in Jesus Christ is not merely one but rather THE decisive event for the history of Israel*' (p. 97).

The message of the New Testament is that Jesus lived, died and rose again for all who believe in him and this message is presented by showing that Jesus is the fulfilment of the Old Testament, both its end and its goal. Therefore the New Testament points Christians to the Old, where they may see examples of God's judgment and grace toward his people. These examples are relevant because in both Old and New Testaments God's people live in time and history and in both Testaments they encounter God in Christ within that situation. The Old Testament however is not simply helpful in understanding the Christian life; it is essential to apprehend God's revelation in Jesus Christ, which cannot be known without the Old Testament (pp. 98–101).

4.2 Critique

a. Method

Vischer insists on a historical and linguistic approach to the Old Testament and claims that his thesis is based on sound scholarly method (1934: 14–17, 27–33). Yet one of the main criticisms directed against his work is that he does not take history seriously and substitutes guesswork for scholarship in his exegesis.[3] Now it is true, as his reviewers have pointed out at length, that some of Vischer's interpretations are open to question and others are plainly fanciful, though these are the exception rather than the rule. It is also true that he evades the

---

[3]*E.g.* Thielicke (1948: 105–106); Porteous (1951: 339); Kraeling (1955: 226).

question of historicity and is more concerned to expound the text in its final form than to study its literary history. Nevertheless, in spite of these qualifications, Vischer's work is essentially what he intends it to be: exegesis based on the principles of modern historical and linguistic scholarship.[4]

Another common criticism of Vischer's work is that he uses unacceptable methods of interpretation such as typology and allegory.[5] Yet Vischer explicitly rejects these methods, apart from typology in the sense of 'example' or 'pattern' (see 1964: 99–100; cf. below: ch. 7.2.a), and insists on scholarly study of the text. His view of the relationship between the Testaments and his exegeses of Old Testament texts depend not on allegory – nor on typology as popularly understood – but on historically based scholarship (cf. Bright 1967: 86–87).

b. Jesus as the Old Testament Christ

One of the most important aspects of Vischer's understanding of the relationship between the Testaments is his assertion that Jesus is the Christ of the Old Testament (1934: 11–14). This proposition is fundamental: any Christian theology presupposes that Jesus is the Christ, and it is naturally the Old Testament which defines the concept 'Christ'.[6] However it is only one side of the truth, and we need also to account for the element of surprise in the coming of Jesus of Nazareth as the Christ. There is no doubt that Jesus, according to the testimony of the New Testament, was the fulfilment of the Old Testament promises of a Messiah;[7] but there is equally no doubt that in many ways the fulfilment was so radically different from the expectation that Jesus can only be understood to be the Christ of the whole Bible (cf. Baumgärtel 1952: 91). The New Testament does not only identify the Christ, it explains his nature and function in much more detail than is done in the Old Testament (Porteous 1951: 337–338).

---

[4]Cf. Hertzberg (1936); Jacob (1945: 76); Filson (1951: 144–145); Congar (1949: 11–12).

[5]E.g. Baumgärtel (1952: 93); Köhler (1953: 251–253); Harrington (1973: 314).

[6]Cf. Brunner (1934); Cullmann (1957). On the Old Testament and Christ, cf. also van Ruler (1955: 34–68; see below: ch. 5).

[7]Promise and fulfilment will be discussed in greater detail below: ch. 8.

c. Christological Old Testament interpretation

It follows from the preceding point that Vischer develops a Christological interpretation of the Old Testament. Following good exegetical procedure he takes account of the context of the passage in question and for him this context is the whole Bible. He dismisses the possibility of giving a theological interpretation of the Old Testament in the Christian church without reference to Christ:

> The hallmark of Christian theology is that it is Christology, a theology that can affirm nothing of God except in and through Jesus Christ ... (John 1:18) ... From this it is clear that all the knowledge of God which resides in the Old Testament scriptures is mediated through Jesus Christ. Consequently, the theological exposition of these writings within the Church can be nothing other than Christology (1934: 28–29).

Such a method lays Vischer open to the criticism that he reads New Testament meanings into Old Testament passages (Porteous 1951: 338). But it is consistent with his presupposition of the theological identity of the Testaments which enables him to move freely in the whole Bible to find analogies and explanations for clarification on difficult passages.

Vischer does not claim that Jesus Christ was present in Old Testament times and may be found and expounded directly in the texts of the Old Testament (contrast A. T. Hanson 1965), but simply that Old Testament interpretation must take seriously the fact that Christians believe the Old Testament to have been fulfilled in the New (cf. 1934: 27–28). Immanuel, for instance, is not identical with Jesus Christ: on the contrary, Immanuel is a sign (a person, thing or event that has an essential correspondence with something greater in the future and thus points to it and confirms it though it is not yet known; 1954a: 52). For Vischer, Christological interpretation means that every Old Testament text points toward the death of Christ and cannot be fully understood without reference to him (cf. Filson 1951: 145; Bright 1967: 86–88). 'The witnesses of the Old Testament and those of the New stand facing each other like the two sections of an antiphonal choir looking towards a central point ... Immanuel' (Vischer 1934: 25; cf. Goldingay 1981: 34).

Vischer's Christological interpretation has provoked a good deal of interest and disagreement (cf. Baumgärtel 1952: 93–95);

but it is a natural corollary of his view that the Old and New Testaments have the same – Christian – theology.[8]

d. A timeless revelation

Another significant aspect of Vischer's work is its conception of revelation (*cf.* Thielicke 1948: 100–117). On the basis of the unity of the Bible he argues that 'the events which happened in the life of Christ as temporal history form an eternal *now* . . . In every generation every true Christian is contemporaneous with Christ' (1934: 21). But while it may be agreed that God himself is outside time, God's plan is enacted within history and it is there that his revelation is to be found (*cf.* de Vaux 1952). There is a danger of obscuring the dynamic nature of divine revelation in the biblical documents by abstracting it into timelessness in this way (*cf.* Porteous 1951: 327, 339). Though Vischer starts from a very different point, the end result of this view has a certain similarity to Bultmann's existential view of revelation (*cf.* above: ch. 3.2.a).

A corollary to this view of a timeless revelation is that 'in its nature and essence *salvation under the old covenant was in no way different from ours*' (1934: 21). Vischer qualifies this by indicating differences in the way salvation was administered, in earthly forms in the Old Testament and spiritual ones in the New. But he virtually ignores the fundamental difference, that in the New Testament Jesus Christ has come and brought blessings, such as new birth and eternal life, unknown or unexpected in the Old Testament (*cf.* Porteous 1951: 337; Baumgärtel 1952: 91–92).

e. A relationship of identity

The title of the present chapter sums up Vischer's thesis: the Old and New Testaments are equally Christian Scripture. It follows that for him the theological relationship between the Testaments is a relationship involving not only 'unity' but 'identity'.[9] Of course, Vischer is aware of the differences between the Old and the New: his starting-point ('the Old Testament tells us *what* the Christ is; the New, *who* He is'; 1934: 7)

---

[8]On Christological interpretation of the Old Testament, see also Glen (1951); M. Barth (1954); Fohrer (1970); Boyd (1975: 136–137); Mildenberger (1975); Wainwright (1982) and Escobar (1983).

[9]*Cf.* Eichrodt (1938: 75–76); Thielicke (1948: 104); Kraeling (1955: 220 *cf.* 225–226).

makes that clear. Nevertheless, his basic presupposition is that the two Testaments have the same theology and the same Christology. The implications of this include Christological interpretation of the Old Testament and a timeless view of revelation and salvation.

In a sense this solution to the problem of the relationship between the Testaments is not new: it dates back to the earliest days of the church. In fact it may be considered the traditional Christian approach to the Old Testament, apart from that of Marcion and his followers, until the rise of historical criticism in the eighteenth and nineteenth centuries (*cf.* Florovsky 1951: 173–174; Bright 1967: 79–84). The Fathers and Reformers affirmed in different ways their basic conviction that the Old Testament is Christian Scripture and therefore to be interpreted Christologically. Their view of the relationship between the Testaments was essentially that the two are identical in their value, inspiration and theology (*cf.* above: ch. 2.1 – 2.4). Thus Vischer is really restating the traditional view in a twentieth-century context, aware of the results of historical criticism of the Bible and sensitive to the historical situation in which he lived.

There is no doubt that a Christian solution to the problem of the relationship between the Testaments must take account of Vischer's work. He has reminded us that the New Testament identifies Jesus of Nazareth as the Christ promised in the Old Testament, though we should note that the full meaning of the word 'Christ' is ascertainable only from the whole Bible. The Old Testament is not a self-contained revelation but has a conclusion outside itself, in the New Testament revelation of Christ, and therefore Christian Old Testament interpretation must not forget that the Christ is made fully known only in Jesus of Nazareth. Vischer has also pointed out that thousands of years of history can be contemporaneous to an eternal God, without neglecting the temporal nature of his revelation and salvation.

4.3 Comparison: other 'scriptural' solutions

Many other writers have advocated an understanding of the Old and New Testaments as equally Christian Scripture, generally with Jesus Christ as the key which unites the two. We shall now examine four of these 'scriptural' solutions.[10]

a. Karl Barth

In a lecture during the early period of his life Barth stated his view thus:

> The Old Testament mainly concerns us through its relation to the New Testament. If the Church is represented as the successor of the synagogue, then the Old Testament witnesses to Christ before Christ (but not apart from Christ). The Old and New Testaments are related to one another as prophecy to its fulfilment, and the Old Testament should always be regarded in this light . . . The Old Testament, though a completely Jewish book, none the less refers to Christ . . . The Old Testament looks forward, and the New Testament speaks of the future while looking back, and both look to Christ (n.d.: 93–94).

In later works, especially *Church Dogmatics*, he continued to maintain that the Old Testament is a witness to Christ (1938b: 70–101, 489) and that the Old Testament points forward while the New Testament points back to Christ as the centre of the Bible (1938b: 481; 1955: 822). Like Vischer,[11] Barth emphasizes that Jesus of Nazareth is the Messiah of Israel (1938b: 448; 1942: 198; 1945a: 239, 276; 1953: 166) and recognizes the 'essential identity of Old Testament and New Testament' (1938b: 74; *cf.* 1940: 364–367; 1950: 216; 1953: 167). For Barth the two Testaments are one in their witness to God's revelation, in their message about God, his creation, his sovereignty and his grace.[12]

---

[10]Others which could be considered in this category include Otto Procksch (1933; 1950); Hans Hellbardt (1937); S. de Diétrich (1945); Joseph Coppens (1948); Hermann Diem (1955); C. Larcher (1962) and Ronald Clements (1978).

[11]Although Vischer was influenced by Barth's thought, most of Barth's works considered here are later than Vischer's major work (1934) and he quotes Vischer with approval (*e.g.* 1938b: 80; 1942: x).

[12]1938b: 80–101; 1940: 381–382; 1945a: 63–64, 202–203; 1950: 178–183; 1955: 822. Barth's view of the relationship between the Testaments has been summarized briefly here on the basis of a few relevant passages from his works. For a more detailed study of his position, see Bächli (1987); also Thielicke (1948); Davis (1965); Kelsey (1975: 39–50); Ford (1979).

b. Edmond Jacob

Although he never discusses it at length, Jacob's view of the relationship between the Testaments can be seen from a number of his works. In his *Theology of the Old Testament* (1955) he states, in words that could almost have been written by Vischer:

> A theology of the Old Testament which is founded not on certain isolated verses, but on the Old Testament as a whole, can only be a Christology, for what was revealed under the old covenant, through a long and varied history, in events, persons and institutions, is, in Christ, gathered together and brought to perfection . . . a perfectly objective study makes us discern already in the Old Testament the same message of . . . God . . . which characterizes the Gospel (p. 12; *cf.* 15, 17, 328).

Christ is therefore at the centre of the Bible and the Old Testament is the road which led to Jesus Christ and can only be interpreted as such, although it should not be Christianized (1950: 156–157; 1955b: 84). Jacob recognizes that there are obvious differences between the Old Testament and the New, but nevertheless affirms that the two are essentially united in their language, structure and message.[13]

c. George A. F. Knight

Knight has the distinction of being the author of a 'Christian' Old Testament theology (1959). In it he makes no secret of his presupposition that 'the Old Testament is nothing less than Christian Scripture' (p. 7; *cf.* 1953: 51; 1962: 9–10, 13–14). This does not mean, however, that the Old Testament is a collection of prophecies of Christ. Rather there is a close parallel between God's acts through his son Israel and those through his son Jesus (1959a: 8, 225–247; *cf.* 1953: 71–73). Knight's thought here has a certain similarity to the idea of typology as 'patterns' (see 1960a:

---

[13]1955a: 31–32, 61–62, 112; 1966b: 393; 1968b: 431–432. Like Vischer, Jacob has been criticized for inconsistencies in method (Bright 1962), and for giving inadequate consideration to the history of salvation (Rhodes 1959). Perhaps in response to such criticism, Jacob later emphasized the importance of historical method and affirmed his work to be a theology of the history of salvation (1966a: 126n.; 1968a: vii–ix).

57; *cf.* below: ch. 7.2.a). Moreover, he argues, the Old and New Testaments are equally revelation and have fundamentally the same theology (1959a: 8; 1953: 27, 36–37, 66; 1962: 61–65). This explains the adjective 'Christian' in the title of his theology: it is not individual passages but the Old Testament as a whole which is messianic, looking forward to Christ (1959a: 286; *cf.* 285–320). A corollary is that there is an 'essential identity between the Israel of old and the Church which has come into existence through Christ' (1959a: 335; *cf.* 336–343).[14]

d. Brevard S. Childs

Childs' basic thesis is that 'the canon of the Christian church is the most appropriate context from which to do Biblical Theology' (1970: 99). On the basis of this thesis he has developed what may be described as the 'canonical approach', one of the most significant new approaches to biblical interpretation of the nineteen-seventies. In this Childs acknowledges his debt to Karl Barth, whose exegesis he describes as consistently rooted in the theological context of the Christian canon (*cf.* pp. 110–111).

The Christian canon of Scripture

Childs elaborates the meaning of his thesis as follows (1970: 99–103):

● the Old and New Testaments together constitute Christian Scripture, in accordance with the confession of virtually all branches of the Christian church;
● these Scriptures must be interpreted in relation to their function within the community of faith that has treasured them and expects to encounter God through them;
● the biblical tradition is not merely illustrative but is normative for the life of the church;

---

[14]There have been many reviews and discussions of Knight's 'Christian' Old Testament theology (*e.g.* Ackroyd 1962; Durham 1970; Harrington 1973: 34–40). Some scholars acknowledge this to be the natural approach of a Christian, but others complain that he has failed to produce a distinctively Christian theology and that the result is little different from other Old Testament theologies. Examples of his biblical interpretation, which is rather similar to that of Vischer, may be found in his many commentaries on Old Testament books (*e.g.* 1950; 1955; 1961; 1976; 1984; 1985).

● the biblical text must be interpreted in its canonical form, because it is in this form and not in its pre-history that it is normative for Christian faith; nevertheless

● the text of Scripture must not be separated from the reality of which it speaks, for it points faithfully to the divine reality of Christ.

In this canonical context, the two Testaments cannot be considered identical, since they speak of Christ in different ways; and yet neither can they be separated nor can one be subordinated to the other. The Christian canon of Scripture consists of both Old Testament and New Testament.

A relationship of witness

Childs argues that the recognition of both Old and New Testaments as Christian Scripture is based on the conviction that both Testaments are witnesses to God's redemptive activity; and at the same time he points out that this involves a proper understanding of the historical and cultural context in which that witness was originally given (pp. 112–113). 'The Old Testament within the context of the canon is not a witness to a primitive level of faith, nor does it need to be Christianized. Within its historical context it is a witness to Jesus Christ' (p. 111). Unlike Vischer's idea of a timeless revelation, Childs emphasizes the historical nature of the biblical witness;[15] however he argues that this involves not only historical-critical study but also study of the canonical shape of the literature which reflects Israel's unique history (cf. 1978; 1979: 71).

Thus Childs rejects any suggestion that the Old Testament is simply background material for the New or indeed that the New Testament is simply an appendix to the Old:

The Christian church confesses to find a witness to Jesus Christ in both the Old Testament and the New

---

[15]McEvenue (1981: 233–236) claims that Childs' canonical interpretation involves the relativization of historical perspectives and the timeless applicability of Scripture. However this claim ignores Childs' specific statements that 'The Bible does not function in its role as canon to provide a collection of eternal ideas' (1970: 101) and that God's will has been revealed 'not in timeless universal truths but in concrete manifestations of himself, restricted in time and space, and testified to by particular witnesses' (p. 105). Moreover McEvenue produces very little evidence that Childs does this in practice in his works.

> ... By reading the Old Testament along with the New as Christian scripture a new theological context is formed for understanding both parts which differs from hearing each Testament in isolation (1979: 671; *cf*. 1970: 109).

However this does not mean that the two Testaments are to be considered identical or harmonized, rather that they both witness independently and together to the one purpose of God (1964: 440–441).

A relationship of continuity

The early Christians were convinced of the continuity between the Old and New Testament witnesses. Childs demonstrates this on the basis of New Testament quotations of Old Testament texts, making three main points (1970: 202–209):

- the Christian God was identified with the God of Israel;
- the Old Testament idea of God was understood to be consistent with faith in the person of Jesus Christ, indeed Old Testament texts were used in the development of Christology; and
- attempts to separate Christ and the Old Testament were rejected by affirming the dynamic, personal and practical unity between God and Christ.

It might be asked whether this continuity is really representative of the relationship between the Testaments as a whole; whether there is not an essential discontinuity in the tension between monotheism and trinity, old creation and new creation, old covenant and new covenant. Childs admits the force of such an objection, but considers that even in this undeniable discontinuity there is a fundamental continuity of divinity, creation and covenant (pp. 211–216). Thus Childs emphasizes the essential continuity between the Testaments, though he does not deny that there are also elements of discontinuity (*cf*. 1958: 268–270).

The Old Testament as Scripture

Childs has worked out his 'canonical approach' on a grand scale in his later works, particularly in his commentary on Exodus (1974) and his *Introduction to the Old Testament as Scripture* (1979).[16]

---

[16]The former was described by a reviewer as 'a commentary whose

In the former he aims 'to interpret the book of Exodus as canonical scripture within the theological discipline of the Christian church' (p. xiii; *cf.* 1964) and he pursues this aim with a format for each section reminiscent of, but distinct from, that of the *Biblischer Kommentar* (*cf.* above: ch. 2.7.b):

- *text* (translation, textual and philological notes);
- *prehistory of the text* (literary, form-critical and tradition-historical problems);
- *Old Testament context* (exegesis of the text in its final [canonical] form);
- *New Testament context* (New Testament understanding of the text in the light of its confession of Jesus Christ);
- *history of exegesis* (analogous to the section on prehistory, which deals with the period before the text took its canonical form, this section is concerned with interpretation after the formation of the text ['posthistory'?]); and
- *theological reflection* (in the context of the Christian canon).

Childs explains that the first and second sections are directed primarily to the technical scholar, and the fifth section stands on its own as part of intellectual history, but it is the sections on Old and New Testament context and theological reflection which form the heart of the commentary and are intended for all readers. This is, of course, consistent with his stated aim of interpreting the text in its final form, that is in the context of the Christian canon of Scripture.

---

challenges and contributions are so large that it claims and deserves the attention of a more diverse readership than any commentary published in this century' (Wharton 1975); and the *Journal for the Study of the Old Testament* devoted an entire issue in 1980 to seven major reviews of the latter work — mostly acknowledging it to be original and exciting, imaginative and pioneering — followed by a response by Childs himself. By no means all reviewers agreed with Childs' canonical approach, but none could dispute that he had thrown down a major challenge to the disciplines of Old Testament exegesis and introduction which could not be ignored.

He has since continued the same approach in an introduction to the New Testament as canon (1984a). For a full bibliography of his works, see Childs Fs: 329–336.

In his Old Testament introduction, Childs has a slightly different programme. Here he is concerned 'to describe the form and function of the Hebrew Bible in its role as sacred scripture for Israel' (1979: 16). The introductory chapters discuss the understanding of canon and emphasize the importance of interpreting the final form of the biblical text in the light of its function for a community of faith (*cf.* 1978: 53–55). The majority of the work is devoted to an analysis of each of the books of the Hebrew Bible, consisting of three main sections:

● historical-critical problems;
● the canonical shape of the book; and
● theological and hermeneutical implications.

The sections on theological and hermeneutical implications summarize and reflect on the significance of each book in the canonical context of the Hebrew Bible, but do not generally consider its significance in the broader context of post-biblical Judaism or of the Christian canon of Scripture which includes both an Old and a New Testament. As Barr (1983: 152) points out, the Old Testament is interpreted as Scripture, but not as *Christian* Scripture, in quite a different way from Barth who emphasized a consistently Christian interpretation of the Old Testament. Childs is not unaware of this and touches on it in the final chapter, where he argues for a fundamental continuity between the Hebrew Scriptures and the Christian Bible. However the question remains: why in his commentary does he interpret Exodus as Christian Scripture but in his introduction pursue only the more limited aim of understanding the Old Testament as *Israel's* Scripture?

The canonical form of the text

Childs' most vehement critic has been James Barr (1983). The most important question he raises is that of how far the canonical form of the text should be considered normative (pp. 75–104).[17] Barr argues that the later form of a text is not

---

[17]Barr also demonstrates that in many respects Childs' programme is little different from that of the 'Biblical Theology Movement' which it purports to replace and may in fact be seen as completing the quest of that movement (1983: 130–139). Unfortunately Barr's critique is marred by his description of Childs' approach as 'canonical criticism', a term specifically repudiated by Childs (1978: 54; 1979: 82); by his caricature of several of Childs' arguments; and by his failure to provide a clear

necessarily superior to earlier forms, and that there may even be a deterioration in traditions over the course of time. While we are perfectly entitled to read the text as it stands, it is another matter to claim that it is this form which is determinative for theology.

This raises the important question of truth: which form of the text represents the truth about God most clearly and accurately? Does the recognition of certain writings as canonical Scripture mean that truth is to be found in them and nowhere else (*cf.* McEvenue 1981: 236)? How far has historical criticism, which Childs considers to be of only secondary importance, discovered the truth about the Bible (*cf.* Barr 1983: 118–119)? Should we be looking for truth behind the texts themselves, in the basic facts of the gospel or the history of salvation (*cf.* Childs 1970: 102)? To formulate the question in a different way, is biblical truth to be sought in:

● the text in its final, canonical, form? or
● earlier stages in the development of the text, as discovered by historical-critical scholarship? or
● the events that happened and words that were spoken which gave rise to the text?

Perhaps all of these have their place, so long as the interpreter makes clear his or her intention and does not claim a monopoly of truth. Moreover, as Melugin (1988) has argued, even the 'final' canonical form of the text has a continuing history of interpretation: its meaning is not located once and for all in the canonical text but is discovered afresh in each historical situation in which the church reads the text (*cf.* Clements 1978: 15–19).

Childs has clearly stated his priority as the interpretation of biblical texts in their final form, that is, in the context of the canon of Scripture, and his work should therefore be evaluated on this basis rather than because of its failure to do something else.[18] He does not claim that this is the only valid method of

---

statement of what approach to biblical interpretation he himself proposes. Childs (1984b) has replied to Barr's criticisms in a major review of the latter's book.

[18]John Barton (1984a: 77–103) describes the canonical approach well and indicates its positive achievements, while drawing attention to the fundamental theological problem of *which* of the available canons of Scripture should be its basis. He also demonstrates the (apparently unintentional) affinities of the canonical approach with the 'new criticism' of twentieth-century secular literary studies, and argues that many

interpretation, simply that he is standing within the tradition of the church which has recognized these writings in their canonical form to be normative for its faith, 'a channel of life . . . through which God instructs and admonishes his people' (1970: 99). 'This understanding of the Scripture's uniqueness remains a statement of faith' (p. 104), but it has at least as much claim to be taken seriously as statements which give priority to the interpretation of earlier forms of the text, a process which is fraught with many more difficulties and whose 'truth' is no easier to prove than Childs' canonical approach (*cf.* Ellul 1970: xvii–xviii).

Bibliography (4)

Ackroyd, P. R. 1962: 'G. A. F. Knight's "A Christian Theology of the Old Testament"', *ExpT* 73:164–168.

Bächli, O. 1987: *Das Alte Testament in der Kirchlichen Dogmatik von Karl Barth*, Neukirchen-Vluyn.

Barth, K. n.d.: *Prayer and Preaching*, ET London, 1964 (French, 1953 & 1961; originally a course of lectures delivered when Barth was 'comparatively young', p. 64).

—1918/21: *The Epistle to the Romans*, ET: Oxford, 1933 (German, 1918, [2]1921, [6]1928).

—1938b: *Church Dogmatics* I.2, ET: Edinburgh, 1956 (German, 1938, [3]1945).

—1940: *Church Dogmatics* II.1, ET: Edinburgh, 1957 (German, 1940, [2]1946).

—1942: *Church Dogmatics* II.2, ET: Edinburgh, 1957 (German, 1942).

—1950: *Church Dogmatics* III.3, ET: Edinburgh, 1961 (German, 1950).

—1953: *Church Dogmatics* IV.1, ET: Edinburgh, 1956 (German, 1953).

—1955: *Church Dogmatics* IV.2, ET: Edinburgh, 1958 (German, 1955).

Barth, M. 1954: 'The Christ in Israel's History', *Theology Today* 11:342–353.

Bright, J. 1962: 'Edmond Jacob's "Theology of the Old Testament"', *ExpT* 73:304–307.

Childs, B. S. 1964: 'Interpretation in Faith: The Theological Responsibility of an Old Testament Commentary', *Int* 18:432–449.

—1974: *Exodus: A Commentary*, London.

of the arguments against the latter may also apply to the former (pp. 140–179). Whether or not that is the case depends to a large extent on how far the Bible is correctly described as 'literature': the inadequacies of the new criticism for understanding secular literature do not necessarily transfer to the canonical approach to sacred Scripture, which sets out to understand a diverse collection of writings (law, history, poetry, liturgy, prophecy, *etc.*), most of which were not written primarily with literary aims nor are they read now primarily because of their literary interest.

—1978: 'The Canonical Shape of the Prophetic Literature', *Int* 32:46–55.

—1984a: *The New Testament as Canon: An Introduction*, London.

—1984b: Review of Barr (1983) in *Int* 38:66–70.

Congar, Y. M. J. 1949: 'The Old Testament as a Witness to Christ' in *The Revelation of God*, ET: London/New York, 1968: 8–15 (originally in *La Vie Intellectuelle* 17, 1949: 335–343).

Cullmann, O. 1957b: *The Christology of the New Testament*, ET: London, 1959 (German, 1957): 111–136.

Davis, L. 1965: 'Typology in Barth's Doctrine of Scripture', *Anglican Theological Review* 47:33–49.

Diem, H. 1955: *Dogmatics*, ET: London/Edinburgh, 1959 (German: *Theologie als kirchliche Wissenschaft: II. Dogmatik*, 1955): chs 5 & 9.

Diétrich, S. de 1945: *Le dessein de Dieu: Itinéraire biblique*, Neuchâtel.

Durham, J. I. 1970: 'George A. F. Knight, *A Christian Theology of the Old Testament*' in Laurin (1970): 171–190.

Eichrodt, W. 1938: 'Zur Frage der theologischen Exegese des Alten Testamentes', *ThBl* 17:73–87.

Escobar, S. 1983: 'Our Hermeneutic Task Today' in Branson & Padilla (1983): 3–10.

Fohrer, G. 1970: 'Das Alte Testament und das Thema "Christologie"', *EvTh* 30:281–298.

Ford, D. F. 1979: 'Barth's Interpretation of the Bible' in *Karl Barth: Studies of his Theological Method* (ed. S. W. Sykes), Oxford: 55–87.

Glen, J. S. 1951: 'Jesus Christ and the Unity of the Bible', *Int* 5:259–267.

Hellbardt, H. 1937: 'Die Auslegung des Alten Testaments als theologische Disziplin', *ThBl* 16:129–143.

Herntrich, V. 1936: *Theologische Auslegung des Alten Testaments? Zum Gespräch mit Wilhelm Vischer*, Göttingen.

Hertzberg, H. W. 1936: Review of Vischer (1934) in *TLZ* 61:435–439.

Jacob, E. 1945: 'A propos de l'interpretation de l'Ancien Testament: Méthode christologique ou méthode historique?', *ETR* 20:76–82.

—1950: 'L'Ancien Testament et la prédication chrétienne', *Verbum Caro* 4:151–164.

—1955b: 'Considérations sur l'autorité canonique de l'Ancien Testament' in Boisset (1955): 71–85.

—1966b: Review of Miskotte (1963) in *RHPR* 46:392–394.

—1968a: New preface to *Théologie de l'Ancien Testament* ([2]1968). The rest of the book is cited as 1955a (see general bibliography).

—1968b: 'La Théologie de l'Ancien Testament: état présent et perspectives d'avenir', *ETL* 44:420–432.

Kittel, B. *et al.* 1980: Reviews of B. S. Childs' *Introduction to the Old Testament as Scripture* by B. Kittel, J. Barr, J. Blenkinsopp, H. Cazelles, G. M. Landes, R. E. Murphy & R. Smend with a response by Childs in *JSOT* 16:2–60

Knight, G. A. F. 1949: *From Moses to Paul: A Christological Study in the Light of Our Hebraic Heritage*, London.

—1950: *Ruth and Jonah: The Gospel in the Old Testament*, London, [2]1966 ([1]1950).

—1953: *A Biblical Approach to the Doctrine of the Trinity*, Edinburgh/ London (*SJT* Occasional Papers 1).
—1955: *Esther, Song of Songs, Lamentations: Introduction and Commentary*, London.
—1959a: *A Christian Theology of the Old Testament*, London, ²1964 (¹1959).
—1960a: 'New Perspectives in Old Testament Interpretation', *The Bible Translator* 19 (1968): 50–58 (inaugural address at McCormick Seminary, Chicago, 1960).
—1961: *Prophets of Israel (1): Isaiah*, London.
—1976: *Theology as Narration: A Commentary on the Book of Exodus*, Edinburgh.
—1984: *Servant Theology: A Commentary on the Book of Isaiah 40 – 55*, Edinburgh/Grand Rapids (ITC).
—1985: *The New Israel: A Commentary on the Book of Isaiah 56 – 66*, Edinburgh/Grand Rapids (ITC).
Larcher, C. 1962: *L'actualité chrétienne de l'Ancien Testament, d'après le Nouveau Testament*, Paris (Lectio Divina 34).
McEvenue, S. E. 1981: 'The Old Testament, Scripture or Theology?', *Int* 35:229–242.
Melugin, R. F. 1988: 'Canon and Exegetical Method' in Childs Fs: 48–61.
Mildenberger, F. 1975: 'The Unity, Truth, and Validity of the Bible: Theological Problems in the Doctrine of Holy Scripture', *Int* 29:391–405.
Procksch, O. 1933: 'Christus im Alten Testament', *Neue Kirchliche Zeitschrift* 44:57–83.
—1950: *Theologie des Alten Testaments*, Gütersloh.
Rad, G. von 1935: 'Das Christuszeugnis des Alten Testaments: Eine Auseinandersetzung mit Wilhelm Vischers gleichnamigen Buch', *ThBl* 14:249–254.
Rhodes, A. B. 1959: Review of Jacob (1955a) in *Int* 13:468–470.
Vaux, R. de 1950: Review of Vischer (1934) in *RB* 57:284–285.
—1952: Review of Vischer (1942) in *RB* 59:282–283.
Vischer, W. 1938: 'The Significance of the Old Testament for the Christian Life' in *Proceedings of the Fourth Calvinistic Congress, held in Edinburgh 6th to 11th July 1938*, Edinburgh: 237–260.
—1944: *Psalmen: ausgelegt für die Gemeinde*, Basel, n.d. (preface, 1944).
—1954c: 'Return, Rebel Sons! A Sermon on Jeremiah 3:1,19 – 4:4', *Int* 8:43–47.
—1955a: 'The Vocation of the Prophet to the Nations: An Exegesis of Jeremiah 1:4–10', *Int* 9:310–317.
—1958: *Valeur de l'Ancien Testament: Commentaires des livres Job, Esther, l'Ecclésiaste, le second Esaïe, précédés d'une introduction*, Geneva.
—1959: 'Perhaps the Lord will be Gracious: A Sermon', *Int* 13:286–295 (on Am. 5).
—1961a: 'God's Truth and Man's Lie: A Study of the Message of the Book of Job', *Int* 15:131–146.
—1961b: 'The Love Story of God: A Sermon', *Int* 15:304–309 (on Hosea).
—1971: 'Nehemia, der Sonderbeauftragte und Statthalter des Königs:

Die Bedeutung der Befestigung Jerusalems für die biblische Geschichte und Theologie' in von Rad Fs: 603–610.

Wainwright, A. 1982: *Beyond Biblical Criticism: Encountering Jesus in Scripture,* London.

Wharton, J. A. 1975: 'Splendid Failure or Flawed Success?' *Int* 29:266–276.

Zimmerli, W. 1940: 'Auslegung des Alten Testamentes', *ThBl* 19:145–157.

See also works by Vischer, Barth, Jacob, Knight and Childs in the general bibliography.

5

The Old Testament as the essential Bible

5.1 Arnold A. van Ruler

An alternative possibility to the proposals of Bultmann and Vischer is to see the relationship between the Old Testament and the New Testament as a relationship of 'priority'. It is, of course, obvious that the Old Testament was formed before the New Testament and that the Old Testament was prior to the New Testament historically. However, to claim that in the Christian era the Old Testament also has *theological* priority over the New Testament is a different matter. A notable Dutch Reformed scholar, the late Arnold A. van Ruler of Utrecht, has claimed this and in the following pages his claim will be examined.

A lively debate about the Christian interpretation of the Old Testament was provoked by the launching of a major new commentary on the Old Testament in Germany in the 1950s (*Biblischer Kommentar*, see above: ch. 2.7.b). Van Ruler set out to make a contribution on the part of systematic theology to this debate and he put forward a provocative thesis that stimulated much further debate. The most important statement of the thesis is his book *The Christian Church and the Old Testament*, published originally in German (1955) and since translated into English.[1]

---

[1]Van Ruler's Dutch manuscript was translated into German by Hermann Keller and published as *Die christliche Kirche und das Alte Testament*

The vital question about the Old Testament for van Ruler is how it may be recognized as the Word of God. He points out that the Old Testament is decisively important since it determines one's understanding of Christianity, yet from the earliest times the church has found difficulty in using it and today the question needs to be thought through once more.

a. The Old Testament itself

In the first chapter van Ruler deals with four preliminary questions about the Old Testament.

Are both Testaments about the same God?

A more precise way of putting this question would be to ask whether it is *YHWH*, the God of Israel, who is also the Father of the Lord Jesus Christ (pp. 13–16/15–18). It is a very important question in determining the church's attitude to the Old Testament: a positive attitude to the Old Testament is dependent on a positive answer to this question. Both faith and scholarship are involved here and, although faith will reply first, it is also the responsibility of scholarship to search for an answer. Van Ruler's own answer is clear in his presupposition throughout the whole book that both Old and New Testaments are about the same God.

Revelation and scholarship

The question of the identity of the God of the Old Testament leads on to the question of revelation, and van Ruler asks how revelation may be perceived in the Old Testament literature (pp. 16–21/18–24). He believes that the primary prerequisite for recognizing revelation is faith, and that the decision of faith to find revelation in the Old Testament is not an arbitrary one since Jesus Christ establishes its authority. Scholarship supports this decision of faith by demonstrating the uniqueness of the Old Testament's understanding of life. In other words, the

---

(1955). The German edition was then translated into English by Geoffrey W. Bromiley (1966, and again 1971, an identical edition which does not mention the former). There are a number of significant errors in the English translation, and so both versions are referred to in the present book, with the German and English page numbers given in that order: *e.g.* 1955: 11/13, or simply p. 11/13.

Most of his other writings are only available in Dutch (*e.g.* 1945; 1947), though two expositions of Old Testament passages have been translated into English (1960; 1962).

function of scholarship is to determine what the Old Testament says and the function of faith is to decide whether or not what it says is revelation.

This simple distinction between the roles of faith and scholarship is nevertheless inadequate, because it leaves unsolved the problem of whether the recognition of the Old Testament as revelation affects scholarly exegesis. Does scholarship study only the human aspect of revelation or can it study revelation itself? The fundamental problem is that of the relation between revelation and the Bible: van Ruler's view is that the Bible is not only a record of revelation, nor even a witness to revelation, but is itself a means of revelation. The hermeneutical problem of relating the exegete and his method to the author and his subject involves a tension between establishing the meaning of the text and receiving it as revelation. Theological scholarship will not therefore be satisfied with investigation of the text on a purely human level, but will attempt to understand that revelation.

What does the Old Testament mean by 'revelation'?

Revelation in the Old Testament, according to van Ruler, refers to the self-communication or presence of God among his people in concrete historical events (pp. 22–27/24–30). 'The dimension of history is of predominant significance for what the Old Testament understands by revelation' (p. 23/25) and for van Ruler history is a vital part of the revelation itself, not just the sphere in which it takes place (p. 25n./28). This understanding of revelation as God's active presence in Israel's history has at least two implications. First, although it contains religious and theological ideas, the quintessence of the Old Testament is not to be found in these but in God himself who is present in the history of Israel. Secondly, the concept of progressive revelation, which implies that human beings gradually come to know more of God, is inappropriate since revelation is concerned not with what we know but with what God does among us. Human knowledge naturally becomes fuller with the progress of time but God's presence, and therefore revelation, cannot be said to be more or less real in different instances. It follows that the Old Testament and New Testament are equally revelation: there is no progress in revelation from the Old Testament to the New Testament[2]

---

[2]Van Ruler admits a progress in salvation history, but this is a historical, temporal progress rather than a spiritual, intellectual progress as is implied by the term 'progressive revelation'.

but God is actively present in Jesus Christ, as in Israel, and in both cases his presence needs to be authenticated and clarified by signs and witnesses.[3]

Van Ruler next asks for what purpose and in what way God is present in Israel, and answers briefly that God's purpose is not simply redemption but the establishment of his kingdom, the theocracy. He also argues that the manner in which God is present in Israel is forceful, in contrast to his treatment of other nations to whom he gives comparative freedom, and this forceful aspect of God's presence among his people comes to a climax when he becomes man for them in the incarnation.

Christian preaching of the Old Testament

The above understanding of revelation raises a problem for the Christian who preaches from the Old Testament: how can revelation which is so inextricably tied to the history of Israel be revelation for the Christian church (pp. 28–33/30–36)? Or, in the words of Wolff (1952:97), 'What is the message that the text has for us in the name of God today if it is still to be the message of the Old Testament text, even though God has now uttered his definitive word in Jesus Christ?' If the Old Testament is to be revelation for Christians, and van Ruler assumes that it will be, they must either be Israel or be related to Israel in such a way that what happened to Israel applies to them also. It might be suggested that 'tradition' is the key: that is, Christians stand in the same tradition as Israel, so that salvation is 'passed on' from the Jews to the Gentiles. However, since the Old Testament revelation is rooted in the history of Israel, it can only be passed on fully if there is a 'repetition' of Israel. This takes place as 'around Christ and by the Spirit we are appointed and made Israel'. It means that Christians are involved in the sanctification of life and the world as well as in the sanctification of the church, and that the final prospect for the world is the presupposition of Israel: theocracy.

Christian preaching of the Old Testament is thus not simply preaching of Christ as he may be found in the Old Testament but also preaching of the kingdom. The concrete earthly things which this involves are in fact the most important, since God's ultimate purpose is the sanctification of the earth. At first the

---

[3]He refers to the resurrection, Spirit and apostles in the New Testament, which are perhaps intended to correspond to the Exodus, the prophetic word and the historical confessions (the *credos* and the histories of which they are the core) in the Old Testament.

New Testament appears more spiritual than the Old Testament, but this is a negative rather than a positive attribute. 'If the church's preaching is to be full preaching of the kingdom, in which all reality is set in the light of the Word and counsel of God, the Old Testament is quite indispensable. The New Testament is not enough' (pp. 32n./34–35). Thus the Old Testament stands as an independent source for Christian preaching, which includes preaching not only of the gospel but also of the kingdom.

b. The Old Testament and Christ

It may seem that the problem of Old Testament interpretation focuses on the idea of 'Christ in the Old Testament' (p. 13/15). However, van Ruler deliberately postponed discussing this and first established the validity of the Old Testament as the Word of God independently of any Christological interpretation. Revelation in the Old Testament, he has claimed, is the active presence of the one God – who is Father of our Lord Jesus Christ – in the history of Israel, and it becomes revelation for Christians as they become Israel. Therefore preaching of this revelation will be preaching of the presence of God, and this is manifested above all in his kingdom. Now van Ruler turns to ask whether it is *also* valid to use the Old Testament to preach Christ; in other words, is it possible to preach a Christian message from an Old Testament perspective? This can only be so if the Old Testament itself 'sees' Christ.

Jesus Christ as an act of God in his history with Israel

Van Ruler first remarks that the Old Testament in its entirety is not a single promise of Christ, but contains a history which is continually moving from promise to fulfilment, within the Old Testament itself (pp. 34–37/37–40). This is a real history, with concrete promises fulfilled in visible ways, each fulfilment pointing further into the future so that the history is never finished. It is here in the history of Israel itself that the basis of typology is to be found, not only in its relationship to Christ but in the pattern of promise and fulfilment which links later events to earlier ones. Jesus Christ is one act in this history of God with his people, and thus fulfils promises of the Old Testament in a similar way to the fulfilments within the Old Testament itself. In this way, and only in this way, Jesus Christ becomes theologically significant for the history of Israel, and thus for the Old Testament.

This act inaugurates a new but not yet final phase of that history

The question follows whether Jesus Christ is only one act among others or whether this act has a special character: does it bring about a *new* phase in God's dealing with Israel or the *final* phase of ultimate fulfilment (pp. 38–40/41–43)? On the one hand, it is certain that the New Testament is more than an extension of the Old Testament, since it speaks of a completely new act of God in Christ which brings the end of the law and the old covenant and inaugurates the last time in a revolutionary way by introducing Jesus Christ as the centre of history. On the other hand, the New Testament does not devalue the Old Testament, and promise and expectation are still important as Christians look into the future to the consummation of history. Van Ruler concludes therefore that the New Testament is more than a new phase, but not yet the final phase in the history of God with his people.

Attempts to harmonize the Testaments

Christian theologians, in particular those involved in the *Biblischer Kommentar*, often try to understand this integration of the New Testament events into God's history with Israel by means of the concepts of promise and expectation (pp. 40–46/43–49). They say, for instance, that since God is free to interpret and fulfil his promises, Jesus Christ may be seen as God's fulfilment of his promises to Israel in the Old Testament. There are many of these promises, some of them contradictory to others and some nebulous, but all of them are fulfilled in Christ. The expectation in the Old Testament is concerned with the coming Lord himself rather than with those to whom he will come, and he is expected as the one who comes to kill and make alive. This very pattern is fulfilled in the New Testament when God himself comes to mankind in Jesus Christ, whose life centres on his death and resurrection.

Van Ruler does not deny that there is some truth in these observations but he thinks that they oversimplify the issues. The people Israel has an essential place in Old Testament expectation, and the fulfilment of Old Testament promises is not in every case to be found in Christ by the spiritualization of promises belonging to Israel. There is a 'plus' in the Old Testament compared with the New Testament, a remainder which is not a factor in the New Testament fulfilment. Moreover, although death and resurrection are the focal point in the New Testament they are not the fundamental purpose of the revelation, which is the same as in the Old Testament: that men may live rightly and to the glory of God.

Incongruity between the Testaments

Van Ruler rejects such harmonizing attempts to integrate the

New Testament into God's dealing with his people Israel and argues that incongruities and differences of emphasis occur at some vital points (pp. 49–57/46–53):

- God himself comes as the Messiah in the New Testament, whereas in the Old Testament the Messiah is only a man;
- the New Testament is concerned above all with forgiveness but the Old Testament with kingship;
- the dominant event of the New Testament (the rejection of the Messiah by the chosen people) is not even foreseen by the Old Testament;
- suffering and the love of God are the keynotes of the New Testament in contrast to the wrath and glory of God in the Old Testament;
- the New Testament has one way of atonement but the Old Testament many; and
- in the New Testament the apostles are sent to the nations whereas in the Old Testament the nations have to come to Israel for salvation.

Allegory

One way of seeing 'Christ in the Old Testament' is to renew allegorizing, a method that has often been popular in the history of the church (pp. 53–58/57–62). This appears to solve many problems by giving the entire Old Testament to the church, which is therefore free to interpret it. But allegorical interpretation is arbitrary, often taking words out of context in order to find Christ in the Old Testament, and it implies that God inspired the Old Testament in a mysterious way and thus deliberately obscured the meaning. Moreover, van Ruler argues, if the Old Testament were an allegory it would not matter what it actually said since the real meaning would be something other than what it said. Its bond to the history of Israel would be irrelevant and the Old Testament would no longer be revelation in the sense of God's presence in the history of his people. Allegorical exegesis is superficially attractive since it evades the problem of the historical reliability of the Old Testament, but in ignoring God's history with his people it inevitably fails to understand the nature of revelation and finds in the Old Testament not the historical Christ but a subjective or other-worldly Christ.

Van Ruler recognizes a difference between intellectual knowledge and spiritual understanding of the Bible, and argues that scholarship, if it is to take the Bible seriously as God's revelation, should attempt to penetrate beyond the study of the actual words to an understanding of God's purpose in revelation. However, this is no justification for allegorical exegesis, since God has chosen to express himself in ordinary words and therefore it is through these that his purpose may be understood. Allegorizing must be rejected and historical-grammatical study remains fundamental, according to van Ruler; nevertheless scholarship alone is insufficient to understand God's words and true exegesis is possible only in and by the Holy Spirit.

Typology

Another way of finding 'Christ in the Old Testament' is typological interpretation, a method which was being revived in the 1950s (in the *Biblischer Kommentar*, for example). Van Ruler analyses the way the method was being used thus (pp. 58–68/62–72):

● earlier historical facts are related to later ones (in particular Old Testament facts to those in the New Testament), both kinds of facts being recognized as acts of God, so that features of the earlier time recur or have parallels or are continued or developed in the later time;

● it is stressed that typology concerns the whole Old Testament and not just the messianic prophecies;

● it is asked whether the typological relationship is only perceived in retrospect or whether it is fixed by God from the beginning;

● it is conceded that the real meaning of a text may not originally have been understood;

● it is considered that Christian theologians must understand the Old Testament from the New, although this cannot be made into a strict method; and

● Jesus Christ is seen as 'the final goal of the way of God' with his people Israel, and thus secretly present in the Old Testament.

Van Ruler's critical comments on this typological method bring him right to the heart of his thesis, defining the place of Jesus Christ in God's plan and the authenticity of the Old Testament as the canonical Word of God.

His first comment is concerned with the centrality of Jesus Christ in God's plan. He argues that, contrary to what is usually thought, it is less the case that God's history with Israel is directed toward Jesus Christ than that God's act in Jesus Christ is for the benefit of Israel. Similarly, God's history with Israel is for the benefit of the peoples of the earth and God's purpose in salvation is for his creation, not the other way round. 'We are not men in order that we might be Christians; we are Christians in order that we might be men' (p. 65/68). It was Jesus' sacrifice that solved the problem of guilt and therefore he is the centre of God's purpose, but this is different from saying that God is concerned exclusively with him. God's concern is not only with reconciliation but with sanctification, not only with the Messiah but with the Spirit. From the beginning God's plan is for his kingdom, and

> Jesus Christ is an emergency measure that God post-poned as long as possible (*cf.* Mt. 21:33–46). Hence we must not try to find him fully in the Old Testament, even though as Christian theologians we investigate the Old Testament in orientation to God (p. 65/69).

Secondly, van Ruler advocates a more cautious use of typology, limiting the types to those authenticated by God (in the New Testament, presumably). Types can be recognized only in retrospect and therefore Jesus Christ fulfils the Old Testament by putting into effect what it says, not because the Old Testament foresees what he will do and speaks about it. So the Old Testament speaks about Jesus only in the sense that he fulfils it.

Thirdly, according to van Ruler, Jesus Christ fulfils the Old Testament above all by solving its root problem, the broken relationship between God and mankind.[4] It follows that it is not what is typologically related to Christ that is most important, but Israel, the world and God himself, the very things dealt with pre-eminently in the Old Testament. 'The Old Testament is and remains the intrinsic Bible (*die eigentliche Bibel*). In it God has made known himself and the secret he has with the world' (p. 68/72). Thus van Ruler states explicitly the underlying theme of his whole book, that it is the Old Testament which is the original, essential and canonical Word of God and the New

---

[4]Here he says that forgiveness and expiation are a fundamental part of the Old Testament, in apparent contradiction to his previous statement that forgiveness is the characteristic of the New Testament in contrast to the Old Testament (pp. 48/51–52).

Testament is its interpretative glossary (*erklärendes Wörterver-zeichnis*). So the Old Testament must not be interpreted simply in terms of the gospel of Jesus Christ: it must be interpreted in its own terms, the life of individuals and the history of the people of God.

c. The Old Testament and the church

Finally van Ruler considers the question of why and in what way the Old Testament is necessary for the Christian church.

Six concepts

In the first place, the Old Testament is necessary for the Christian church as a *legitimation* of Jesus as the Christ (pp. 69–71/75–77). The Old Testament shows that Jesus is in harmony with God's relationship to his people and thus that he has been sent by God, and it witnesses to Jesus' claim to do the works of God by showing what those works are. Its attestation of Jesus' messiahship links the Old and New Testaments as it combines the Old Testament concept of the kingdom of God and the New Testament concept of the deity of Jesus.

It is also possible to look at the relationship between the Testaments in the opposite way: not only does the Old Testament legitimate Jesus as the Christ but Jesus himself authenticates the Old Testament, in van Ruler's terminology he is its *foundation* (pp. 71–74/77–80). In Jesus Christ God's promises are fulfilled, God's relationship with Israel, humanity and the world has been ratified, and the kingdom of God has been founded on earth. Therefore the Old Testament is necessary for the Christian church because Jesus has confirmed the validity of what it says. A corollary is that only the Christian church can understand the Old Testament. Although it is indeed Israel's book, it became evident through the coming of the Messiah and the Spirit that the Old Testament is not only concerned with Israel but with the whole world. The promises and the kingdom of God are passed on from Israel to the church in the incarnation and rejection of Christ.

The third way in which the Old Testament is necessary for the Christian church is for *interpretation* of the gospel, since the New Testament can only be understood historically on the basis of the Old Testament (pp. 74–77/80–82). Without the Old Testament the kingdom is lost from sight, as is the historical, worldly, theocratic element of Christianity, and so systematic theology should take the Old Testament more seriously and use it to help express the significance of Jesus being the Christ.

Next van Ruler refers to the Old Testament's importance for *illustration* (pp. 77–79/83–85). It is not simply that the imagery of the Old Testament has a lasting value, but that Jesus Christ cannot be understood other than in terms of the Old Testament. Apart from the basic fact that Jesus is Israel's Messiah, his close involvement in the difficult situation in which Israel had got entangled, his answer to the problem of guilt (expressed in the language of Jewish 'blood-theology') and the fact that the church is now 'Israel' are important instances of the necessity for preaching Christ by means of Old Testament expressions and concepts.

Fifthly, *historicization*: the Old Testament shows Jesus Christ to be part of God's history with Israel and thus a genuinely historical fact (pp. 79–82/86–87). Although it is obvious to ordinary people, the fact that history is central to Christianity has been continually evaded by theologians. In this situation the Old Testament with its unmistakable concern for history is essential as a reminder that God's revelation is inextricably linked to historical facts.

Lastly, the church's need of the Old Testament is expressed by the concept of *eschatologization*, by which van Ruler means that initially, finally and therefore all the time it is God and the world that are fundamentally important (pp. 82–85/88–91). This is seen more clearly in the Old Testament (which is positively concerned with creation, kingdom, law, sanctification, culture, marriage, the state, *etc.*) than in the New (where it is recognized but obscured by the details of revelation, the incarnation of the Messiah and the indwelling of the Spirit). So the Old Testament has a surplus over the New Testament, not only in the ceremonial sphere, but in its social and political ideal of the sanctification of the earth. This is an ideal which the church has lost through a false deduction from the necessity for Christ's death that nothing more can be done with the earth.

Some further implications

Van Ruler's book ends with two questions and two problems (pp. 85–92/92–98). 'Should the church preach only Christ?' is answered in the negative, since preaching of the kingdom – for the sake of which Christ came – is more fundamental. 'What should follow the recognition of the Old Testament as canon?' is that the church is bound to the Old Testament, not the Old Testament to the church, as is so often the case.

The problems of the relationship between the Old and New Testaments as Christian canon, and the Old Testament as Israel's book today, are outlined but not solved. What is clear is that both Old and New Testaments are to be recognized as authorities and that, although the Old Testament becomes valid for Gentiles through Jesus Christ, the people of Israel still exists and has an important part in God's history with the world.

5.2 Critique

a. Incongruity between the Testaments

Van Ruler draws attention to a number of incongruities between the Old Testament and the New (pp. 49–57/46–53).

First, he distinguishes between the Old Testament idea of the Messiah as a man and the New Testament teaching that he is God; but in doing so he ignores the fact that the Old Testament looks forward to the coming not only of a human Messiah but of the Lord himself (*e.g.* Mal. 3:1) and the New Testament recognizes the genuine humanity of Jesus (*e.g.* Jn. 1:14; Rom. 9:5).

Secondly, he claims that the Old Testament emphasizes kingship and the New Testament guilt and atonement. Yet a dominant theme throughout the Law, Prophets and Writings is the guilt and need for forgiveness of individuals and nations faced with a holy God;[5] and the idea of the kingdom of God is fundamental to the teaching of Jesus (Mk. 1:15) and Paul (1 Cor. 15:24–28).[6]

Thirdly, van Ruler suggests that the Old Testament does not envisage the dominant event of the New Testament, the rejection of the Messiah (*cf.* Bright 1953: 198–208; Eichrodt 1933: 510–511; P. Richardson 1969). This may be countered on the one hand by referring to the prophetic expectation that the Servant would be rejected (Is. 53) and the common rejection of God's messengers in the Old Testament (Is. 6:9–10; Je. 11:19; Ezk. 3:7; Am. 7:12–13; *cf.* Steck 1967; Crenshaw 1971: 94–99)

---

[5]*E.g.* in the Old Testament the word 'sin' (*ḥāṭā'*) occurs 593 times, 'iniquity' (*'āwōn*) 223 times, 'atonement' (*kipper*) 101 times and 'forgive' (*sālaḥ*) 50 times. *Cf.* in the New Testament the word 'sin' (*hamartia* and compounds) occurs 149 times and 'forgive' (*aphiēmi*) 46 times. Even van Ruler admits elsewhere (p. 67/71) that the root problem of the Old Testament is the broken relationship between God and mankind, *i.e.* the need for expiation and forgiveness.

[6]The word 'kingdom' (*basileia*) occurs 157 times in the New Testament, usually accompanied by the explanation 'of God' or 'of heaven'; whereas in the Old Testament the words for 'king' (*melek*) and 'kingdom' (*mamlākâ*) although very common are not often related to God.

and on the other by questioning whether the rejection of the Messiah is really the dominant event of the New Testament. The resurrection is at least as important in the New Testament as the crucifixion, and the New Testament's interest in the cross is more in the fulfilment of God's plan than in human rejection of it (Acts 2:23; cf. Mk. 8:31; Lk. 18:31; Acts 3:18; 4:28; 13:29; 1 Pet. 1:19–20; Rev. 13:8[7]).

Then van Ruler claims that the Old Testament has many ways of atonement but the New Testament only one. There is some truth in this contrast, but his further claim that the idea of substitution emerges clearly only in the New Testament cannot be accepted. On the contrary, substitution is an important concept in the Old Testament: 'Israel knew very well what substitution and atonement meant; what it did not know was the way of their final realization in Jesus of Nazareth' (Stamm 1956: 208).

There is also some truth in van Ruler's distinction between the Old Testament expectation of the nations coming to Israel for salvation and the New Testament apostolate which evangelizes the nations. Nevertheless both Testaments recognize the fundamental point, which is that salvation is possible for the Gentiles as well as for Israel (cf. Stamm 1956: 209; see also Rowley 1944b; Jeremias 1956; Martin-Achard 1959a). World mission and blessing for all nations through the chosen people were implicit in Abraham's call (Gn. 12:1–3). Jonah was sent to Nineveh to preach his message and his reluctance to fulfil this mission was due to jealousy and small-mindedness rather than ignorance of God's plans to save the nations (Jon. 4:1–2). Further evidence that the faith of Israel had a missionary aspect is to be found in the proselytes that Paul found throughout the Roman Empire in the first century, showing that Judaism had in fact made many converts (Acts 2:10; 6:5; 13:43; cf. Mt. 23:15; see Bright 1953: 160–161). On the other hand, the Old Testament expectation of the nations coming to Israel for salvation is not entirely forgotten in the New Testament: at the birth of Jesus 'wise men from the East came to Jerusalem, saying, "Where is he who has been born king of the Jews?"' (Mt. 2:1–2); and at Pentecost it was the 'nations' who came to Jerusalem to hear the gospel preached for the first time after the resurrection (Acts 2:5–11).

In conclusion, although there are obvious differences in

---

[7]Translate: '. . . the Lamb slain before the foundation of the world'; so Caird (1966); Morris (1969).

emphasis and content between the two Testaments, the contrast is not nearly so sharp as van Ruler claims.

b. The surplus

One major aspect of the relationship between the Testaments, according to van Ruler, is that the Old Testament has a surplus over the New:

> To the very depths of Old Testament expectation, the people of Israel as a people, the land, posterity and theocracy play a role that cannot possibly be eliminated. This role cannot be altered by regarding Christ and his church as the fulfilment, in other words, by spiritualizing. There is a surplus (*zu viel*) in the Old Testament, a remnant that cannot be fitted into the New Testament fulfilment (pp. 42–43/45).

At this point Stamm (1956: 206–208) criticizes van Ruler, arguing that fulfilment should be seen in the context of the whole and not in terms of individual promises, since Jesus – admittedly to the surprise of contemporary Jews – claimed to fulfil all the different messianic promises. But van Ruler has more to say:

> In the Old Testament what matters is everyone sitting under his vine and fig tree, in other words, earthly possessions and inhabiting the earth where righteousness dwells – all to God's praise. The element of the earth is not eliminated, not even when the cross of Jesus Christ is planted in that earth. Here too is a surplus in the Old Testament as compared with the New (p. 46/49; *cf.* pp. 83–85/89–91).

It is indeed true that these things are characteristic of the Old Testament, perhaps more so than of the New Testament.[8] But it should not be assumed that the New Testament is disinterested in

---

[8]Liberation theologians have placed a particular emphasis on the Old Testament, finding its 'earthly realism' (Fierro 1977: 480) and its depiction of 'God the liberator' in the Exodus event (Segundo 1976: 485) to be particularly relevant to their political concerns. Indeed Hanks (1983: 85–96) finds many points of similarity between Judaism and liberation theologies.

ordinary life on earth,[9] nor that the Old Testament is disinterested in spiritual things.[10] Van Ruler's mistake is oversimplification: his characterization of the Old Testament as 'earthly' and the New Testament as 'spiritual' must be rejected (see Wolff 1956a: 176–179).

c. Jesus Christ as God's 'emergency measure'

From the Old Testament standpoint Jesus Christ is either of theological significance only as an historical fact – as an act of God in the history with his people, Israel – or he is of no significance at all (van Ruler 1955: 37/40; *cf.* 34–40/37–43; also 80/86).

Indeed, for van Ruler, Jesus Christ is not even an essential part of this history but an emergency measure which God delayed and eventually found necessary in order to establish his kingdom (p. 65/69). The implication of this is presumably that Jesus will no longer be needed once his rescue mission has been accomplished (*cf.* 1 Cor. 15:28; see Moltmann 1973: 259–266).

Now it is not to be disputed that Jesus Christ, as his title testifies, came as the Messiah of Israel: this is a fundamental fact for any evaluation of the relationship between the Testaments. But van Ruler's formulation is dependent on a questionable view of revelation and history (*cf.* Barr 1966: 65–102), and does not adequately account for the radical newness of God's act in the incarnation, life, death and resurrection of his Son (*cf.* von Rad 1960: 382–383; Thomas 1966). To make Jesus Christ only an emergency measure, although it contains an element of truth and warns against a premature Christological interpretation of the Old Testament, ignores the New Testament claim that Jesus Christ was part of God's plan from the beginning (*cf.* Jn. 1:1–18; Col. 1:15–20).

d. Creation and salvation

Van Ruler presupposes that the doctrine of creation is more fundamental than the doctrine of salvation, and hence that

---

[9]See Mt. 13; Lk. 1:53a; Jn. 10:10b; Acts 2:44–46; Rom. 12–13; 1 Cor. 7:16; Phil. 4; Col. 3:18–25; James; Rev. 21; *cf.* Wilder (1955).

[10]See Gn. 6:8; 15:6; Nu. 16:30; Dt. 29:18–19; 1 Sa. 2:26; Jb. 19:25–27; Ps. 16:9–11; Is. 43:1–7; Je. 31:31–34; Ezk. 37; Dn. 12:2–3; *cf.* Eichrodt (1933: 210–220); Vriezen (1966: 153–175).

sanctification is greater than reconciliation (pp. 63–65/67–69, 82–85/88–91). According to him the Old Testament is concerned with creation and the New Testament with salvation, therefore the Old Testament has priority over the New Testament. This is apparent in his devotional study, *God's Son and God's World* (1960): unlike many books which deal first with the Old Testament and then progress to the New Testament, Part One is devoted to the New Testament (the 'I am' sayings, 28 pp.) and Part Two to the Old Testament (Ps. 104, 39 pp.). 'The intention of the gospel of Christ is that we do rejoice in the world ... Through the gift of Jesus Christ we are able again to love the world and be glad in it' (p. 5).

There is indeed a certain logic in this. If God's purpose is for the world, then salvation may be understood as a remedy to heal the world's sickness, and health is obviously more important than healing. Moreover, it may be urged that 'for those who believe their God to be Lord of all, the supreme act of the past is the act of creation itself' (Foulkes 1958: 31). Undoubtedly this is one aspect of the truth, and may be a necessary corrective to any ideas of salvation that fail to take account of what is to be saved and for what purpose it is to be saved. In line with van Ruler, Bonhoeffer (1951) counters those who advocate Christianity simply as a religion of salvation in these terms:

> Is there any concern in the Old Testament about saving one's soul at all? Is not righteousness and the kingdom of God on earth the focus of everything? ... It is not with the next world that we are concerned but with this world as created and preserved and set subject to laws and atoned for and made new (pp. 94–95).

and

> The Christian hope sends a man back to his life on earth in a wholly new way which is even more sharply defined than it is in the Old Testament ... This world must not be prematurely written off (p. 112; *cf.* 50, 93).

Vriezen (1956: 221), however, points out that 'the earth as creation cannot be truly loved without the deep confession of sin which desecrates it, and without knowledge of the power of God which has broken the power of sin and prepares a new future for the earth. Sanctification without redemption is impossible.'

The basic problem is that van Ruler does not deal adequately with the fact of sin and the theology of salvation which are fundamental to the whole Bible, not just the New Testament.[11] A balanced Christian appreciation of the whole biblical message must recognize that creation and salvation are each of fundamental importance and neither exists without the other.[12] Indeed Jesus the saviour is also the one who inaugurates the new creation (Jn. 14:2; 2 Cor. 5:17; 1 Jn. 3:2; *cf*. Moltmann 1973: 263). Even if it is conceded that there are different emphases in the Old and New Testaments, that 'creation' is a more dominant note in the former and 'salvation' in the latter, both Testaments have the same ideal of a sanctified earth and both acknowledge that this can only be brought about by the activity of God who not only created the world but also provided for its salvation (*cf*. also Bonhoeffer 1951: 126–127; Barr 1966: 149–170; 1970).

e. Kingdom of God

The theme of the kingdom of God underlies the whole of van Ruler's book (*cf*. his popular exposition of Zechariah, 1962, of which this is also true). This is closely related to the idea that the doctrine of creation is more important than the doctrine of salvation, and van Ruler argues on this basis that the purpose of God's revelation is not only redemption but more particularly the setting up of his kingdom, the theocracy.[13] Israel starts as a theocracy, the church becomes the theocracy and the theocracy is the final expectation for the world (p. 32/34). Thus for van Ruler Israel is more important than the church (*cf*. below: ch. 9.3) and the Old Testament is more important than the New. He argues that one reason why the Old Testament is necessary for the Christian church is because its concern for the kingdom

---

[11]See above: ch. 5.2.a; *cf*. Festorazzi (1967); Grogan (1967a); Hill (1967); Gunneweg (1977: 113).

[12]*Cf*. Toombs (1969: 310–312); Gutiérrez (1971: 153–160); Westermann (1978); Goldingay (1987: 200–239).

[13]1955: 26–27/28–29; *cf*. 1947: 29–47. The isolation of the concept of theocracy as central to the Old Testament is not new. The word was originally coined by Josephus (*Against Apion* 2:164–167). Smend (1970: 39–44) traces the use of the concept of theocracy as the 'centre' of the Old Testament since the seventeenth century, showing that it belongs with the idea of God as the Lord (*e.g.* Wellhausen 1878: 411–425).

brings out the aspect of kingship in the concept of Messiah which would be lost from sight if Jesus was understood only through the New Testament (p. 75/81). So also the Old Testament should be interpreted not Christologically but eschatologically, which for van Ruler means theocratically (pp. 82–83/ 88–89; cf. Vriezen 1956: 219–220; Plöger 1959).

Undoubtedly, the concept of the kingdom of God is fundamental to biblical theology[14] and van Ruler's work provides a balance to others which stress the importance of concepts such as 'covenant', 'communion with God', 'salvation history' and 'people of God'. Moreover, it is true that God saves people in order that they may live under his rule, that Jesus came in order to set up God's kingdom and that in this sense theocracy is more ultimate to the biblical message than soteriology.

However van Ruler's 'theocratic theology' (cf. Hommes 1967) is inadequate insofar as it does not take sufficient account of the variety of biblical theology and in particular because of the outstanding failure of the Israelite attempt at theocracy. Not one of the forms of statehood experienced by Israel – wilderness community, tribal league, monarchy, post-exilic community – succeeded in being theocracies, and it was not until the coming of Jesus that the kingdom of God was at last inaugurated. Van Ruler's claim that the theocracy is the presupposition of Israel must therefore be challenged (see Vriezen 1956: 216–222). No doubt many Israelites assumed that they lived in a theocracy and the false prophets encouraged them in their complacency, but the burden of the canonical prophets was to proclaim the eschatological kingdom of God, a theocracy to be established on the 'day of the Lord' (Is. 9:7; Ezk. 20:33; 37:24–28; Ho. 3:5; Ob. 21; Zc. 14:9, 16–17). Nor are Christians called to establish a theocracy on earth in the Old Testament sense, though there have been tendencies towards this in both traditional Catholicism and militant Protestantism (Gunneweg 1977: 107–111).

One of the stumbling-blocks of the preaching of Jesus is that the kingdom comes in an unexpected way, through the death and resurrection of the Son of God. So Vriezen (1956: 218) can say:

> It had been demonstrated in Israel that theocratic preaching could not save Israel, that Israel could not

---

[14]On the concept of the kingdom of God in biblical theology, see Bright (1953); Ladd (1974); Bruce (1968a: ch. 2); Klein (1970); Gray (1979); Goldsworthy (1981); Willis (1987). It is one of the key themes of liberation theology (see Kirk 1979: 136–140; Dussel 1979; Hoesl 1982).

be transformed into a theocracy without the suffering and sacrificial death of the Servant of God. Theocracy could become a living reality in Israel only through the cross, as in fact it can be realized in any way at all only through the cross ... Jesus Christ is the locus of the breaking through of the kingdom of God in the world.

Although the Old Testament envisages the kingdom of God, it is the New Testament which portrays its coming. Thus it is a fallacy to make the Old Testament superior to the New Testament on the ground that it deals with the kingdom rather than redemption (*cf.* Wolff 1956a: 196n.): both Testaments are vital to maintain the biblical understanding of the kingdom of God.

f. A relationship of priority

All these five propositions – that there are fundamental incongruities between the Testaments, that the Old Testament has a surplus compared with the New, that Jesus Christ is an emergency measure in God's history with Israel, that the doctrine of creation is more important than the doctrine of salvation, and that the kingdom of God is the central concept of the Old Testament – are aspects of van Ruler's basic thesis that the Old Testament is primarily and inherently the Bible and the New Testament is its interpretative glossary. It follows that the relationship between the Testaments is a relationship of priority: the Old Testament has historical and theological priority with respect to the New Testament. In van Ruler's words:

> The Old Testament is and remains the intrinsic Bible. In it God has made known himself and the secret he has with·the world. All goodness and also all truth and beauty – the fully redemptive knowledge of being – shines out before us in this book. It is the book of humanity ... Both exegetically and homiletically one must continually begin afresh and remain occupied with the text of the Old Testament itself ... The Old Testament itself remains the canonical Word of God, and it constantly confronts us with its own authority (p. 68/72).

This is true up to a point. God's intentions for the salvation and sanctification of humanity and the world are set out first of all in the Old Testament, and the New Testament records the fulfilment of those intentions. Jesus Christ is part of God's dealings in history with his chosen people and his church is spiritually Israel. God's ultimate purpose is that his kingdom should be established over all creation.

This much may be learnt from van Ruler, and the most fundamental criticism of his thesis concerns not so much what he says but what he fails to say. He does not take account of the failure of the Israelite theocracy. Moreover he underestimates the radical nature of God's act in Jesus Christ, which is not simply the final stage of God's activity in Israel but also a new event that inaugurates God's kingdom. From the Old Testament point of view Jesus Christ is the final act, but from the point of view of the New Testament he has become the centre of history (Cullmann 1946). The New Testament is, therefore, not merely a glossary to interpret the real meaning of the Old Testament, but equally the record of God's activity in the history of his people Israel and thus God's self-communication or 'revelation'. Van Ruler's interpretation of the Old Testament is stimulating and educative, drawing attention to aspects of it which are often ignored. Nevertheless, his understanding of the relationship between the Testaments overestimates the importance of the Old Testament and must finally be rejected.

5.3 Comparison: other 'Old Testament' solutions

We shall now discuss the work of another Dutch scholar, Kornelis H. Miskotte, whose solution to the problem of the relationship between the Testaments is somewhat similar to that of van Ruler, and some other views which imply the theological priority of the Old Testament over the New Testament.

a. Kornelis H. Miskotte

Kornelis H. Miskotte was a prolific writer in the fields of literature and philosophy as well as that of theology, but it was particularly in *When the Gods are Silent* (1963)[15] that he expounded his view of the Old Testament. This book was called the

---

[15]Published originally in Dutch (1956), in a revised form in German (1963) and then translated into English (1967). The subtitle ('On the Significance of the Old Testament') has been omitted in the English translation, except on the dust-cover. Miskotte has written several other

theological book of the decade in Germany and remains one of the most important works on the significance of the Old Testament of the modern era, though it still awaits a serious reaction from biblical scholarship. This is not the place for a full-scale study and only Miskotte's view of the relationship between the Testaments will be considered here.

A relationship of priority

In many respects Miskotte's work implies the theological priority of the Old Testament over the New Testament, and it has a number of similarities to that of van Ruler. Like him, Miskotte rejects any suggestion that the New Testament is about a different God or has a different message from the Old Testament (1963: 131–132, 143) and finds the essence of the Old Testament in its testimony to God himself, to whom he refers by means of the term 'the Name' (pp. 65–71, 114–119, 257–264). He recognizes that there are differences between the Testaments (p. 107; cf. above: ch. 5.2.a) but rejects formulae such as 'provisional and definitive', 'law and gospel', 'promise and fulfilment' as inadequate descriptions of these differences (pp. 108–110). The difference is not to be understood systematically but as part of the human aspect of the Scriptures: whereas the Bible is united because of its testimony to one God and one Christ, the humanity of the Scriptures means that 'though the one Word is the same in the Old Testament as in the New, it is nevertheless very decidedly different' (p. 153). The unity of the Bible pervades the text, yet it is never visible or demonstrable as something 'given' (1948: 84).

The theocracy is the basis of Israel and the ideal of the church, and the kingdom is God's ultimate purpose for the world (1963: 138, 207–214, 216, 274–275, 279, 292–294, 298, 301, 417; cf. above: ch. 5.2.e). Miskotte agrees with van Ruler in accepting Bonhoeffer's view of the Old Testament as presenting a 'worldly Christianity' (pp. 80–81; cf. 273) but he diverges on the question of the relationship between salvation and creation (cf. above: ch. 5.2.d). Here Miskotte argues that salvation is part of God's plan in creation and that 'the Creation is already a part of God's redemptive history, that the existence of salvation is superior and antecedent to that of Being'.[16] This may be compared with

---

works on the Old Testament and its relationship to the New (e.g. 1948; 1959; 1966), but unfortunately none has been translated into English.

[16] 1963: 118; cf. 471, 475; cf. also von Rad (1936a); B. W. Anderson (1955: 6–10, 19–20); Barr (1966: 18–19).

the statement of Nixon (1963: 5): 'in the Old Testament the Exodus has pride of place even over the Creation'.

The surplus

The Old Testament has both a deficit and a surplus compared with the New Testament, but the relative importance of the latter in Miskotte's view is shown by the fact that he devotes half a page to the deficit and 132 pages to the surplus (1963: 169–302; on 'surplus', cf. above: ch. 5.2.b)! In using the word 'surplus' Miskotte refers to elements in the Old Testament which:

> are not surpassed in the New Testament, nor are they denied; but there they have receded into the background. We observe that when the essential substance and tendency of the Old and the New Testament are balanced there remains a margin of ideas . . . which includes scepticism, rebellion, erotics, politics (themes which are hardly mentioned in the New Testament) (pp. 170–171; cf. 252–257, 264–282).

He rejects the traditional disparagement of the primitive mentality of the Old Testament: according to him anthropomorphism is not a failing but a surplus (p. 173; cf. 128–129; 1959: 40), an idea developed by several other scholars (Vischer 1949; Jacob 1955a: 39–42; Mauser 1970; Clines 1973). Miskotte argues that if the New Testament is expounded without reference to the Old Testament there is the danger that naïvety will be replaced by abstraction, which is really a flight from the reality of God (1963: 177–179). Other aspects of the surplus are the Torah (pp. 228–246), suffering and poverty (pp. 246–252), the presence of God (pp. 262–263), expectation (pp. 283–288) and prophetism (pp. 288–295).

We may cautiously concede that these things have a more prominent place in the Old Testament than in the New, but it does not follow that the New Testament has nothing relevant to say. Before these things are accepted in the Christian church they must be confronted with the message of the New Testament: only in the light of Jesus Christ's fulfilment of the Old Testament can they be valid for Christianity (Vriezen 1966: 97–98).

'Let the Old Testament speak for itself'

So far Miskotte's view of the Old Testament has been seen to be similar to that of van Ruler. But there is one aspect in which Miskotte emphasizes the priority of the Old Testament over the

New Testament even more clearly, and that is in his consistent plea that the Old Testament should be allowed 'to speak for itself' (1963: 104–105, 225–226, 239, 243, 262, *etc.*; *cf.* von Rad 1960: 333; Bright 1967: 112). 'Everything' is in the Old Testament, according to Miskotte, and it follows that the New Testament is in the Old Testament, not in detail but in the sense that the Old Testament has already said everything essential. It is therefore a mistake to read the New Testament message of Christ into the Old Testament: on the contrary, 'we need constantly to be learning from the Old Testament what is the meaning and the intent of that which we call "Christ"' (1963: 159; *cf.* Jacob 1965: 48). 'The New Testament used in isolation needs to be corrected on the basis of the fundamental words of the Old Testament' (1963: 461). 'The testimony in the Old Testament proclaims a knowledge of salvation which, in that it becomes an event, already includes within it the fulfilled salvation as its own presupposition' (p. 467).

Thus Miskotte views the Old Testament as an independent witness to 'the Name' and the New Testament as its Christian sequel, the Talmud being its Jewish sequel. One corollary is that the New Testament use of the Old Testament cannot be said to be binding: such a proposition is based on the false presupposition that the New Testament performs exegesis on the Old Testament. It is not that the New Testament explains the Old Testament but that the Old Testament – which speaks for itself as a witness to the Name – is used by New Testament writers to explain Christ (pp. 468–469). The question arises here, however, whether the Old Testament was really accepted and understood in the early church as easily as Miskotte implies: Acts 15, Romans 14 and similar passages suggest that it was not (so Vriezen 1966: 48n.).

A relationship of identity?

There are also similarities between Miskotte's thought and that of Vischer and Barth. Although he will have nothing of Christological interpretation of the Old Testament (1959: 119) it is clear that for Miskotte Christ is at the centre of the biblical witness:

> The testimony of the Old Testament goes out into the time of expectation, that of the New Testament into the time of recollection. Both are relative to the time of revelation itself. What they have in common is their relationship to, their orientation toward one and the same Object, one and the same Name, one and

the same Event, one and the same Salvation (1963: 113; *cf.* 143).

In other words, every part of the Bible points to the unique and definitive event of revelation in Jesus Christ, though every part views it from a distance, looking forward to what God would do or back to what he had done in the past. In this way the Old Testament is an indirect witness to Christ (pp. 132, 144; *cf.* 159, 467), speaking not only through the New Testament but '"for itself" as a fully valid witness of Him who has come' (p. 105). A further link with Vischer and Barth is Miskotte's recognition that the two Testaments have essentially the same theology (*e.g.* 1963: 131–132, 257, 411–412; also x, 160; *cf.* 1948a: 80–86; Jacob 1966). But in spite of these resemblances, the dominant aspect of Miskotte's view of the relationship between the Testaments is the priority of the Old Testament over the New Testament rather than their identity, and therefore it is classified here with that of van Ruler as an 'Old Testament' solution.

b. James Barr

James Barr is a British scholar whose series of lectures on *Old and New in Interpretation* (1966) is an important study of the relationship between the Testaments. He rejects formulations which understand the Old Testament 'in the light of the New Testament', arguing that 'in the minds of the apostles ... the relation was the opposite: the problem was not how to understand the Old Testament but how to understand Christ' (p. 139). It is often assumed that Christ is a known quantity and that it is the place of the Old Testament in the church which is the problem. But in the early church there was no doubt about the Old Testament: the problem was to identify the Christ. So also today, the church's strategy should not be to take Christ as the 'key' to the meaning of the Old Testament, but 'rather, taking the Old Testament as something we *have* in the Church to ask in what way the guidance it affords helps us to understand and discern and obey the Christ more truly' (p. 140). This means that a Christian formulation of the relationship between the Testaments must be related to the Old Testament from the beginning (p. 149) and the interpretation of Old Testament texts is not automatically dependent on New Testament interpretation (pp. 154–155; *cf.* 141–146), though Barr dismisses as naïve any attempt to let 'the Old Testament speak for itself' (pp. 167, 170; *cf.* above: ch. 5.3.a). He sees at least five levels to the relationship between the Testaments (pp. 134–139, 157–166):

> ● the religion of late Judaism (which developed out of the Old Testament and was the basis for the New Testament, cf. 1968);
> ● the text of the Old Testament (which was the authority of the New Testament);
> ● the mind of Jesus (whose self-understanding was shaped by biblical patterns but who interpreted the Old Testament in an authoritative manner);
> ● the minds of the apostles (who came to understand Jesus as the Christ and used the Old Testament in their preaching, cf. Miskotte 1963: 100–101); and
> ● the relationship between Jews and Gentiles (who were made into one body in the church, cf. below: ch. 9.3).

The priority of the Old Testament with respect to the New Testament, however, does not imply for Barr that the former is more important than the latter:

> The Christian faith stands equally upon the basis of the Old Testament and of the New or, more correctly, upon the basis of the God of Israel and of Jesus of Nazareth. In this sense the importance of Old and New Testaments is in principle more or less equal: and the two have a certain independence, an independence warranted by the newness of that which took place in Jesus ... If for Christians Jesus is the finality and the culmination, which might place the New Testament in the higher position, Jesus himself stands under the God of Israel, which might place the Old Testament in the higher (1973: 166–167).

At the deepest level the relationship between the Testaments is not a matter of common patterns of thought or a balance of their different emphases, but is an aspect of the unity of the one God (1973: 181). The real basis of the relationship between the Old Testament and the New, and thus of the use of the Old in the church inaugurated by the New Testament, is the assertion of faith that the One God of Israel is also the Father of the Lord Jesus Christ (1966: 149–153).

Barr's view is evidently not nearly so extreme as that of van Ruler and Miskotte, and he indicates effectively the theological and historical priority of the Old Testament over the New Testament, while demonstrating that the relationship between the Testaments is a mutual one and that neither is more important than the other.[17]

c. 'Sectarian impatience'

An approach to the Old Testament common among many Christian sects is to treat the Old Testament as directly and completely valid today. Van Ruler (1955: 11–12/13) uses the term 'sectarian impatience' to describe the extreme literalism that often characterizes this attitude to the Old Testament. It may be seen in Seventh-Day Adventism's insistence that Saturday should be observed as the Sabbath (Bear 1956: 56–64; van Baalen 1956: 216–223; Hoekema 1963: 161–169), Mormonism's idea of polygamy (Boyd 1956: 442–443; van Baalen 1956: 160–168, 178) and British–Israelism's application of Old Testament prophecies to modern Britain and America (Baron 1915; van Baalen 1956: 189–203). Perhaps the clearest example is that of the Jehovah's Witnesses, who retain the 'Old Testament' name for God, insist on the unity – as distinct from the trinity – of God, refuse blood transfusions on the basis of Leviticus and forbid the use of Christmas trees on the basis of Jeremiah 10:3–4 (Stuermann 1956: 329–330; Hoekema 1963: 249–250). Their use of the Bible may be summarized in Stuermann's words: 'Almost everywhere they subordinate Christian and New Testament themes to those of Judaism and the Old Testament' (1956: 345).[18]

Bibliography (5)

Anderson, B. W. 1955: 'The Earth is the Lord's: An Essay on the Biblical Doctrine of Creation', *Int* 9:3–20.

Baalen, J. K. van 1956: *The Chaos of Cults: A Study in Present-Day Isms*, London, [2]1956 ([1]n.d.).

Baron, D. 1915: *The History of the Ten "Lost" Tribes: Anglo–Israelism Examined*, London.

Barr, J. 1968: *Judaism – Its Continuity with the Bible* (The Seventh Montefiore Memorial Lecture), Southampton.

---

[17]On James Barr's view of the Bible, see further Wells (1980).

[18]This approach may be compared with the emphasis on the direct relevance of the Old Testament among the African independent churches (Mbiti 1969: 235; Loccum report 1977: 62; *cf.* Muzorewa 1985: 115).

—1970: 'Themes from the Old Testament for the Elucidation of the New Creation', *Encounter* 31:25–30.

—1973: *The Bible in the Modern World*, London.

Bear, J. E. 1956: 'The Seventh-Day Adventists', *Int* 10:45–71.

Bonhoeffer, D. 1951: *Letters and Papers from Prison*, ET: London, 1953 (cited from the 1959 reset printing; German, 1951).

Boyd, R. F. 1956: 'Mormonism', *Int* 10:430–446.

Caird, G. B. 1966: *A Commentary on the Revelation of St. John the Divine*, London.

Clines, D. J. A. 1973: 'God in Human Form: A Theme in Biblical Theology', *JCBRF* 24:24–40.

Crenshaw, J. L 1971: *Prophetic Conflict: Its Effect Upon Israelite Religion*, Berlin (Beihefte zur ZAW 124).

Dussel, E. 1979: 'The Kingdom of God and the Poor', *International Review of Mission* 68:115–130.

Festorazzi, F. 1967: 'The Faith of Both Testaments as Salvific Experience: "We are safe." (Jeremiah 7.10)', *Concilium* 3.10:24–31.

Gray, J. 1979: *The Biblical Doctrine of the Reign of God*, Edinburgh.

Grogan, G. W. 1967a: 'The Experience of Salvation in the Old and New Testaments', *Vox Evangelica* 5:4–26.

Hill, D. 1967: *Greek Words and Hebrew Meanings: Studies in the Semantics of Soteriological Terms*, Cambridge, 1967 (SNTS Mon 5).

Hoekema, A. A. 1963: *The Four Major Cults*, reprinted Exeter, 1969 (originally Grand Rapids, Michigan, 1963).

Hoesl, M. 1982: 'The Kingdom: Preferential Option for the Poor', *Missiology* 10:57–68.

Hommes, Tj. G. 1967: 'Sovereignty and Saeculum: Arnold A. van Ruler's Theocratic Theology', Harvard dissertation (not available to me; summary in *HTR* 60:489–490).

Jacob, E. 1966b: Review of Miskotte (1963) in *RHPR* 46:392–394.

Jeremias, J. 1956: *Jesus' Promise to the Nations*, ET: London, 1958 (German, 1956).

Klein, G. 1970: 'The Biblical Understanding of the "Kingdom of God"', ET in *Int* 26:387–418 (German, 1970).

Martin-Achard, R. 1959a: *A Light to the Nations: A Study of the Old Testament Conception of Israel's Mission to the World*, ET: Edinburgh/London, 1962 (French, 1959).

Mauser, U. 1970: 'Image of God and Incarnation', *Int* 24:336–356.

Mbiti, J. S. 1969: *African Religions and Philosophy*, London/Ibadan/Nairobi.

Miskotte, K. H. 1948: *Om het levende Woord: Opstellen over de praktijk der exegese*, The Hague.

—1959: *Zur biblischen Hermeneutik*, Zollikon (ThSt 55).

—1966: *Geloof en Kennis: theologische voordrachten*, Haarlem.

Morris, L. 1969: *The Revelation of St. John: An Introduction and Commentary*, London.

Muzorewa, G. H. 1985: *The Origins and Development of African Theology*, Maryknoll, New York.

Plöger, O. 1959: *Theocracy and Eschatology*, ET: Oxford, 1968 (German, 1959).

Rad, G. von 1936a: 'The Theological Problem of the Old Testament Doctrine of Creation', ET in von Rad (1966): 131–143 (German, 1936).

Rowley, H. H. 1944b: *The Missionary Message of the Old Testament*, London.

Ruler, A. A. van 1945: *Religie en Politiek*, Nijkerk.

—1947: *De vervulling van de wet: Een dogmatische studie over de verhouding van openbaring en existentie*, Nijkerk.

—1960: *God's Son and God's World: Sixteen Meditations on the Person of Christ and the Psalm of Nature*, ET: Grand Rapids, Michigan, 1960 (Dutch, n.d.).

—1962: *Zechariah Speaks Today*, ET: London, 1962 (Dutch, n.d.).

Smend, R. 1970: *Die Mitte des Alten Testaments*, Zürich (ThSt 101).

Steck, O. H. 1967: *Israel und das gewaltsame Geschick der Propheten: Untersuchungen zur Überlieferung des deuteronomistischen Geschichtsbildes im Alten Testament, Spätjudentum und Urchristentum*, Neukirchen-Vluyn (Wissenschaftliche Monographien zum Alten und Neuen Testament 23).

Stuermann, W. E. 1956: 'Jehovah's Witnesses', *Int* 10:323–346.

Thomas, T. G. 1966: 'The Unity of the Bible and the Uniqueness of Christ', *The London Quarterly and Holborn Review* 191:219–227.

Toombs, L. E. 1969: 'The Problematic of Preaching from the Old Testament', *Int* 23:302–314.

Vischer, W. 1949: 'Words and the Word: The Anthropomorphisms of the Biblical Revelation', *Int* 3:3–18.

Wells, P. R. 1980: *James Barr and the Bible: Critique of a New Liberalism*, Phillipsburg, New Jersey.

Wilder, A. N. 1955: *Otherworldliness and the New Testament*, London.

Willis, W. (ed.) 1987: *The Kingdom of God in 20th-Century Interpretation*, Peabody, Massachusetts.

See also works by van Ruler, Miskotte and Barr in the general bibliography.

——————6——————

The Old and New Testaments as one salvation history

6.1 Gerhard von Rad

The key to von Rad's exposition of Old Testament theology and its relationship to the New Testament is found in the concept of 'salvation history'.[1] Israel's history as found in the Old Testament is 'confessional', since essentially it is confession of the saving acts of God: Israel's origin in the patriarchs, oppression in and redemption from Egypt and the gift of the promised land. The whole of von Rad's theology is founded on this 'salvation history', which is therefore the predominent theme in his interpretation of the Old Testament. Cullmann (1965: 54) sums up von Rad's approach thus:

> The progressive reinterpretation of Israel's old traditions is continually awakened by new events in the present. This development of the traditions is itself salvation history and stands in continuity with the original event basic to the traditions.

The structure of von Rad's book is consistent with this basis of saving history, presented and developed in Israel's historical traditions. His first volume deals with the 'historical traditions',

---

[1]Von Rad's major work is his *Old Testament Theology* (I:1957; II:1960) but many of his other writings also touch on the subject of the relation-

under which title he includes the primeval history, patriarchal stories, law, psalms and wisdom literature, the first three being integrated into the 'canonical' saving history and the last two forming Israel's response to God. In the second volume he deals with the one major element of Old Testament thought which does not fit into this structure: the prophetic traditions. The prophets rejected the efficacy of past saving acts for their own time and looked to a new salvation in a new history (1957: vii). Nevertheless, the theology of Israel's prophetic traditions is also based on 'salvation history' and forms a complement to that of the historical traditions.

While much of his writing has implications for the relationship between the Testaments, the most important elaboration of von Rad's solution to the problem is the final section of the second volume of his *Old Testament Theology* (1960). An analysis of this section, which von Rad calls 'The Old Testament and the New', will now be made.

a. Actualization

Von Rad begins by considering 'The Actualisation of the Old Testament in the New' (1960: 319–335). He limits himself to a tradition-historical approach to the problem of the relationship between the Testaments, already taken as the basis for understanding Old Testament theology. He argues that 'the way in which the Old Testament is absorbed in the New is the logical end of a process initiated by the Old Testament itself, and that its "laws" are to some extent repeated in this final reinterpretation' (p. 321). Thus von Rad does not begin with the New Testament use of the Old, but attempts to show how the Old Testament points forward to the New.

The Old Testament, according to von Rad, is oriented towards the future: it 'can only be read as a book of ever increasing anticipation' (p. 319). It presents a dynamic religion, which is never complete or satisfied but continually looks to the future for improvement, fulfilment, or re-formation. At any particular point in time the religion is part of a continual appropriation, reinterpretation and actualization of more primitive forms of the religion. This is seen in the way Yahwism adopts and adapts the pre-Mosaic religion; the way in which the prophets take the election traditions and reinterpret them with

---

ship between the Testaments (*e.g.* 1937; 1952a; 1953b; 1961a; 1963). A full bibliography of his works is given in his Festschrift (1971).

reference to the coming 'day of the Lord'; and in the way the New Testament writers take the Old Testament traditions, accepting, rejecting or revising them in much the same way that the Old Testament writers themselves interpreted and used the traditions at their disposal.

Central to the New Testament is the idea that a new saving event has taken place. It announces the inauguration of the kingdom of God in the person and work of Jesus, the promised Christ. Old Testament traditions are cited as promises which are now fulfilled, and correspondences are noted between God's earlier saving acts and the supreme saving act which has occurred in Christ. There is both contrast and continuity between the Old and the New: on the one hand, the newness of the Christ-event is emphasized; on the other, Old Testament prophecies and parallels are pointed out. The New Testament exhibits great freedom in the way it takes over the Old, showing sometimes the contrast and at other times the continuity between the Testaments. 'Proof from Scripture' is therefore inadequate to describe this method: the Old Testament is used not only for proof but also because the New Testament needs the Old to express its message. The approach of the New Testament is *ad hoc*, presupposing a general understanding of the relationship between the Testaments and on that basis actualizing Old Testament texts by citation or allusion.

The most difficult problem raised by the continued Christian use of the Old Testament is whether or not it was only of temporary value and should have been given to Israel when the church separated from her. No doubt study of New Testament use of the Old may provide an answer to this question, and that is a task for New Testament theology. Christianity, however, is based not only on the New Testament but on the whole Bible, and it is therefore important to consider the Old Testament's view of the matter as well. This von Rad elaborates in the next three chapters, starting with a study of the relationship between 'The Old Testament's Understanding of the World and Man, and Christianity'.

b. The world and humanity

Does the Old Testament remain revelation now that Christ has come? Or, to rephrase the question in a more penetrating way, is the real meaning of the Old Testament brought to light only with the coming of Christ? The church has always recognized the theoretical equality of revelation in the Old and New Testaments, but in practice has usually found the problem to be the interpretation of the Old Testament in relation to the New. It has rarely achieved the New Testament's freedom and insight in biblical interpretation, though even the New Testament does not contain an exhaustive account of its relationship to the Old. Von Rad's attempt to deal with the problem (pp. 336–356) is based on the proposition 'that it is in history that God reveals the secret of his person' (p. 338), a proposition which is admittedly very general and requires closer definition by means of concrete examples.

A study of the Old Testament's understanding of the world, humanity and death follows. In each case von Rad concludes that Israel's view was decidedly secular, in contrast to the mythological views of contemporary nations. The God of Israel is not limited to the realms of myth or the sacred but is active in the world, in history, in everyday life.

The same is true of Christianity, according to von Rad. The message of the New Testament is not mythological, nor primarily didactic, but descriptive of God's action in history by which he renews his relationship with Israel and the world. This similarity between Israel's secular view of the world and Christianity is of course not coincidental: rather, the language and thought of the Old Testament are fundamental to the expression of the New Testament saving event. Israel's unique experience of God prepared her quite specifically for the supreme experience of God made possible in Jesus Christ.

c. The saving event

Von Rad next considers 'The Old Testament Saving Event in the Light of the New Testament Fulfilment' (pp. 357–387).

'The Old Testament is a history book' (p. 357; cf. 1952a: 25). This history, which extends from the creation to the end of time and includes Israel, the nations and the world, is saving history since every part is presented as the activity of God whose will and purpose is to save. In this history God reveals himself by words and acts, and in the Old Testament there are two corresponding kinds of account: theological, where the event is put in a wider interpretative context; and pre-theological, where the account concentrates on the event itself, without interpretation. It is these pre-theological accounts which make the Old Testament characteristically a history book, although they are fewer in number than those accounts which give a theological interpretation to the events they describe. Even the pre-theological accounts, it is true, received new interpretations as they were placed by redactors in wider contexts or adapted to suit the style of a particular strand of the Old Testament, for example in the Priestly Document or the Deuteronomic History. Nevertheless, this continual reinterpretation did not do violence to the stories since 'their intrinsic openness to a future actually needed such fresh interpretations on the part of later ages' (p. 361).

Theologians such as Bengel, Beck and von Hofmann (*cf.* above: ch. 2.4) explained the relationship between the Testaments in terms of a detailed and connected divine plan or 'economy' of salvation. Modern biblical theology, on the other hand, emphasizes the discontinuity both within the Old Testament and between the Old Testament and the New. Von Rad rejects such extreme views of continuity and discontinuity and suggests a unity in the sense that 'the true goal of God's relationship with Israel is the coming of Jesus Christ' (p. 363). He argues first of all that there is a 'structural analogy' between the saving events in the Old and New Testaments (the term 'typology' may also be used to describe this, *cf.* 1952a). Old Testament events are to be understood in the context of God's action in history, which comes to fulfilment in Jesus Christ. Indeed it is only in the Christ-event that analogies and correspondences with earlier events become truly meaningful.

'The coming of Jesus Christ as a historical reality leaves the exegete no choice at all; he must interpret the Old Testament as pointing to Christ, whom he must understand in its light' (p. 374). This raises a double question: how far can Christ elucidate the Old Testament and how far can the Old Testament elucidate Christ? Von Rad answers simply that Christ is necessary to understand the Old Testament and the Old Testament is necessary to understand Christ. This proposition, he argues, has the support of church history and the Old and New Testaments themselves. Without the New Testament saving event, the Old Testament would be understood only incompletely; without the Old Testament, the New Testament witness to Christ would have to be radically reinterpreted.

Von Rad's previous chapter showed the relationship between the understanding of the world and humanity in the Old Testament and in Christianity, but there is more to the relationship between the Testaments than this. 'The chief consideration in the correspondence between the two Testaments does not lie primarily in the field of religious terminology, but in that of saving history' (p. 382). In the Old Testament there is a close relationship between divine words and historical acts as means of revelation, and in Jesus Christ this dual form of revelation comes to its highest expression. Thus von Rad affirms that the central theme of his whole theology, God's salvation in history, is also the fundamental factor in the relationship between the Testaments. There are two aspects to this: first, 'the New Testament saving event appears as the prolongation and conclusion of Israel's history with God' (*cf.* van Ruler, see above: ch. 5.2.c); secondly, 'the New Testament saving event has at the same time to be understood in the sense of a repetition, though . . . on the basis of an entirely new saving event' (p. 383).

d. The law

There are two reasons why biblical studies cannot ignore the question of the relationship between the Testaments. On the one hand, according to von Rad, the most essential characteristic of the Old Testament is that it points forward and it is naturally important to know what it points forward to; on the other hand, the New Testament explicitly refers back into the past so that it is important to consider what is its origin. To understand the law, the third aspect of the relationship between the Testaments considered by von Rad, it is therefore necessary to take full account of its meaning in both Old and New Testaments (pp. 388–409).

First, the significance of the law in early Israel is considered. Von Rad rejects the idea that the law was the primary or essential aspect of the relationship between Israel and God. Israel's relationship to God was not dependent to the law; on the contrary, the law presupposes Israel's relationship to God.

Secondly, von Rad considers attitudes to the law in the preaching of the prophets. In early Israel the law was understood as something which was quite capable of being fulfilled. If it was not fulfilled, the reason was not Israel's inability but her unwillingness to obey. This conception of the law, as also of Israel's relationship to God as a whole, was transformed by the prophets. The early prophets took the law and applied it to Israel in a radical way, showing that disobedience to the law demonstrated the complete failure of her relationship with God and therefore judgment and death were coming to her. Jeremiah and Ezekiel penetrated the situation more deeply still, realizing that Israel was in fact unable to keep the law and announcing that God himself would make possible a new obedience. This process of renewing the law may be understood by means of von Rad's fundamental approach to Old Testament theology, the reinterpretation of earlier traditions: 'confronted with the eschatological situation, the prophets were set the task of taking the old regulations and making them the basis of an entirely new interpretation of Jahweh's current demands upon Israel' (p. 400).

Thirdly, even after the Exile the law was not central to Israel's faith. Salvation in the Old Testament is always based on grace, although von Rad sees the first steps in the direction of a more legalistic religion in parts of the Chronicler's history:

> There is no basis in the Old Testament for the well-known idea which early Lutheranism exalted to almost canonical status, that Israel was compelled by God's law to an ever greater zeal for the Law, and that it was the Law and the emotions it evoked which prepared the way for true salvation in Christ (p. 405; contrast Bultmann, see above: ch. 3.2.c).

Finally, von Rad turns to the question of the early church's understanding of Old Testament law. He argues that the same principle is found here as in the Old Testament prophets: 're-interpretation in the light of a new saving event' (p. 407). There is no normative interpretation of the Old Testament, but many charismatic interpretations, among which that of Paul is central. According to him, the Old Testament law is radically fulfilled in Christ, who himself lived a perfect life before God, took the punishment for other people's disobedience to the law and made possible a more personal relationship between them and God than existed under the old covenant.

6.2 Critique

Von Rad's Old Testament theology is without doubt one of the most original and stimulating works on the Old Testament of the twentieth century, and it is impossible and unnecessary to discuss it fully here.[2] The following discussion concerns only a number of issues which it raises for understanding the relationship between the Testaments.

a. History and historicity

As a starting-point in considering von Rad's solution to the problem of the relationship between the Testaments, we shall

---

[2]There are many critical works on von Rad's approach to Old Testament theology (*cf.* Baker 1976: 276–277). Some of the more important

look at his view of history (*cf.* Honecker 1963; Greig 1974). With great clarity he explains Israel's distinctive idea of history as the sequence of acts which God had performed for her salvation (1960: 99–112). Like Bultmann (*cf.* above: ch. 3.2.b), von Rad assumes a distinction between history as interpreted by the historian (*Geschichte*) and the historical facts which form the material for such history writing (*Historie*). He takes up some of the insights of existential 'kerygma theology', understanding the Bible not as a presentation of general truths nor as a source for historical research but as a witness to God's saving activity in history (Pannenberg 1961b; *cf.* Eichrodt 1961: 515). Thus he expounds the significance of the canonical history of election, oppression, Exodus and the gift of a new land (*Geschichte*), though he can say very little about what actually took place in those 'events' (*Historie*) since he accepts the critical reconstruction of Alt and Noth which denies that most of Israel was ever in Egypt![3] One of the most fundamental criticisms of von Rad's thesis is therefore its failure to provide a real foundation for the 'history' it describes (Eichrodt 1961: 516; de Vaux 1963). Von Rad (1963: 423–425) claims that Israel's view of history has a real historical basis, it is true, but in his actual exposition he gives little content to this 'reality' (*cf.* Davies 1970: 73–77; Pannenberg 1973).

A satisfactory solution to the problem of the relationship between the Testaments must give due consideration to the centrality of 'real' history in the Bible, without neglecting its other aspects. The Bible is a history book, in the sense that it contains detailed and ordered accounts of many past events which are asserted to have really taken place. Chronology is not a dominant concern: sequences of events are often incomplete and occasionally different writers record the same events in different orders. There are some accounts which are not specifically stated to be either fact or fiction and where different interpreters may draw different conclusions (*e.g.* the stories of Job and Jonah; the parable of the good Samaritan). However the biblical writers are clearly convinced that the formative and crucial events of the history of Israel and the life of Jesus really

---

are those of Eichrodt (1961); Pannenberg (1961b); Harvey (1971); Wolff (1973); Greig (1974); Spriggs (1974); L. Schmidt (1975) and Crenshaw (1978).

[3]For the Alt-Noth reconstruction of Israel's history see Alt (1913–56) and Noth (1950). Critiques include Bright (1956) and Wright (1960; *cf.* von Rad 1961b).

happened. The essence of the biblical creeds (as also those of the early church) is the statement of certain events which are affirmed to have taken place (*e.g.* Dt. 26:5–10; 1 Tim. 3:16). It is true that the significance of these events lies not so much in the fact that they have taken place (historicity) as in their function within the sequence of divinely-planned and prophetically-interpreted history. Nevertheless, the conviction that the foundation events really took place is the basis of both Old Testament and New Testament faith, and without such events there would have been no faith. If there had been no Abraham and Moses, there would have been no Israel; if there had been no crucifixion and resurrection, there would have been no Christian church.

b. History and story

The idea that the Bible is a history book has been disputed by James Barr (1976), who argues that the narrative corpus of the Old Testament is more accurately designated 'story' than 'history'. He admits that it has certain historical features (*e.g.* continuity and chronology), that parts of it constitute a fairly reliable source of historical evidence, and even that some sections could almost be described as history-writing. On the other hand he claims that large elements of the narrative are myth or legend, human and divine causation are not clearly distinguished, the writers often had motives other than that of writing history (*e.g.* aetiology or analogy), and there is no critical evaluation of sources and reports. Thus the Old Testament story 'spirals back and forward across history, sometimes coming closer to it, sometimes going farther away from it' (p. 8).

Barr's proposal should be seen in the context of the new emphasis on the literary character of the Bible that was characteristic of the nineteen-seventies (see above: ch. 2.7.c). During that decade many scholars were concerned with understanding the biblical text in its final form and found 'story' to be a useful category for this purpose, which throws light on many of the literary characteristics of the narrative without demanding decisions on the historicity or otherwise of what is narrated (*cf.* Hasel 1985: 35–37; Moberly 1986). In fact it has not been only biblical interpreters who have been interested in the role of 'story', but many other theologians who have recognized the importance of stories in human life and the effectiveness of communicating theological truth through them (*e.g.* C. S. Song 1984; D. P. Niles 1985; *cf.* Lischer 1984).

Without disparaging the achievements of literary study of the biblical narratives, we may nevertheless question whether the term 'story' is in fact a more appropriate term than 'history' for most of these narratives. According to the *Concise Oxford Dictionary*, 'history' is a 'continuous methodical record of public events; study of growth of nations; whole train of events connected with nation, person, thing, *etc.*'. On that definition it is not inappropriate to call the narrative from Genesis 12 to the end of Kings 'history'. Opinions will differ as to how accurate that history is, but there is little doubt that the Old Testament writers intended to write a continuous methodical record of public events connected with the growth of their nation. Inevitably they had different presuppositions, methods and emphases than modern historians, but that does not mean that they were not writing history.

The Old Testament history was written on the presupposition that God was in control of events on earth and that he had revealed himself to his people Israel in a variety of ways; whereas many modern historians would dispute the validity of such a presupposition and consider matters of divine causation to be outside the scope of historical enquiry.[4] However this presupposition would have been perfectly acceptable in ancient Palestine, since everyone in those days (as still the majority of the world's population!) believed in gods who really affected everyday life. The biblical writers chose to record certain events and omit others, and their evaluation of what was important was no

---

[4]Barr argues that the mingling of human and divine causation of events in the Old Testament story is an indication that the writer did not have primarily historical aims (1976: 7). 'History is about what really happened. It may not be able to tell us precisely, definitively or incontrovertibly what really happened; but what really happened is the assumed standard by which it operates' (1980: 41). But why shouldn't a historian who believes in God consider whether or not there really was divine intervention in certain events? No doubt it is not easy to determine objectively when divine intervention has occurred in human history, but is there any fundamental reason why a historian should not attempt to do so? To rule the attempt out is to decide *a priori* that divine intervention does not really happen, which is no more justifiable a presupposition than that of the biblical writers who believed that it did happen.

For a valuable discussion of approaches to history, see Moltmann (1964: 172–182). He points towards a more adequate approach which is based not merely on the principle of analogy (which tends to exclude extraordinary events), but which can grasp the whole of history (including unique events such as the resurrection of Christ).

doubt different from that of a modern historian writing a history of ancient Israel. That does not mean that they could not write history, simply that their presuppositions and emphases were different from those of modern historians. We do not argue that Paul did not write theology because his presuppositions and methods were different from those of modern theology; nor that the 'laws' of the Pentateuch are not really laws because they are not expressed with the rigour of modern legal science. It is unrealistic to use the modern humanistic conception of historical-critical research as the standard by which to evaluate the work of ancient writers who could not possibly have had such a conception.

To sum up, we may recognize that in terms of literary form the biblical narratives have many of the characteristics of 'story'. However, in terms of aim and content, most of the writers were not using this literary form in order to entertain or to create something beautiful but for the purpose of recording events which they believed had really happened and were of historical importance for their nation. Irrespective of our views on the historicity of those events, and acknowledging that authorial intention is not necessarily the final arbiter of the meaning of a text, there is no reason to deny that the biblical writers set out to write history.

c. Tradition history

One of the most important contributions to modern study of Old Testament tradition history is von Rad's monograph, 'The Form-Critical Problem of the Hexateuch' (1938). His argument is essentially that the Hexateuch (Genesis – Joshua) is an elaboration of one simple idea, namely God's grace to Israel shown in election of the patriarchs, exodus from Egypt and settlement in Palestine. This idea is expressed in Israel's earliest creeds, among which Deuteronomy 26:5b–9, Deuteronomy 6:20–24 and Joshua 24:2b–13 are the most important. One of the most revolutionary features of von Rad's study is his claim that these creeds do not mention the events of Sinai and that therefore the Sinai tradition was originally independent of the Exodus tradition proper. The combination of these two traditions was the work of the Yahwist, according to von Rad, and he gathered together many scattered traditions around the central co-ordinating conception of the ancient creeds. Subsequent redaction added many other elements to form the Hexateuch, but always in subjection to the one central idea. In a similar way the Deuteronomic and Chronicler's histories have certain fundamental bases – going back originally to the Hexateuchal traditions – which have been expanded to form the present works.

This reconstruction of the origin of the Hexateuch naturally provoked considerable interest and reaction.[5] Whatever conclusions we draw about the accuracy of von Rad's reconstruction, we need to be aware that it is the basis of his whole understanding of Old Testament theology and its relationship to New Testament theology. In the preface to the first volume of his Old Testament theology (1957), von Rad writes:

> If there is any truth in the recognition that the whole of the Hexateuch is built upon a very few ancient credal statements which became constitutive for the Israel of all ages, then this is so important that a theology of the Old Testament would practically have to start out from this fact.

On this basis von Rad develops his theology, using the methods of form criticism and tradition history.

Von Rad's use of the tradition-historical method is particularly significant in his presentation of the relationship between the Testaments. He considers that the Bible contains a few fundamental traditions which are continually reinterpreted to make them relevant to the contemporary situation. Repeatedly Israel is addressed as the people of God and claims the old saving history as her own (1963: 413): 'Not with our fathers did the LORD make this covenant, but with us, who are all of us here alive this day' (Dt. 5:3; cf. 1957: 193; 1960: 109, 268). In the Deuteronomic and Chronicler's histories the same traditions are taken up and applied to the election of David and his throne (1957: 306–354; cf. Rost 1947). The message of the prophets does not belong to the basic theology of the Old Testament, according to von Rad; but understood in terms of tradition history it is seen to be a reinterpretation of the salvation history, initially as condemnation and later as a new salvation (1957: 66; 1960: 3–5). This new salvation, although it contains the implication that the old salvation has come to an end, is expressed in the language of the old: there is to be 'a new David, a new Exodus, a new covenant, a new city of God' (1960: 323; cf. 239–240). Such continual reinterpretation is made possible and

---

[5]See e.g. Beyerlin (1961); Vriezen (1963b); Huffmon (1965); Davies (1970: 71–73); Hyatt (1970) and Nicholson (1973).

valid by the fact that the Old Testament traditions are 'open to the future' (1960: 319–321, 360–362; *cf.* 1961a: 10–11). Moreover the same fact makes it possible to understand the relationship between the Testaments in terms of tradition history:

> We said earlier that the prophets do not improvise, that they show themselves to be bound to definite traditions, that they move about within the realm of older witnesses to Jahwism in an extraordinarily dialectic fashion, that they take their own legitimation from these and at the same time, because of new content which they give them, go beyond them and even break them up, that, while they certainly select from among the traditions, at the same time they keep them as the broad basis of their arguments – does not this also describe the relationship of the Apostles and the writers of the Gospels to the Old Testament? (1960: 327; *cf.* pp. 321–333, 367–369, 384–386).

Tradition history is therefore an important clue to understanding von Rad's solution to the problem of the relationship between the Testaments.[6] Even more important, however, is a conception which in von Rad's theology is closely related to tradition history and sometimes hardly distinguishable from it (*cf.* D. A. Knight 1973: 133–136): the conception of salvation history.

d. Salvation history

It was mentioned above (ch. 2.4.e) that von Hofmann's idea of 'salvation history' (*Heilsgeschichte*) has influenced modern studies of this theme and this is true in particular of von Rad's theology (see *e.g.* 1960: vi). Both of these writers were concerned to find a genuinely theological way to understand the Old Testament, in contrast to the widespread 'history of religions' approach (Greig 1974: ch. 1). The major difference between the two is that von Hofmann was interested in an objective saving history, von Rad

---

[6]D. A. Knight has written a valuable survey of tradition-historical study of the Old Testament (1973) and edited an important symposium on the subject (1977). See also Noth (1948); Barr (1957b); Childs (1962); Zimmerli (1971b); Clements (1975) and Goldingay (1981: 125–133).

in an existential one (*cf.* Pannenberg 1961b: 91). For von Rad, the basis of Israel's salvation history is in her early creeds (Dt. 26:5b–9; *etc.*) and is essentially confessional (concerning what Israel believed to have happened) rather than factual (concerning what could be proved to have happened). The question of salvation history has been the topic of wide-ranging debate,[7] but discussion here will be limited to one or two aspects of von Rad's use of salvation history to express the relationship between the Testaments.

It may be asked whether salvation history is an adequate structuring concept for a theology of the Old Testament and its relationship to the New. Does it do justice to the creation story, sagas, law, poetry and wisdom literature of the Old Testament to fit them into the category of historical traditions? Barr (*e.g.* 1963; 1966: 72–76) has repeatedly argued that it does not, that the Old Testament contains more than salvation history (*cf.* Spriggs 1974: 40–42). Christopher Barth (1963: 368–369) has challenged von Rad's treatment of the psalms and wisdom literature as Israel's answer to God's history of salvation: he considers the whole Bible to be both God's word and Israel's answer. David Burdett (1974), on the other hand, attempts to show that the wisdom literature is an integral part of the history of redemption, as a demonstration of the ideal character of a citizen in the messianic kingdom.

Be that as it may, a more fundamental question still demands an answer: is the creed of 'salvation in history' really the kernel of Old Testament theology? Barr (1962: 144) claims:

> There is no evidence that von Rad treats this concept critically, and it is obvious that he feels he can use it as an ace of trumps against all other ideas of the planning of an Old Testament theology, or of the treatment of certain details within it.

Barr has overstated the case, for von Rad does recognize at least some of the limitations of his work. In the introductions to both volumes he emphasizes that he does not consider he has written a complete and comprehensive Old Testament theology (1957: vii; 1960: vi). He points out that the idea of salvation history was

---

[7]*E.g.* Steck (1959); Richardson (1964b: 133–139); Feiner and Löhrer (1965–); Croatto (1966); Cullmann Fs (1967); Peter (1970); Gutiérrez (1971: 149–187); Hesse (1971); Gunneweg (1977: 173–217); Goldingay (1981: 66–96). See also below: ch. 6.3 (especially Cullmann).

lost in the legalism and apocalyptic of the post-exilic period (1957: 91; 1960: 303–304). Moreover his fundamental proposition, 'the Old Testament writings confine themselves to representing Jahweh's relationship to Israel and the world in one aspect only, namely as a continuing divine activity in history' (1957: 106), is immediately qualified by reference to the obvious fact that it is apparently not true of some parts of the Old Testament. In some cases (*e.g.* some of the psalms) von Rad argues that they presuppose God's historical activity, in others (*e.g.* Job, Ecclesiastes) he suggests that the failure to relate to the salvation history 'is closely connected with the grave affliction which is the theme of both these works'.

There is no one concept that can sum up the meaning of the whole Old Testament nor its relationship to the New Testament. Nevertheless 'salvation history' has the merit of effectively grasping and organizing the material of the Old Testament in such a way as to stress the centrality of elements which are undoubtedly central and the secondary nature of others which are not. Even Barr (1963: 201), while emphasizing that there are other important axes through the biblical material, admits that

> there really is a *Heilsgeschichte* ... we have been generally right in saying that this can be taken as the central theme of the Bible, that it forms the main link between Old and New Testaments, and that its presence and importance clearly marks biblical faith off from other religions.

e. The question of reality

A crucial problem in von Rad's use of the concept of 'salvation history' is the reality of the 'salvation' and the 'history'.[8]

First, is this 'salvation' real, or merely a product of Israel's imagination? Like a pure mathematician who analyses concepts and their interrelationships without asking whether or not they have any connection with the real world, von Rad evades the question. He separates the 'objective' picture of Israel's history obtained by historical criticism on the basis of Troeltsch's principle of analogy from the kerygmatic picture given by Israel's confessions which understood history in terms of God's activity (1957: 107–108; *cf.* C. Barth 1963: 368). Yet the question

---

[8]On the question of reality, see further Wright (1964); Pannenberg (1973) and Brown (1976: especially pp. 13–75).

remains: did God choose and deliver Israel and give them a new land in fulfilment of his promise, or is salvation history an invention or misapprehension? The Old Testament is based on the belief that God really acts in history to save his people, and von Rad's existential presentation is inadequate to the extent that it fails to take account of this (Pannenberg 1961b: 94n.; Spriggs 1974: 57, 81; cf. above: ch. 3.2.a).

Secondly, a closely related question concerns the reality of this 'history' (cf. Hasel 1970). The crux of the matter is that von Rad expounds the saving history not on the basis of the modern scholarly reconstruction of Israel's history but on Israel's own understanding of her history (1957: vi; cf. above: ch. 6.2.a). Undoubtedly such an exposition may be illuminating and, if Israel rather than modern scholarship was right, it would be the best kind of exposition; but since von Rad believes that modern scholarship is right, the validity of his approach is questionable. Logic and honesty demand a theology based on either the historical-critical reconstruction of Israel's history (if that is considered to be correct, cf. Hesse[9]) or Israel's own account of her history (if that is considered to have a real historical basis, cf. Eichrodt 1961: 516; Ladd 1966b). It may well be true that von Rad has drawn too sharply the contrast between the two pictures of Israel's history (cf. Soggin 1964) and more recent scholarship has tended towards a mediating position, namely that historical-critical study has not invalidated the totality of the Old Testament picture of Israel's history (cf. Hasel 1985: 35). Nevertheless the fact that he bases his theology on what he himself considers to be an invalid foundation remains a fundamental weakness in von Rad's work.

f. A relationship of actualization

Martin Noth, in his contribution to the 1952 symposium which launched the *Biblischer Kommentar*, wrote about 'The "Representation" of the Old Testament in Proclamation'. In order to deal with the problem of transition from exegesis to proclamation Noth turns to the Old Testament, in which he finds a process of re-presentation (*Vergegenwärtigung*) of historical events. The festivals of Passover and Tabernacles, for instance,

---

[9]In contrast to von Rad, Hesse refuses to separate salvation history from 'real' history (cf. Hasel 1972a: 31–34). The real course of Israel's history is therefore more important for Christian theology than Israel's own conception of her history, which according to Hesse is fragmented and inaccurate (1960a: 24–26; cf. 1958; 1969).

came to be understood as re-enactments of events related to the Exodus. The proclamation of the law took place 'in such a way as to make Israel hear the law as if it were for the very first time' (p. 82). Such cultic re-presentation is not entirely unrelated to the ancient Oriental cyclic view of history, Noth admits, but there is also a fundamental difference: 'the "re-presentation" at the periodical feasts of ancient Israel does not involve some timeless myth, but something which by nature is a unique historical event ... the Exodus from Egypt' (p. 85). The Old Testament's re-presentation is distinctive in its historical nature, being concerned not with myth but with the saving acts and moral demands of God. From his brief survey of the Old Testament evidence Noth concludes that a legitimate re-presentation of the Old Testament in modern proclamation cannot use historical individuals, nor can it use specific historical situations, since both of these are unrepeatable; it can only re-present the saving acts of God by 'telling' them.

A closely related idea is expounded in von Rad's theology, *i.e.* that of 'actualization' (*Aktualisierung*).[10] An example of actualization is to be found in Old Testament worship, according to von Rad (1960: 103–110). In the great festivals, for instance, which though originally agricultural were historicized by Israel, the saving events connected with the festivals were 'actualized' in the celebration. Another example of a somewhat different nature is the book of Deuteronomy, which von Rad considers to be 'a unique actualisation of God's will designed to counter specific dangers which appeared at a definite hour in the already lengthy history of Jahwism' (1960: 394). For von Rad it is one of the most basic concepts of Old Testament theology:

> In each specific case, Israel spoke in quite a different way about the 'mighty acts' of her God ... Israel constantly fell back on the old traditions connected with the great saving appointments, and in each specific case she actualised them in a very arbitrary, and often novel, way ... This continual actualisation of the data of the saving history, with its consequence that every generation saw itself anew on the march

---

[10]1960: 319–335. A major study of actualization in the Old Testament has recently been written by Joseph W. Groves (1987). A similar idea is found in liberation theology: the progressive reinterpretation of the Exodus in new historical situations (Kirk 1979: 99–100, 147–148, 157–158; Branson & Padilla 1983: 173).

towards a fulfilment, occupies such a prominent position in the Old Testament that a 'Theology of the Old Testament' must accommodate itself to it (1963: 413–416).

'Actualization' is therefore a very suitable term to express the relationship between the Old Testament and the New:

> The way in which the Old Testament is absorbed in the New is the logical end of a process initiated by the Old Testament itself (1960: 321) . . . The history of tradition showed us how old material could suddenly be put on a new basis and into new theological horizons, and the question therefore is whether the reinterpretation of Old Testament traditions in the light of Christ's appearance on earth is not also hermeneutically perfectly permissible . . . The Apostles clearly take the view that the texts of the Old Testament only attain their fullest actuality in the light of their fulfilment (p. 333).

That there are some fundamental weaknesses in von Rad's work – especially in his view of history and the reality of salvation history – has been shown above and discussed at length by his critics. Nevertheless, von Rad has made a very significant contribution to solving the theological problem of the relationship between the Testaments. Despite all necessary criticisms, he has demonstrated the essential truth of his solution, which is centred on the concepts of tradition history, salvation history and actualization. Two further aspects of von Rad's solution (typology and promise/fulfilment) will be discussed in detail below (chs. 7–8).

6.3 Comparison: other 'salvation history' solutions

The final section of the present chapter is concerned with a number of other solutions to the problem which are related in some way to that of von Rad, subsumed under the general heading of 'salvation history' solutions.[11]

---

[11]There are many other works which could have been considered in this category, *e.g.* W. J. Phythian-Adams (1938); Ethelbert Stauffer (1941); Klaus Schwarzwäller (1966); George Eldon Ladd (1968) and Leonhard Goppelt (1975–76); also many of the works on 'typology' and 'promise and fulfilment' discussed below (chs. 7.1; 8.1).

a. Oscar Cullmann

Many other writers before and after von Rad have explained the relationship between the Testaments in terms of salvation history. One of the most influential has been Oscar Cullmann, who in two major works (1946 and 1965) expressed his view of the centrality of salvation history to New Testament faith.[12] He argues that 'New Testament man was certain that he was continuing the work God began with the election of the people of Israel for the salvation of mankind, which God fulfilled in Christ, which he unfolds in the present and which he will complete at the end' (1965: 13). Although his main concern is to expound New Testament theology rather than to solve the problem of the relationship between the Testaments, Cullmann's work is nevertheless an important contribution to the understanding of the latter question.

b. George Ernest Wright

Another significant contribution to understanding the theological relationship between the Testaments has been made by the American scholar, G. Ernest Wright. In his programmatic monograph – *God Who Acts* (1952) – he maintains that 'Biblical theology is *the confessional recital of the redemptive acts of God* in a particular history, because history is the chief medium of revelation' (p. 13).[13] Such recital is characteristic of the Bible, as von Rad has shown by his tradition-historical study of Old Testament confessions of faith (pp. 70–76; *cf*. above: ch. 6.2.c) and Cullmann and Dodd in their New Testament studies (pp. 66–70). It follows that for Wright the coming of Jesus Christ is to be understood primarily as 'a historical event which was the climax of God's working since the creation. All former history had its goal in him because God had so directed it' (p. 56). Thus Wright's study of biblical theology leads to conclusions similar to those of von Rad, several years before the latter published his Old Testament theology: the relationship between the

---

[12]See also his article in *OTCF* (1964). Critiques of his proposal include Bultmann (1948b); Frisque (1960) and Harrington (1973: 197–201). *Cf*. Hasel (1978: 111–119).

[13]On revelation through history, see Lemke (1982); *cf*. P. D. Hanson (1978).

Testaments is to be understood in terms of salvation history.[14]

c. Samuel Amsler

Amsler's doctoral thesis, *L'Ancien Testament dans l'Église* (1960a), published in the same year as the second volume of von Rad's Old Testament theology, is probably the most important French Protestant work on the relationship between the Old Testament and the New.[15] Its aim is to attempt a definition of principles for reading the Old Testament in the Christian church (p. 11). Amsler's method is first to analyse what the Bible itself says about Christian reading of the Old Testament (*cf.* above: ch. 1.3.c), and secondly to relate this to the results of contemporary Old Testament scholarship. His argument centres on the fact that the Old Testament was the Bible of the primitive church: the early Christians used the Old Testament not simply because in a Jewish context it was convenient to do so, but because they were convinced that the advent, life, death and resurrection of Jesus Christ were the fulfilment of the old covenant and therefore inextricably related to it. The ultimate reason for Christian use of the Old Testament is therefore quite simply that Jesus is the Christ promised by the Old Testament (p. 10).

It is often asked how far can we imitate the New Testament's interpretation of the Old Testament. Amsler rejects a simple adoption of New Testament methods, choosing rather to go beyond them to the fundamental principle by which they are governed (pp. 103–104). Their value lies not in themselves but in their expression of the early church's faith in Jesus Christ, and this faith implies a theological relationship between the old and new covenants which alone can validate Christian reading of the Old Testament. Amsler's work is less well known than that of Cullmann and Wright, so the main points of his argument will now be summarized.

Jesus Christ and salvation history

The central aim of the New Testament is to witness to a

---

[14]Wright has written many other works which are relevant to the question of the relationship between the Testaments (*e.g.* 1951a; 1955; 1964; *cf.* 1970). He has since qualified his view in certain respects (1969: 39–69), but his basic position remains the same. For critiques, see Gilkey (1961) and Kelsey (1975: 33–38).

[15]Other relevant works by Amsler include two articles on typology (1952; 1953) and one on text, and event (1960b).

historical event: the birth, ministry, death and resurrection of Jesus Christ (1960a: 105–121). It is a unique event, since in it God himself has intervened in the world to save mankind; but it is not an isolated event, since it is to be viewed as the centre of a history which extends from creation to the end of time. In so saying, Amsler takes up Cullmann's view that Jesus is the final and definitive meaning of both salvation history and universal history. On the one hand, according to the New Testament, the last days have come in him and the whole history of mankind and creation is henceforth determined by him; on the other hand, the New Testament relates Jesus to past history, showing him to be the final outcome of God's activity in creation and in the history of Israel. To separate the central event of history from the events which lead up to and follow on from it robs the centre and the context of their full significance for revelation and salvation.

The question arises whether this New Testament perspective of salvation history corresponds to that of the Old. Recent Old Testament study leads to the reply that the Old Testament bears witness to the living God who revealed himself to Israel by intervening in her secular history (p. 108). According to the Old Testament, God encounters his people in historical events, and these events are significant not as a succession of incidental facts but as a sequence of interlinked occurrences which together make a history. Amsler argues that the historical works organize the material into a connected narrative, the prophets declare that past and future events play a role in the present, the psalms and liturgical writings concentrate history into the present by means of ceremonial worship, the law expresses the practical consequences of God's historical action in making a covenant with his people and the wisdom literature shows in a negative fashion that the result of abandoning the historical perspective is to lose the key to the biblical revelation (*cf.* above: ch. 6.2.d). In order to interpret the Old Testament, therefore, it is vital to place every event in its historical context, which includes both events that precede it and those that result from it. This orientation to history, Amsler claims, is apparent in the attitude of the Old Testament prophets to time: one stations himself beyond the event (*e.g.* Ezk. 20: 42), another describes a future event as though it had already taken place (*e.g.* Am. 5:2), while another describes past events as though they had yet to happen (*e.g.* Dn. 7:23). It is not only the prophets, however, who interpret events with reference to the future: the whole Old Testament bears witness to a history which is incomplete in itself and is open to the future. So for the Old Testament the interpretation of historical events will be truly possible only at the end of time.

The New Testament affirms that the end of time has already been inaugurated in Jesus Christ, who thus shows the full significance of the events of the old covenant by giving them their complete context. So Christian interpretation of the Old Testament is the direct consequence of faith in Jesus Christ. Every event of the old covenant receives in him the eschatological context by which its full meaning becomes clear, and at the same time contributes to the elucidation of the central event of salvation history. Here Amsler finds the real theological basis for Christian reading of the Old Testament: without the Old Testament salvation history is curtailed and disfigured, and the Christ-event loses its authentic significance.

The old covenant and Jesus Christ

In the Christ-event God has realized the promises and fulfilled the demands of the Old Testament (1960a: 122–134). The relationship between the two covenants is therefore essentially historical, not doctrinal; a relationship between two complementary series of events in the plan of salvation history, not between two collections of timeless truths.

The New Testament adopts the Old Testament idea of salvation history as a chain of events linked by promise and fulfilment, but introduces a new aspect to the concept of fulfilment: Jesus Christ does not simply prolong the old covenant but replaces it by another, that of the eschatological kingdom of God. This decisive fulfilment is not alien to the Old Testament; on the contrary, in it the prophetic linking of events by promise and fulfilment finds its goal. Moreover, Christian interpretation of the Old Testament must be based on this understanding of fulfilment, since only then can it be true to the prophetic interpretation of history.

The witness of the Old Testament

Jesus' fulfilment of the old covenant has two consequences: Jesus Christ shows the real revelatory significance of the old covenant and the events of the old covenant display clearly particular aspects of the event in which they are fulfilled, God's revelation in Christ. Thus the Old Testament functions as a witness to God's saving activity in history (1960a: 135–151). Since the climax of history occurred in Jesus Christ, it is only in the church – among those who believe that Jesus is the Christ – that the Old Testament can play its authentic role as witness to that salvation history. This witness takes two forms, words and events, and according to the New Testament each is fulfilled in

Jesus Christ. Many Old Testament words are quoted in the New and specifically said to be fulfilled in Christ (see further below: ch. 8); and many Old Testament events are referred to, thus implying their typological importance (see further below: ch. 7).

The principle is clear that the words and events of the Old Testament, in their witness to God's provisional revelation in the old covenant, also bear witness to God's definitive revelation in Jesus Christ. Further, the New Testament affirms that the true meaning of the Old Testament is in God's intervention in history to reveal himself and save people, so that every part of this salvation history has its role in bearing witness beforehand to the way God would later reveal himself in Jesus Christ.

It is only from the perspective of the New Testament, according to which Jesus Christ completes the salvation history of the Old Testament, that Old Testament words and events can be recognized as promises and prefigurations of Jesus Christ. This is legitimate, according to Amsler, because the Old Testament itself is aware of an eschatological aspect to both word and event. The New Testament shows the church both the reason and the method for reading the Old Testament: since it has been fulfilled in Jesus Christ all the events of the Old Testament prefigure him in some way and its words bear indirect witness to the meaning of his coming.

A relationship of salvation history

It is evident that Amsler's solution to the problem of the relationship between the Testaments has many similarities with that of von Rad, in particular in its emphasis on salvation history. This is particularly significant since they approach the problem from quite different angles: von Rad from Old Testament tradition history, Amsler from that of New Testament interpretation of the Old Testament. Amsler's work thus gives additional support to this understanding of the relationship between the Testaments, though it is also subject to some of the criticisms applied to von Rad's work (for example, the fact that it fits some parts of the Old Testament better than others). Amsler, it is true, stresses the importance of 'text' as well as 'event' in the Bible (1960a: 135–163; *cf.* 1960b; Barr 1966: ch. 3), but his concern to interpret the whole Old Testament in terms of salvation history is such that like von Rad he is led to a rather negative evaluation of all that does not fit this perspective (*e.g.* the wisdom literature, p. 111). Moreover it may be asked whether there is not more to the Bible than text and event. Human life and personality involves not only words and deeds but also thoughts and feelings. Perhaps more attention should be given to the thoughts and feelings of God and people recorded in the Bible, as well as their words and deeds? God does not only speak and act, according to the Old Testament, he chooses, plans, loves, delights, hates and is faithful and true. So also men and women are not limited to word and deed but frequently engage in worship, obedience or disobedience, love, delight, hate, unfaithfulness and hardness of heart.

d. Wolfhart Pannenberg

In the year following the completion of von Rad's Old Testament theology a programmatic work was published by a group of younger Heidelberg scholars entitled *Revelation as History* (1961). It was edited by Wolfhart Pannenberg,[16] who has since become the chief spokesman of the group, and included essays by him, Rolf Rendtorff, Ulrich Wilckens and Trutz Rendtorff. The programme is summed up in Pannenberg's seven dogmatic theses (ch. 4):

> **1.** God's self-revelation in the Bible is indirect, being mediated through historical acts.
> **2.** Revelation is understood fully only at the end of revelatory history.
> **3.** Revelation is universal, being open to anyone who has eyes to see.
> **4.** Revelation is first realized in the fate of Jesus, insofar as the end of all events is anticipated in that event.
> **5.** The Christ-event is revelation insofar as it is part of God's history with Israel.
> **6.** The universality of the Christ-event is expressed in the Gentile Christian understanding of revelation.
> **7.** The Word relates itself to revelation as foretelling, forthtelling, and report.

A lively debate on the relationship between revelation and history ensued.[17]

The close link between God's history with Israel and the

---

[16]The clearest expression of Pannenberg's view of the relationship between the Testaments is in his essay 'Redemptive Event and History' (1959). Together with a number of other essays that touch on the subject it is translated in *Basic Questions in Theology* (1967). *Cf.* Galloway (1973); Tupper (1974).

[17]See Loretz (1964: 22–42); Moltmann (1964: 76–84); Braaten (1965); Barr (1966: 65–102); Fuller (1966); O'Collins (1966); Robinson & Cobb (1967), and Harder & Stevenson (1971).

Christ-event is implied in Pannenberg's fourth and fifth theses. Like von Rad, Pannenberg uses the category of salvation history to express the relationship between the Testaments (*cf.* J. M. Robinson 1964: 127–129):

> The connection between the Old and New Testaments is made understandable only by the consciousness of the one history which binds together the eschatological community of Jesus Christ and ancient Israel by means of the bracket of promise and fulfilment (1959: 25; *cf.* 1967: 179–181).

However Pannenberg rejects von Rad's separation of salvation history from history as it 'really' happened. The history he refers to is not simply salvation history as believed and confessed by Israel (von Rad): it is 'reality in its totality' (Pannenberg 1959: 21), which includes not only salvation history but the creation and the consummation as well. This may be compared with liberation theology's stress on the unity of history in which salvation history is understood as the heart of human history (*e.g.* Gutiérrez 1971: 153; *cf.* Kirk 1979: 31, 177). Thus Pannenberg establishes the relationship between the Testaments in real history, which he conceives as God's characteristic sphere of self-revelation. This history is, of course, completely intelligible only from the perspective of its end. Nevertheless the end of history is anticipated in the Christ-event, so that at least in an anticipatory sense the meaning of the revelation in history recorded in the Old Testament becomes clear.

In this universal understanding of revelation *apocalyptic* has an important place. According to Koch (1970: 14), Pannenberg reintroduced the apocalyptic understanding of history into systematic theology, though it was Käsemann who effectively brought the concept out of obscurity into the forefront of theological discussion. The latter, in his programmatic essay 'The Beginnings of Christian Theology' (1960), argued that apocalyptic was 'the mother of all Christian theology' (p. 40). It follows from this that apocalyptic is seen to be the chief link between the Testaments.[18] Koch (1970) concludes his study of apocalyptic in these words:

---

[18]*Cf.* also Sauter (1966: 239–251) and Betz (1969). On apocalyptic, see above: ch. 1.2.c.

Our survey has shown sufficiently that late Israelite and early Christian apocalyptic is not one branch of the literature of the ancient world among others, a sector which one may consider philologically and exegetically or leave alone, according to taste. Does the apocalyptic world of ideas not represent the change-over between the Testaments, *i.e.*, does it not reflect that religious movement which, under the impression of the person of Jesus and his destiny, permitted a part of late Israel to merge into early Christianity?

This positive evaluation of apocalyptic stands in sharp contrast to that of von Rad (1960: 301–308).

e. Jürgen Moltmann

Many of the insights of von Rad and Pannenberg are taken up by Moltmann in the development of his *Theology of Hope* (1964).[19] He discusses critically the ideas of God's self-revelation in salvation history, universal history and tradition history (pp. 69–84) and makes much use of the concept of promise and its future fulfilment in his own exposition of history and eschatology (pp. 95–229; see further below: ch. 8). The implications of Christian hope in modern society are expressed in the term 'Exodus Church', by which Moltmann means that Christians constitute the 'pilgrim people of God' – the 'community of eschatological salvation' – who are called to transform the face of the world in which they believe, hope and love (pp. 304–338). This idea is particularly congenial to the liberation theologians, some of whom have been influenced by Moltmann's theology and engaged in debate with him on its political implications.[20]

On apocalyptic, Moltmann (1964: 133–138) argues that the evaluations of von Rad and Pannenberg are both based on the recognition that 'apocalyptic applies cosmological patterns to history, with the result that either "history" comes to a standstill [von Rad] or else "history" becomes intelligible as a summary representation of reality in its totality [Pannenberg]'. He suggests a third way of looking at apocalyptic, by seeing its significance not in 'cosmological interpretation of eschatological

---

[19]On Moltmann's theology, see Bauckham (1987).
[20]*E.g.* Gutiérrez 1971: 160–162, 182, 216–220; Moltmann 1973: 314–340; *cf.* Langley 1978: 967–975.

history', but in 'eschatological and historic interpretation of the cosmos'. Just as in the message of the prophets Israel's 'hope for history' became concerned with world history, so in apocalyptic this hope became concerned with cosmology. Thus, according to Moltmann, apocalyptic points theological eschatology beyond national history and individual existence to the world as a whole; and therefore in effect it is one way in which the Old Testament points forward to the New (*cf.* p. 138).

f. Hartmut Gese

Salvation history is of fundamental significance for biblical theology, but the key to the relationship between the Testaments is to be found in *tradition history*, according to Gese (1977a; *cf.* 1974: 11–30; 1977b). He understands canonization as the final stage in the living process of forming tradition, and argues that the Old Testament was not a closed canon by the time of the New Testament. Rather the New Testament is the end and goal of a single tradition-building process, so that in terms of tradition history there is no gulf or opposition between the Old Testament and the New. New Testament interpretation of the Old Testament is consistent with interpretation of earlier texts found in the later strata of the Old Testament itself. Thus biblical theology is a continuous holistic process which incorporates the whole biblical tradition, the entire history of God's self-revelation to mankind. Clearly Gese emphasizes the unity of the Bible and the continuity between its two constituent parts.

There has been a good deal of criticism of Gese's proposal, particularly concerning his claims about the late closing of the Old Testament canon (see Hasel 1985: 32–33, 40–42). The New Testament often refers to writings which it describes as 'Scripture' and the extent of those writings is almost identical with that of the Hebrew Bible (Childs 1979: 669; *cf.* Guthrie 1981: 953–982). Another criticism concerns Gese's understanding of the unity of the Bible in terms of tradition history and its key concept of 'actualization'. Although his exposition illuminates the process by which the Bible came about, to understand the unity of the Bible solely in this way does not account satisfactorily for those aspects of the Old Testament which were not actualized in Jesus nor for those aspects which found a real continuation in post-Christian Judaism (Goldingay 1981: 131–132).

g. Elmer A. Martens

One of the most distinctive of the many Old Testament theologies published in the past twenty years is that of Elmer Martens (1981). He takes 'God's design' as the central theme and Exodus 5:22 – 6:8 as a pivotal text which states this design in programmatic form. There are four main elements in the design (salvation, the covenant community, knowledge of God and life in the promised land), and Martens traces the four elements in three main periods of Old Testament history (premonarchy, monarchy and post-monarchy). He also indicates briefly the prehistory of the fourfold theme in Genesis and its posthistory in the New Testament.

Martens' exposition is mentioned here in the category of 'salvation history' approaches to the relationship between the Testaments because it has more similarities with these approaches than with those in any of the other three categories. However, unlike von Rad, he is confident of the historicity of the biblical narratives, and so he has no problem relating history as it is recounted with history as it really happened. Unlike Gese, Martens shows little interest in the history of traditions, and focuses his attention almost entirely on the canonical form of the biblical text. Perhaps his most important contribution is to show that the biblical presentation of God's purpose in history does not merely concern salvation in the sense of deliverance (whether it be from enemies, oppression or sin), but also includes the positive benefits of a relationship with God (through cultic worship and personal experience), a relationship with other people (through the covenant community) and a relationship with the created world (through the land).

h. Hans-Ruedi Weber

Finally, we mention briefly a recent work by a teacher at the Pacific School of Theology in Fiji, previously director of biblical studies at the World Council of Churches. Weber (1989) takes the theme of power as the focus for a biblical theology, concentrating on six biblical traditions of faith: exodus, kingship, wisdom, holiness, poverty and apocalyptic. He expounds each tradition in both the Old and New Testaments and shows its particular relevance to the theme of power. Rather like Gese, Weber understands biblical theology to be 'a converging bundle of traditions of faith' which are in tension with each other but converge in Jesus Christ (p. 22). Thus in preference to the common category of 'promise and fulfilment' (*cf.* below: ch. 8), he suggests that the relationship between the Testaments be described in terms of 'trajectories of faith' and their 'convergence' on Jesus of Nazareth.

Bibliography (6)

Alt, A. 1913–56: *Kleine Schriften zur Geschichte des Volkes Israel*, Munich, three volumes, I:1953; II:1953; III:1959 (collection of essays originally published 1913–56; ET of selection: *Essays on Old Testament History and Religion*, Oxford, 1966).

Amsler, S. 1960b: 'Texte et événement' in Vischer Fs: 12–19.

Barr, J. 1957: 'Tradition and Expectation in Ancient Israel', *SJT* 10:24–34.

—1962: 'Gerhard von Rad's Theologie des Alten Testaments', *ExpT* 73:142–146.

—1963: 'Revelation Through History in the Old Testament and in Modern Theology', *Int* 17:193–205.

—1976: 'Story and History in Biblical Theology', reprinted in *Explorations in Theology 7: The scope and authority of the Bible*, London, 1980: 1–17 (originally in *JR* 56 [1976] 1–17).

—1980: 'Historical Reading and the Theological Interpretation of Scripture' in *Explorations in Theology* 7:30–51.

Barth, C. 1963: 'Grundprobleme einer Theologie des Alten Testaments', *EvTh* 23:342–372.

Bauckham, R. 1987: *Moltmann: Messianic Theology in the Making*, Basingstoke.

Betz, H. D. 1969: 'The Concept of Apocalyptic in the Theology of the Pannenberg Group', *JTC* 6:192–207.

Beyerlin, W. 1961: *Origins and History of the Oldest Sinaitic Traditions*, ET: Oxford, 1966 (German, 1961).

Braaten, C. E. 1965: 'The Current Controversy on Revelation: Pannenberg and His Critics', *JR* 45:225–237.

Bright, J. 1956: *Early Israel in Recent History Writing: A Study in Method*, London.

Brown, C. (ed.) 1976: *History, Criticism and Faith: Four exploratory studies:* Leicester.

Bultmann, R. 1948b: 'History of Salvation and History', ET in *Existence and Faith* (1961): 226–240 (German, 1948).

Burdett, D. 1974: 'Wisdom Literature and the Promise Doctrine', *Trinity Journal* 3:1–13.

Childs, B. S. 1962: *Memory and Tradition in Israel*, London.

Crenshaw, J. L. 1978: *Gerhard von Rad*, Waco, Texas.

Croatto, J. S. 1966: *La Historia de la Salvacion*, Buenos Aires.

Davies, G. H. 1970: 'Gerhard von Rad, *Old Testament Theology*' in Laurin (1970): 63–89.

Eichrodt, W. 1961: 'The Problem of Old Testament Theology', excursus added to ET of *Theology of the Old Testament*, I:512–520.

Feiner, J. & Löhrer, M. (ed.) 1965–: *Mysterium Salutis: Grundriss heilsgeschichtlicher Dogmatik*, five volumes.

Frisque, J. 1960: *Oscar Cullmann: Une théologie de l'histoire du salut*, Tournai (Cahiers de l'actualité religieuse 11).

Fuller, D. P. 1966: 'A New German Theological Movement', *SJT* 19:160–175.

Galloway, A. D. 1973: *Wolfhart Pannenberg*, London.

Gese, H. 1974: *Vom Sinai zum Zion: Alttestamentliche Beiträge zur biblischen Theologie*, Munich (Beiträge zur evangelischen Theologie 64, reprints of 1958–73 articles).

—1977a: 'Tradition and Biblical Theology' in Knight (1977): 301–326.

Gilkey, L. B. 1961: 'Cosmology, Ontology and the Travail of Biblical Language', *JR* 41:194–205.

Greig, A. J. 1974: '*Geschichte* and *Heilsgeschichte* in Old Testament Interpretation with Particular Reference to the Work of Gerhard von Rad', Edinburgh dissertation.

Groves, J. W. 1987: *Actualization and interpretation in the Old Testament*, Atlanta, Georgia (SBL Dissertation Series 86).

Harder, J. G. & Stevenson, W. T. 1971: 'The Continuity of History and Faith in the Theology of Wolfhart Pannenberg: Toward an Erotics of History', *JR* 51:34–56.

Harvey, J. 1971: 'The New Diachronic Biblical Theology of the Old Testament (1960–1970)', *BThB* 1:5–29.

Hasel, G. F. 1970: 'The Problem of History in Old Testament Theology', *Andrews University Seminary Studies* 8:23–50.

Honecker, M. 1963: 'Zum Verständnis der Geschichte in Gerhard von Rads Theologie des Alten Testaments', *EvTh* 23:143–168.

Huffmon, H. B. 1965: 'The Exodus, Sinai and the Credo', *CBQ* 27:101–113.

Hyatt, J. P. 1970: 'Was There an Ancient Historical Credo in Israel and an Independent Sinai Tradition?' in May Fs:152–170.

Käsemann, E. 1960: 'The Beginnings of Christian Theology', ET in *New Testament Questions of Today* (1969): 82–107 and *JTC* 6 (1969): 17–46 (German, 1960).

Knight, D. A. 1973: *Rediscovering the Traditions of Israel: The Development of the Traditio-Historical Research of the Old Testament, with Special Consideration of Scandinavian Contributions*, no place of publication given (SBL Dissertation Series 9).

Ladd, G. E. 1966b: 'History and Theology in Biblical Exegesis', *Int* 20:54–64.

—1968: *The Pattern of New Testament Truth*, Grand Rapids, Michigan.

Langley, M. 1978: 'Jesus and Revolution' in *The New International Dictionary of New Testament Theology* (ed. C. Brown), Exeter/Grand Rapids, 3:967–982.

Lemke, W. E. 1982: 'Revelation through History in Recent Biblical Theology: A Critical Appraisal', *Int* 36:34–46.

Lischer, R. 1984: 'The Limits of Story', *Int* 38:26–38.

Loretz, O. 1964: *The Truth of the Bible*, ET: London/New York, 1968 (German, 1964).

Moberly, R. W. L. 1986: 'Story in the Old Testament', *Themelios* 11:77–82.

Nicholson, E. W. 1973: *Exodus and Sinai in History and Tradition*, Oxford.

Niles, D. P. 1985: 'Story and Theology – A Proposal', *EAJT* 3:112–126.

Noth, M. 1948: *A History of Pentateuchal Traditions*, ET: Englewood Cliffs, New Jersey, 1972 (German, 1948).

O'Collins, G. G. 1966: 'Revelation as History', *The Heythrop Journal* 7:394–406.

Pannenberg, W. 1961a: 'Dogmatic Theses on the Doctrine of Revelation' in *Revelation as History* (ed. W. Pannenberg), ET: New York, 1968 (German, 1961): ch. 4.

—1961b: 'Kerygma and History', ET in *Basic Questions in Theology* I, London, 1970: 81–95 (German, 1961).

—1965: 'The God of Hope', ET in *Basic Questions in Theology* II, London, 1971: 234–249 (German, 1965).

—1967b: 'On Historical and Theological Hermeneutic', ET in *Basic Questions in Theology* I, London, 1970: 137–181 (German, 1967).

—1973: 'Glaube und Wirklichkeit im Denken Gerhard von Rads' in Wolff *et al.* (1973): 37–54.

Peter, J. 1970: 'Salvation History as a Model for Theological Thought', *SJT* 23:1–12.

Phythian-Adams, W. J. 1938: *The Fulness of Israel: A Study of the Meaning of Sacred History*, Oxford (Warburton Lectures 1935–37).

Rad, G. von 1938: 'The Form-Critical Problem of the Hexateuch', ET in von Rad (1966): 1–78 (German, 1938).

—1961a: 'Ancient Word and Living Word: The Preaching of Deuteronomy and Our Preaching', *Int* 15:3–13.

—1961b: 'History and the Patriarchs', *ExpT* 72:213–216.

Robinson, J. M. & Cobb, J. B. (eds.) 1967: *New Frontiers in Theology, Volume III: Theology as History*, New York/Evanston/London.

Rost, L. 1947: 'Sinaibund und Davidsbund', *TLZ* 72: 129–134.

Schwarzwäller, K. 1966: *Das Alte Testament in Christus*, Zürich (ThSt 84).

Soggin, J. A. 1964: 'Geschichte, Historie und Heilsgeschichte im Alten Testament: Ein Beitrag zur heutigen theologisch-hermeneutischen Diskussion', *TLZ* 89:721–736.

Song, C. S. 1984: *Tell us our names: Story Theology from an Asian Perspective*, Maryknoll, New York.

Spriggs, D. G. 1974: *Two Old Testament Theologies: A Comparative Evaluation of the Contributions of Eichrodt and von Rad to our Understanding of the Nature of Old Testament Theology*, London, 1974 (SBT II.30).

Stauffer, E. 1941: *New Testament Theology*, ET: London, 1955 (German, [5]1948, [1]1941).

Steck, K. G. 1959: *Die Idee der Heilsgeschichte: Hofmann – Schlatter – Cullmann*, Zollikon (ThSt 56).

Tupper, E. F. 1974: *The Theology of Wolfhart Pannenberg*, London.

Vaux, R. de 1963: Review of von Rad (1957–60) in *RB* 70:291–293.

Vriezen, Th. C. 1963b: 'The Credo in the Old Testament' in *Studies on the Psalms: Papers read at 6th Meeting of OTWSA*, Potschefstroom: 5–17.

Wolff, H. W. *et al.* 1973: *Gerhard von Rad: Seine Bedeutung für die Theologie*' Munich.

Wright, G. E. 1951a: 'The Unity of the Bible', *Int* 5:131–133, 304–317.

—1955: 'The Unity of the Bible', *SJT* 8:337–352.
—1960: 'Modern Issues in Biblical Studies: History and the Patriarchs', *ExpT* 71:292–296.
—1970: 'Historical Knowledge and Revelation' in May Fs: 279–303.
Zimmerli, W. 1971b: 'Alttestamentliche Traditionsgeschichte und Theologie' in von Rad Fs: 632–647.

See also works by von Rad, Cullmann, Wright, Amsler, Pannenberg, Moltmann, Gese, Martens and Weber in the general bibliography.

Part 3

Three key themes

───────── 7 ─────────

Typology

7.1 Typology in modern study

It is necessary first of all to consider what is meant by the word 'typology'. There is a world of difference between the use of the word *typos* ('type') in the Bible and many of the fanciful interpretations in the early church which have been called 'typology', or between the use of typology in modern biblical scholarship and in modern church life. Two main conceptions of typology are to be found today. Since the nineteen-fifties many biblical scholars have used the term 'typology' to express one aspect of the 'salvation history' approach to the relationship between the Testaments. Alongside this there are those who perpetuate fanciful forms of biblical interpretation closely related to allegory and symbolism, referring to them as typology. The place of typology in the theological relationship between the Old Testament and the New Testament depends entirely therefore on what is meant by 'typology'.

A term with such diverse connotations stands in need of replacement or more precise definition. Of those scholars who have chosen the former alternative, some have rejected the idea of typology for the modern church,[1] while others have suggested substitutes. W. J. Phythian-Adams (1944: 11), for

---

[1]*E.g.* Baumgärtel (1952: 78–85, 138–143); van Ruler (1955: 62–73); Barr (1966: 103–148).

example, developed the idea of 'homology', and this was taken up by A. G. Hebert (1947: 218–222). The concept of 'analogy' was important for Barth,[2] as also for von Rad (1960: 363–364) and Wolff (1956a: 167–181). Rowley (1953: 19–20) rejected the term 'typology' but recognized common patterns in the two Testaments (cf. Hooke 1961), and A. T. Hanson (1965: 162) wrote of 'parallel situation'.

On the other hand, although there are problems in retaining the word 'typology', a term originating in the Bible and well-recognized in modern scholarship cannot easily be dropped simply because it has been misused in some periods of history and is popularly misunderstood today. Whether we like it or not the term 'typology' is firmly established in theological vocabulary, and in the present chapter the latter alternative is chosen in an attempt to define the word more precisely. After an analysis of modern study of biblical typology, a synthesis will be attempted on the basis of the meaning of *typos* and its cognates in biblical Greek and the meaning of 'type' in modern English. It will be seen that this results in a more satisfactory understanding of typology, which is consistent with the nature of the biblical literature and illuminates the theological relationship between the Old and New Testaments.

a. Modern definitions of typology

In modern scholarship many definitions of typology have been proposed, and they fall into two main categories.

The first category comprises definitions centring on the idea of 'prefiguration', and these date mainly from the first half of the twentieth century. An example is the definition given by C. T. Fritsch (1947: 214): 'a type is an institution, historical event or person, ordained by God, which effectively prefigures some truth connected with Christianity'.

The second category comprises definitions centring on the idea of 'correspondence', and these date mainly from the second half of the century. An example is G. W. H. Lampe's definition (1953: 202) of typology as 'primarily a method of *historical* interpretation, based upon the continuity of God's purpose throughout the history of his covenant. It seeks to demonstrate the

---

[2]See 1932: 243–244; 1950: 49–51, 102; cf. Smart (1961: 125–129); also von Balthasar (1951: 93–181); Pannenberg (1953); Pöhlmann (1965).

correspondence between the various stages in the fulfilment of that purpose.'

Both kinds of definition have in common a historical basis, and both are clearly distinguished from fanciful interpretation. Although modern scholars have many differences of opinion on details, there is general agreement that typology is to be understood as a form of historical interpretation, based on the Bible itself.[3]

b. Typology in the Old Testament

Many scholars point out that typology originated in the Old Testament itself. Some see typology within the Pentateuch, so that the life of Abraham is a type of obedient faith (Gn. 12:1–9; 15:6; 22:16–18), whereas Lot is typical of wrong attitudes (Gn. 13:10–13; cf. Nu. 11:5; 14:2–4). Moses is a type of the prophets (Dt. 18:15, 18), and the story of the manna has the typological significance that God gives to each according to his needs (Ex. 16:9–27). In the Deuteronomic history David is a type of the ideal king (1 Ki. 9:4; 11:4, 6; 14:8; 15:11; cf. Ps. 132:1–4), and Solomon a type of the ideal wise man (1 Ki. 3:3–12, 28; 4:29–34; 10:1–3, 23–24). Typology is especially clear in the prophetic writings: Isaiah uses the garden of Eden as a type for the new paradise (Is. 9:1; 11:6–9), and Gideon's victory over Midian as a type for God's final victory (Is. 9:4; 10:26); Hosea predicts another period in the wilderness (Ho. 2:13–14; 12:10; cf. Je. 31:2); Second Isaiah expects a new Exodus (e.g. Is. 43:16–21; 48:20–21; 51:9–11; 52:11–12; cf. 11:15–16; Je. 16:14–15); and many of the prophets see David as typical of the king who is to come in the future (Is. 11:1; 55:3–4; Je. 23:5; Ezk. 34:23–24; Am. 9:11).

Von Rad's programmatic essay on 'Typological Interpretation of the Old Testament' (1952) has been one of the most influential factors in the revival of typology in modern scholarship. In it he argues that:

> We see everywhere in this history brought to pass by God's Word, in acts of judgement and acts of

---

[3]Stek (1970) contrasts the use of typology by Fairbairn (1864) and by von Rad (1960). He concludes that for Fairbairn typology is 'a divine *pedagogical instrument* for progressive revelation of a system of spiritual truths about heavenly and earthly realities', whereas for von Rad it is 'a useful *theological method* by which men appropriate for themselves and

redemption alike, the prefiguration of the Christ-event of the New Testament ... This renewed recognition of types in the Old Testament is no peddling of secret lore, no digging up of miracles, but is simply correspondent to the belief that the same God who revealed himself in Christ has also left his footprints in the history of the Old Testament covenant people (p. 36).

Francis Foulkes (1958: 7) sets out to show that the 'theological and eschatological interpretation of history' which is called typology originates in the Old Testament. He argues that the concept of God's acts in history being repeated is fundamental to the Old Testament, since the prophets assumed that God would act in the future in the same way that he had acted in the past (*e.g.* the call of Abraham; the Exodus; the reign of David). However, Israel hoped not simply for a repetition of God's acts but for a repetition of an unprecedented nature (*e.g.* a new Temple; a new covenant; a new creation). This hope was fulfilled in the New Testament and was the basis of the New Testament's typological interpretation of history.

Horace Hummel (1964) asserts even more emphatically that typology has its basis in the Old Testament, stating that 'the *typical* is a dominant concern of the O.T., its historiography, its cultus, its prophecy, etc.' (p. 40). He surveys 'typical' thinking – which he identifies with typological thinking – in the Old Testament, and finds examples in the presentation of historical events (*e.g.* the Exodus), individuals (*e.g.* Abraham; Moses; David), groups (*e.g.* the righteous; Israel; the wise man), laws (*e.g.* Pss. 15; 24), nations (*e.g.* Israel; Edom; Babylon; Gog and Magog), places (*e.g.* the holy land; Jerusalem; the Temple), legends (creation; flood; Jonah), and the cult (in its very nature: re-enaction of God's redemptive acts). Thus Hummel defends his proposition that 'Israel's fundamental concern behind all the personages, events, and scenes of her history was typical, and intended to point to the basic realities of all existence' (p. 47).

c. Typology in the New Testament

In the New Testament the typical element is even clearer than in the Old, especially in its interpretation of the Old Testament.

---

proclaim to others their experiences of the self-revelation of God in history'.

The standard work on the subject is still Leonhard Goppelt's *Typos: The Typological Interpretation of the Old Testament in the New* (1939). Goppelt examines in detail those passages of the New Testament which involve a typological use of the Old Testament, against the background of the contemporary Jewish understanding of Scripture and in contrast to the 'typology' of the letter of Barnabas. His conclusion is simple and important: typology is the dominant and characteristic method of interpretation for the New Testament use of the Old Testament (pp. 198–205; *cf.* Grant 1963/84: ch. 4). It is not only when the Old Testament is actually cited that this is apparent, but in all the New Testament allusions to the Old, many of which do not refer to specific texts. The New Testament writers recall Old Testament parallels to Jesus and the salvation which came through him, depicting both the similarities and the differences.

The purpose of this, according to Goppelt, is not primarily to expound the meaning of an Old Testament text. Typology is not a system for interpretation of the Old Testament, but a way of thinking. Its concern is with the understanding of the New Testament, both with respect to individual passages and to theological ideas. It is an aspect of the New Testament's own awareness of being part of the history of salvation: the New Testament is both a typological fulfilment of the Old Testament salvation history and a typological prophecy of the consummation to come. In contemporary Jewish biblical interpretation typology is relatively unimportant, and where it does occur it is comparatively superficial. In the letter of Barnabas 'typology' is used to make the Old Testament into a collection of Christian teaching. In the New Testament, however, the Old Testament is viewed as a unity which is valid in its own right, and typology is used in a historical rather than a mystical sense.

d. Typology in the relationship between the Testaments

Hans Walter Wolff (1956a: 167–181) develops the idea of typology as the analogy between the Old and New Testaments, centring his argument on the special starting-point of Old Testament interpretation.

First, he rejects any suggestion that ancient near Eastern religion is this starting-point. The Old Testament is quite different from its ancient near Eastern environment: in spite of parallels in detail, the substance is essentially different. Its distinctive characteristics – including its divine law and prophecy, and especially the unique nature of the God of Israel – show that the Old Testament is a stranger in the ancient Orient. It follows that the essence of the Old Testament cannot be understood by analogy to its religious environment.

Secondly, he asks, if studies of the ancient near East are not the key to the Old Testament, will Rabbinic studies unlock its meaning? There is an apparent continuity between the Old Testament and Judaism, but the fact is that from the Christian standpoint Judaism has not properly understood the Old Testament. Whether the synagogue reads its Bible as law or as the source of all wisdom, the full meaning of the Old Testament is to be sought elsewhere.

Thirdly, the question of whether the New Testament can show the meaning of the Old Testament remains for consideration. Wolff points out that Paul addresses the church as the Israel of God (Gal. 6:16), and throughout the New Testament Israel is a type of the church of Jesus Christ (e.g. Mk. 3:14; Rom. 11:17ff.; Jas. 1:1; Rev. 21:12–14). Here he says is a fundamental analogy: 'the Church of Jesus Christ can understand itself aright only as the eschatological Israel of God' (p. 174). There is also an analogy between the basis and the method of salvation in the two Testaments. Although there are obvious differences, the fundamental pattern is the same: the people of God is formed through God's saving activity, the covenant is kept intact only through the forgiveness of sins, and God's kingship over the members of his people demands their obedience to his law. Finally, there is a third analogy between God's gifts in the Old and New Testaments. In both cases there are material and spiritual gifts, and although there are differences the analogy is dominant: 'the new covenant in Christ corresponds to the covenant will of Yahweh as its fulfilment in the same way that marriage corresponds to engagement' (pp. 179–180). Wolff concludes in these words:

> The old Oriental environment and the Jewish successors of the Old Testament Israel, while presenting us with numerous aids to understanding details, still do not provide anything comparable to the essential total meaning of the Old Testament. *Only the New Testament offers the analogy of a witness of faith to the covenant will of God – a witness founded on historical facts – who chooses out of the world a people for himself and calls it to freedom under his Lordship* (p. 180).

This analogy he calls 'typology'.

Wolff (pp. 181–199) gives a number of examples of how this

idea of analogy can be used in biblical interpretation and some will be mentioned here. The Sermon on the Mount and Paul's exhortations give insight into the Old Testament law as God's covenant gift, the concept of 'witness' in Luke and John illuminates that in Ezekiel, and God's salvation of his people by the judges may be seen as one aspect of his continual saving activity throughout their history. Moreover, the primeval history witnesses to God's intention for the world, without which Jesus Christ would not be properly understood; the Day of Atonement ritual shows God's principles in dealing with sin, which are the presupposition for the coming of Jesus and apart from which his death would be inexplicable; and Exodus 14 and Ezekiel 37 show the nature of the divinely-constituted people of God and thus the self-understanding of the church.[4]

7.2 The basis of typology

In the first section of the chapter it has been shown that in the opinion of many modern scholars typology is by no means a fanciful method of interpretation to be dismissed as an illegitimate way of understanding the Bible. On the contrary, it is historically based and originates in the Bible itself. In order to define more precisely the role of typology in understanding the relationship between the Testaments, a semantic, theological and hermeneutical study of its basis and nature will now be attempted.

a. Example and pattern

A more precise definition of the biblical meaning of 'typology' necessitates an examination of the biblical use of the word *typos* ('type') and cognates *typikōs* ('typical'), *antitypos* ('anti-type') and *hypotypōsis* ('type'). There is no biblical equivalent to the word 'typology' for the simple reason that the biblical authors did not analyse or systematize types. For the same reason, 'typical' is a more appropriate translation of *typikōs* than 'typological'.

'Type' is a common word today but in the Septuagint and Greek New Testament *typos* is used only 17 times. In both cases there is one basic meaning. The word *typos* in the Greek Bible usually means 'example' or 'pattern' (12 times); and the occasional meanings 'mark' (Jn. 20:25, twice), 'image' (Am. 5:26; Acts 7:43) and 'to this effect' (Acts 23:25) are

---

[4]A major study of typology which came to hand after the present work was completed is that of R. M. Davidson (1981).

closely related in meaning. Its cognates also relate in every case to the meaning 'example' or 'pattern'. To show this clearly the biblical occurrences of *typos* and its cognates are set out in full below. The basic text is the RSV and the translations in brackets are from the RSV, NEB and NIV respectively (except for the Septuagint: RSV, NEB and Bagster).

The use of the *typos* word-group in the Greek Bible

typos

Ex. 25:40	'the (pattern, design, pattern) . . . shown you on the mountain'
Am. 5:26	'your (images, images, images)'
Jn. 20:25	'(print, mark, marks) of the nails'
Jn. 20:25	'(mark, place, where [the nails] were) of the nails'
Acts 7:43	'(figures, images, idols) which you made to worship'
Acts 7:44	'the (pattern, pattern, pattern) that he had seen'
Acts 23:25	'a letter (to this effect, to this effect, as follows)'
Rom. 5:14	'Adam, who was a (type, foreshadows, pattern)'
Rom. 6:17	'obedient . . . to the (standard, pattern, form) of teaching'
1 Cor. 10:6	'these things are (warnings, symbols to warn, examples) for us'
Phil. 3:17	'as you have an (example, model, pattern) in us'
1 Thes. 1:7	'an (example, model, model) to all the believers'
2 Thes. 3:9	'an (example, example, model) to imitate'
1 Tim. 4:12	'set the believers an (example, example, example)'
Tit. 2:7	'show yourself . . . a (model, example, example) of good deeds'
Heb. 8:5	'the (pattern, pattern, pattern) . . . shown you on the mountain'
1 Pet. 5:3	'being (examples, an example, examples) to the flock'

typikōs

1 Cor. 10:11	'happened to them as (a warning, symbolic, examples)'

antitypos

Heb. 9:24	'a (copy, symbol, copy) of the true one'
1 Pet. 3:21	'Baptism, which (corresponds) to this' (RSV)
	'This water (prefigured, symbolizes) baptism' (NEB, NIV)

hypotypōsis

1 Tim. 1:16	'(example to, typical of, example for) those who . . . believe'
2 Tim. 1:13	'Follow the (pattern, outline, pattern) of the sound words'

The *typos* word-group is closely related in meaning to the word-group which includes *deigma* (Jude 7) and its cognates *deigmatizō* (Col. 2:15), *paradeigma* (Ex. 25:9; 1 Ch. 28:11–12, 18–19), *paradeigmatizō* (Mt. 1:19; Heb. 6:6) and *hypodeigma* (Jn. 13:15; Heb. 4:11; 8:5; 9:23; Jas. 5:10; 2 Pet. 2:6). Here again, apart from Hebrews 6:6 where the meaning of *paradeigmatizō* is 'to hold up to contempt', the meaning is 'example' or 'pattern' in every case.

In no case is any of these words used as a technical term. It is sometimes thought that the word *typos* has a technical sense in Romans 5:14 and 1 Corinthians 10:6 (*cf.* v. 11) (*e.g.* Goppelt 1969: 251–253).

However translators generally agree that the meaning is 'foreshadow' (NEB), 'prefigure' (JB) or 'pattern' (NIV) in Romans 5:14 and 'example' (NIV) or 'warning' (RSV, JB) in 1 Corinthians 10:6, 11. In both cases the usual biblical meaning 'example, pattern' is entirely appropriate and it is unnecessary to suggest a technical use. It is presumably to prevent any implication of a technical term that the modern versions avoid the translation 'type' for *typos*. KJV and NIV do not use the word 'type' at all. RSV does so only at Romans 5:14. Vischer (1960: 120) rejects the word 'typology' partly because it has poorly understood the meaning of *typos*, which he argues is 'example'. The conclusion is straightforward: the evidence of biblical terminology suggests the meaning 'example, pattern' for 'type'.

b. Analogy and correspondence

Typological thinking is part of all human thought, arising out of our attempt to understand the world on the basis of concrete analogies, as von Rad points out.[5] It follows that there is nothing surprising about the application of this method to the biblical world. Archbishop Trench (1870: 12–14) once wrote:

> The parable or other analogy to spiritual truth appropriated from the world of nature or man, is not merely illustration, but also in some sort proof. It is not merely that these analogies assist to make the truth intelligible ... Their power lies deeper than this, in the harmony unconsciously felt by all men, and which all deeper minds have delighted to trace, between the natural and the spiritual worlds, so that analogies from the first are felt to be something more than illustrations, happily but yet arbitrarily chosen ... They belong to one another, the type and the thing typified, by an inward necessity; they were linked together long before by the law of a secret affinity.

It is the conviction that there is such a 'secret affinity' within God's created order, shared by the biblical writers and many of

---

[5]1952a: 17; 1960: 364. Contrast Bultmann (1950b) who rejects typology because he considers it to be based on the idea of repetition. According to him this is derived from the cyclic view of history of the ancient near East and classical Greece, whereas the Old Testament has a linear view of history, a history whose course is divinely-directed and moves toward a definite conclusion. Von Rad (1952a: 20) disputes the validity of this view.

their interpreters throughout the centuries, which lies at the root of the idea of typology. Some use typology cautiously, others use it extravagantly, but all base their use of typology on the conviction that there is a 'secret affinity' between the natural and spiritual orders, as well as between different events in the same order.

Thus it was natural for those in biblical times to see an analogy between the tabernacle and the heavenly pattern shown to Moses (Ex. 25:40; Acts 7:44; Heb. 8:5), between the life of Christ or a Christian leader and the way Christians ought to live (1 Tim. 1:16; Phil. 3:17; 1 Pet. 5:3), between events in Israel's history and events in the life of the church (1 Cor. 10:6, 11; 1 Pet. 3:21), between an idol and the spiritual reality it symbolizes (Am. 5:26; Acts 7:43), and between the man who brought sin into the world and the man who took it away (Rom. 5:14). In each case the presupposition is that God acts consistently so that there are correspondences between different parts of his created order.[6] Typology rests on the basic assumption that 'the history of God's people and of his dealings with them is a single continuous process in which a uniform pattern may be discerned' (Lampe 1953: 201; *cf.* Wenham 1987: 257–258).

c. Illustration

It has been shown that understanding of the relationship between the Testaments in terms of typology is based on the biblical meaning of *typos* ('example, pattern') and the consistency of God which leads to analogies and correspondences within creation and history. Yet there is something even more basic about the idea of typology: it is the way in which almost any biblical text – Old Testament or New Testament – addresses the church. Much of the Bible consists not of propositions but of stories, and these are relevant primarily in the sense of being typical (see Miskotte 1963: 199–207; *cf.* 388–404). Old Testament characters such as Abraham and Moses, David and Elijah,

---

[6]There are two main kinds of correspondence here: vertical (archetype and antitype, *i.e.* the relationship between heavenly and earthly realities) and horizontal (prototype and antitype, *i.e.* the relationship between earlier and later historical facts). In practice, however, the Bible is more interested in horizontal than vertical typology, as is most modern writing on the subject. On this distinction, see Hummel (1964: 39) and Fritsch (1966). On analogy and correspondence, see further Mildenberger (1964: 78–83); Sauter (1965: 184–207).

were human beings 'of like nature with ourselves' (Jas. 5:17) and encountered the same God as the Christian does. One of the main reasons their experiences were recorded was because they are typical of the sort of thing that happens to believers in God and therefore are still relevant today.

At the end of John's Gospel it is noted that 'Jesus did many other signs in the presence of the disciples, which are not written in this book; but these are written that you may believe that Jesus is the Christ . . .' (Jn. 20:30–31). The implication is that certain signs were recorded because they were typical. In chemistry a 'type' is a 'compound whose structure illustrates that of many others' (*Concise Oxford Dictionary*). Hydrochloric acid, for example, is a type of the acids. It is no more an acid than any other, but is typical because it shows clearly the essential nature of an acid in its structure: H-Cl. Sulphuric acid (H_2SO_4) and acetic acid (CH_3COOH) have the same basic structure, but it is not so clear. The structure of hydrochloric acid is also a pattern for such compounds as NaCl and HBr and so it may be termed a type of the haloids too. In a similar way, certain signs are recorded in John because they illustrate some aspect or aspects of the gospel message especially well and thus can serve as types.

This provides at least one reason why so much is made of the affair between David and Bathsheba. There is no question of revelling in the sins of others: it is rather that the temptation, sin, attempt to conceal, rebuke, repentance, forgiveness, punishment and restoration are recorded because they are typical of what happens frequently in the life of a believer. Jonah may be chosen as a type of the Christian, because like so many he was led from sin through despair to eventual salvation. He is also a type of Christ who bore the sins of the world, was brought to the point of feeling abandoned by God and descended to the lowest state possible before he was raised from death to life.[7]

7.3 The nature of typology

a. False ideas of typology

Before attempting a precise definition of the nature of typology

---

[7]On typology as the study of what is typical, see Röhr (1973: 290); *cf.* Bozzo (1974).

it is necessary to distinguish a number of incorrect uses of the word.

Typology is not exegesis

The biblical text has essentially one meaning, its literal meaning, and this is to be found by means of grammatical-historical study. If the author intended a typical significance it will be clear in the text; and if we see a typical significance not intended by the author it must be consistent with the literal meaning. Typology is not an exegesis or interpretation of a text, but the study of relationships between events, persons and institutions recorded in biblical texts.

Typology is not prophecy

Typology and prophecy are related, since both presuppose continuity and correspondence in history; but typology is retrospective whereas prophecy is prospective. Of course, recognition of the fulfilment of prophecy is retrospective, but this is concerned with the fulfilment of *words* in the Old Testament, whereas typology discerns a relationship between the *events, persons* and *institutions* recorded in the Bible.

Typology is not allegory

The distinction between typology and allegory was formulated as early as 1762 by J. Gerhard: 'Typology consists in the comparison of facts. Allegory is not concerned with the facts but with the words from which it draws out useful and hidden doctrine' (quoted by Goppelt 1939: 7). Modern scholars have generally accepted this distinction, laying stress on the historical nature of typology in contrast to the fanciful nature of allegory which often entirely ignores the historical situation.[8] Typology requires a real correspondence between the events, persons and institutions in question, whereas allegory can find 'spiritual' significance in unimportant details or words.

---

[8]A few scholars disagree: Barr (1966: 103–111) denies the validity of the distinction; Jewett (1954) thinks they are much the same thing; and Bright (1967: 79) points out that it is difficult to distinguish between the two in the Fathers. But they have not invalidated the fundamental distinction that typology is generally historical, whereas allegory tends to be fanciful (so Goppelt 1939: 5–18; Florovsky 1951: 173–176; Lampe 1957: 29–35; Lys 1967: 54–75; and many others). Goldingay (1981: 102–107) puts it slightly differently: typology studies events, allegory interprets words.

Typology is not symbolism

Symbolic interpretation involves understanding objects as expressions of a general truth, whereas typical interpretation is concerned to see relationships between historical facts.

Typology is not a method or system

In the church Fathers an elaborate typological method was developed, but in the Bible the typical approach is so unsystematic that it does not even have a fixed terminology. The Bible gives no exhaustive list of types and implies no developed method for their interpretation. On the contrary, there is a great freedom and variety in the outworking of the basic principle that the Old Testament is a model for the New.

b. Suggested characteristics of types

There have been numerous attempts to define the characteristics of types, many of which make the mistake of treating typology as a fixed system of interpretation rather than a basic approach to the Bible.

It is suggested, for instance, that an essential characteristic of a type is that it is designed by God (Goppelt 1939: 18; Moorehead 1939). At first sight this is plausible and it may even be thought that it is self-evident. But surely Christian faith affirms that the whole Bible was designed by God? 'If David could have been placed where he was, and been what he was, without God's design, he would still have been typical. But, of course, without God's intervention, neither he nor his dispensation could have come into existence'.[9]

Another suggestion is that the limits of typology should be defined by giving a series of standards to which a type must

---

[9]Davidson (1903a: 237). *Cf.* Calmet (1837: II.769): 'Whether certain histories which happened in ancient times were designed as types of future events, it is not easy to determine: but observe, (1.) it is likely that such histories are recorded (being selected from among many occurrences) as might be useful lessons, &c. to succeeding ages. (2.) That there being a general conformity in the dispensations of providence and grace, to different persons, and in different ages, instances of former dispensations may usefully be held up to the view of later times, and may encourage, or may check, may direct, or may control, those placed in circumstances, &c. similar to what is recorded, though their times and their places may be widely separated. We have New Testament authority for this.'

conform (Moorehead 1939; Amsler 1952: 81) or limiting types to those found in the New Testament (Wright 1952: 66). But although it is possible to describe what is meant by 'typical', it is arbitrary to limit its occurrence in the Bible by a set of rules. The New Testament gives guidelines, but does not give a definition nor an exhaustive list of types. Since typology is concerned not only with certain parts of the Old Testament but with the whole Bible, there are an unlimited number of possible types. It is not a matter of finding types in a fixed system: rather, many events and persons may usefully serve as typical for one purpose or another.

It is sometimes suggested that types are always concerned with Christ (Amsler 1952: 79) or with God's redemptive activity (Fritsch 1947: 220; Woollcombe 1957: 75). But then much of the Bible is concerned with God's redemptive activity and thus with Christ! It is not surprising that this is the dominant concern of types in the Bible; but the Bible is interested in creation and the kingdom of God as well as redemption, and these have typical aspects too.

A further suggestion is that types prefigure something future (Moorehead 1939; Berkhof 1950: 145). But this implies that they have some meaning other than that which is apparent at the time. It is only in retrospect that an event, person or institution may be seen to be typical. The existence of types necessitates there being other events, persons or institutions – earlier or later – of which they are typical.

It is often suggested that there is a 'heightening' (Goppelt 1939: 18, 199–202) or 'progression' (A. B. Davidson 1903a: 240) from the type to its antitype. But this is simply an aspect of the progression from Old Testament to New Testament, and not a necessary characteristic of a type. The essence of a type is that it is exemplary, and it is also possible for something which is more advanced to be typical of something which is less advanced. Moreover, it is possible for one thing to be a type of its opposite: for example, the entry of sin into the world by the first Adam is said to be typical of the entry of grace by the second (Rom. 5:14).

c. Confusion of typology with fanciful interpretation

One of the basic problems concerning typology is that both in the past and present it has frequently been misunderstood and misused as a fanciful kind of biblical interpretation.

Sometimes, for instance, the word 'typology' has been used for what is really allegorical or symbolic exegesis. There are, of course, some biblical texts which were intended by their authors to have allegorical or symbolic significance and are therefore not to be interpreted literally, such as parts of Ezekiel and Revelation. However, such methods should be used with care and only where it is clear that a text was not intended to be understood in a more straightforward way. For example, there is no need for an allegorical approach to Genesis 37–50 which finds its real meaning to be prefiguration of Christ, when the text has a clear literal meaning and historical function as preparation for the account of the Exodus. Moreover, its relevance for today can be seen by means of typology, without resort to allegory, if Joseph is recognized as a typical character whose life reveals certain basic principles of God's activity which are also true for the life of Christ and Christians.

Perhaps the most common misuse of typology is to find correspondences in trivial details. Rahab's scarlet cord has been said to be a type of the death of Christ and the axe Elisha retrieved from the river a type of Jesus' cross (1 Clement 12; Justin, *Dialogue*: 86), but there is no historical or theological correspondence between these things. There is a consistency in God's created order which makes it possible for there to be red or wooden objects in both Old and New Testaments; but that does not mean that these things have any typical or exemplary importance for the Christian!

However the fact that the term 'typology' has been confused with allegorical and symbolic exegesis, and applied to trivial correspondences, does not invalidate it as a principle if properly used. Also, while the modern church should certainly not imitate such exegetical methods, neither should it despise those who used them: it was the allegorical school in the early church who preserved the Old Testament for Christianity (*cf.* Grant 1963/84: ch. 5).

d. A note on the 'fuller meaning'

During the second part of the twentieth-century, encouraged particularly by the encyclical 'Divino afflante Spiritu' (1943) of Pius XII, a deep interest in the interpretation and theology of the Bible has developed in the Roman Catholic Church. An important aspect of this has been the discussion and use of the concept of a 'fuller meaning' (*sensus plenior*), introduced in 1927 by Andrés Fernández but only widely used after the Second World War. It is defined by Brown (1968) as 'the deeper meaning, intended by God but not clearly intended by the human author, that is seen to exist in the words of Scripture when they are studied in the light of further revelation or of development in the understanding of revelation'. Its implication for understanding the relationship between the Testaments is that the Old Testament is considered to have a deeper meaning of which the human authors were not aware but which becomes clear in the light of the New Testament. In the pages of the Old Testament, 'God so directed the human author's choice of language that future generations should see there "the mystery of Christ" ... This choice of language, the secret of which is revealed in the New Testament, shows in a very clear manner the unity of the two Testaments'.[10]

The fuller meaning should not be confused with the 'spiritual meaning' (*sensus spiritualis*), which is essentially a mystical idea based on the interpretation of the Fathers (*e.g.* de Lubac 1950). It should also be distinguished from typology, at least as the latter is defined here. For example, the fuller meaning of an Old Testament text may include reference to Christ and this is considered to be part of the 'real' meaning of the text, even though the author was unaware of it. Typology, in contrast, does not claim to elucidate the meaning of a text, but cites it to point to an example or pattern ('type') of God's activity in the history of his people. The author may well have been aware of this, indeed in some cases this was precisely the reason he wrote the text.

e. Principles and definitions

So far our argument has taken the form of negative criticism. It has been shown that typology is not to be understood as exegesis, prophecy, allegory, symbolism or a system. The suggestions that divine design, specific limits, connection with Christ and redemption, prefiguration of the future and progression from type to antitype are necessary characteristics of typology have been rejected. Typology has also been dis-

---

[10]Sutcliffe (1953: 343). On Roman Catholic biblical interpretation since 1943, see McKenzie (1964); H. H. Miskotte (1966) and Scharleman (1972). The theory of the 'fuller meaning' has generated a vast quantity of literature and only a few basic works can be mentioned here: Coppens (1948; 1958); Sutcliffe (1953); Brown (1953; 1968). Some Catholic scholars have rejected the idea of a fuller meaning, *e.g.* Vawter (1964). See also Amsler (1960a: 183–186); J. M. Robinson (1965); Harrington (1973: 293–304); Lasor (1978).

tinguished from the theory of a 'fuller meaning'. To turn to the positive side, there are two basic principles of typology which must be adhered to if it is not to result in fanciful or trivial biblical interpretation.[11]

First, *typology is historical*. Its concern is not with words but with historical facts: events, people, institutions. It is not a method of philological or textual study, but a way of understanding history.[12] The fundamental conviction which underlies typology is that God is consistently active in the history of this world – especially in the history of his chosen people – and that as a consequence the events in this history tend to follow a consistent pattern. One event may therefore be chosen as typical of another, or of many others.

Secondly, *typology implies a real correspondence*. It is not interested in parallels of detail, but only in an agreement of fundamental principles and structure. There must be a correspondence in history and theology or the parallel will be trivial and valueless for understanding the Bible.

On the basis of these two principles some working definitions may be suggested:

- a *type* is a biblical event, person or institution which serves as an example or pattern for other events, persons or institutions;
- *typology* is the study of types and the historical and theological correspondences between them;
- the *basis* of typology is God's consistent activity in the history of his chosen people.

---

[11]*Cf.* Goppelt (1939: 17); Berkhof (1950: 145); Amsler (1952: 79–80); Woollcombe (1957: 75).

[12]It follows that typology does not imply any particular doctrine of the inspiration of the Bible: its basis is God's direction of history (so Amsler 1952: 78; but contrast Gundry 1969). The question may be raised whether Jonah or Job, for instance, must be historical in order to be typical. It may be suggested that although typology is essentially historical it is possible to have correspondences between an imaginary person and a real person. Even if such a type is somewhat artificial it could still have educative value. There is an undoubted correspondence between Macbeth or Hamlet and real people: the significance of these characters is not lessened by the fact that they are fictional. Likewise, whether or not they ever lived, there remains a fundamental correspondence between the lives of Jonah and Job as portrayed in the biblical story and those of Christians.

f. Types and paradigms

This understanding of typology may be compared with the exposition of the Exodus-event as a paradigm (example, pattern) of God's saving activity which has been influential in the development of liberation theology (*e.g.* Gutiérrez 1971: 159; *cf.* Kirk 1979: 99–104). Typological interpretation of the Exodus is of course not new: it is found in both Old and New Testaments (*cf.* Anderson 1962; Daube 1963; Nixon 1963). Similar ideas are expressed in hymns such as 'Guide me, O Thou Great Jehovah' and the classic Negro spiritual, 'Let my people go!', the former referring to spiritual and the latter to political salvation. In liberation theology the Exodus is understood as 'the prototype of divine revelation, the privileged moment in which God once manifested himself and now continues to do the same' and 'a liberative revolution . . ., a socially subversive act comparable to slave rebellions or other struggles of oppressed peoples against imperialism' (Fierro 1977: 474). The emphasis has often been on social justice and political liberation rather than spiritual experience and freedom from sin, though the latter aspect is not completely overlooked (*cf.* Branson & Padilla 1983: 163, 173–174; Yewangoe 1987: 296–304).

Such an interpretation of the Exodus as the archetypal event of salvation history gives it paradigmatic rather than normative significance. Thus Fierro (1977: 478–479) argues that its relevance today is not to tell Christians what they must do but to give an example (model, paradigm) of what they might do. Indeed

> the same holds true for other facts and events in the Bible. They are not normative; they are sources of inspiration and liberation. They give rise to a possibility, not to a necessary obligation. In presenting certain actions performed by our forefathers in the faith as an integral part of history in which God is a participant, the biblical account authorizes us to take analogous action on the basis of our faith.

It follows that the function of types and paradigms is not to establish doctrine or ethics, but to suggest possibilities and inspire action. This is consistent with the pragmatic nature of liberation theology, which is more concerned with praxis than dogma (see above: ch. 2.7.c).

However the paradigmatic interpretation of the Old Testament is not limited to liberation theology. For example, Paul Hanson (1978: 86–87) describes the Exodus and the life of Jesus as paradigmatic events which form the nucleus of the confessional heritage of the Christian community of faith. And Christopher Wright (1984: 16–18) proposes a paradigmatic approach to the use of the Bible in social ethics, explaining that a paradigm is a particular case which functions as a model or example to explain a general principle. In the study of languages a paradigm refers to a pattern verb which is learnt not in order to imitate the verb but to apply the pattern. So also the laws and institutions of Old Testament Israel are paradigmatic, not simply to be imitated but providing a pattern which enables those who live in a quite different society to think and behave in a way consistent with the basic principles of the Old Testament. Wright argues that paradigmatic application protects us from the opposite dangers of literal imitation of Israel, and of limiting the validity of Old Testament laws and institutions to historical Israel so that they are irrelevant in modern secular society.

All these paradigmatic approaches to biblical interpretation are based on the principle of God's consistent activity in salvation history, and are essentially the same as what has here been described as 'typology'.

g. A relationship of analogy

We have argued that typology is not a method of exegesis or interpretation, but the study of historical and theological correspondences between different parts of God's activity among his people in order to find what is typical there. The function of typology is therefore not to give a procedure for using the Old and New Testaments, but to point to the consistent working of God in the experience of his people. Thus parallels may be drawn between different events, persons and institutions, and individual events may be seen as examples or patterns for others. Often the narrator has recorded only a bare event, but in this very lack of interpretation it may have typical and thus theological significance (von Rad 1952a: 38). Typology cannot be used for exegesis, because its concern is not primarily with the words of the text but with the events recorded in it. The exegete has to find the meaning of the text and its witness to an event by means of grammatical-historical study. To relate that event to other events recorded in the Bible is the task of the biblical theologian and historian; and to relate it to modern

Christian experience is the task of the preacher. For these typology has its value, so long as it is used judiciously and in accordance with the principles outlined above.

The contribution of typology to understanding the relationship between the Testaments is to point to the fundamental analogy between different parts of the Bible. Every part of the Bible is an expression of the consistent activity of the one God. This means that the Old Testament illuminates the New and the New Testament illuminates the Old. The relationship between the Testaments does not consist only of the Old Testament's expectation of the New and the New Testament's quotation of the Old; there is also a fundamental analogy between the Old and New Testaments as witnesses to God's activity in history. Thus typology, although it is not a method of exegesis, can supplement exegesis by providing comparisons to throw further light on the meaning of specific texts. The discipline most closely related to the study of the Old Testament is therefore the study of the New Testament: ancient Oriental and Jewish studies clarify details of the Old Testament but lack the intrinsic analogy of New Testament studies to Old Testament studies. The corollary is that the discipline most closely related to the study of the New Testament is that of the Old Testament: Jewish and Hellenistic studies are important but do not have a fundamental analogy to New Testament studies in the way that Old Testament studies do. This shows a double aspect to the relationship between the Testaments:

● on the one hand, correct understanding and use of the Old Testament depends on the New Testament; and
● on the other hand, one of the primary uses of the Old Testament is to be the basis for correct understanding and use of the New Testament.

A corollary to this is that typology is an aid to interpretation of the Bible in the Christian church. It has been shown that the essence of the biblical concept of 'type' is 'example' or 'pattern', and one of the primary values of the Bible for the Christian is that it presents examples and patterns of the experience of men and women with God which correspond to the experience of modern men and women. Events, persons and institutions present types for the Christian life. For example, the flood (*cf.* 1 Pet. 3:20–21), the oppression and Exodus (*cf.* 1 Cor. 10), and the Exile and restoration (*cf.* Je. 23:7–8) are typical of God's saving activity among his people, and thus patterns of the salvation which the Christian experiences in Christ. Noah and Job (*cf.* Ezk. 14:14, 20), Moses (*cf.* Heb. 3:2) and David (*cf.* 1 Ki. 3:14; 15:3, 11) are examples of how the believer should live. Balaam (*cf.* 2 Pet. 2:15; Jude 11; Rev. 2:14) and Jeroboam (*cf.* 1 Ki. 15:26, 34; 16:2–3, 19, 26, 31), in contrast, are examples of how he or she should not live. These instances could easily be multiplied (*cf.* Heb. 11). The correspondence between Israelite and Christian institutions (*e.g.* Passover and Lord's Supper; psalms and hymns) and the spiritual application of Old Testament material realities (*e.g.* the Temple and the Christian church as divine dwelling-places, *cf.* 1 Cor. 3:16; sacrifices and offerings, and the Christian's 'living sacrifice', *cf.* Rom. 12:1) are further ways in which typology may aid practical use of the Bible.

All these examples – and many others which could be given – apply to the Christian, but most apply also and especially to Christ himself, which is why typology is often thought to be concerned with types of Christ. But what is more important is that Jesus Christ himself is our supreme example and pattern (Mt. 11:29; Jn. 13:15; Phil. 2:5; 1 Pet. 2:21). Perhaps the concern of typology should therefore be not so much to look for types of Christ as to understand Christ himself as the supreme type for Christians and the world.

Bibliography (7)

Balthasar, H. U. von 1951: *Karl Barth: Darstellung und Deutung seiner Theologie*, Cologne.

Barth, K. 1932: *Church Dogmatics* I.1, ET: Edinburgh, [2]1975 (German, 1932).

—1950: *Church Dogmatics* III.3, ET: Edinburgh, 1961 (German, 1950).

Berkhof, L. 1950: *Principles of Biblical Interpretation (Sacred Hermeneutics)*, Grand Rapids, Michigan: 142–148.

Bozzo, E. G. 1974: 'Jesus as a Paradigm for Personal Life', *JES* 11:45–63.

Brown, R. E. 1953: 'The History and Development of the Theory of a Sensus Plenior', *CBQ* 15:141–162.

—1968: 'Hermeneutics' in *JBC* II:605–623.

Bultmann, R. 1950b: 'Ursprung und Sinn der Typologie als hermeneutischer Methode', *TLZ* 75:205–212.

Calmet, A. 1837: 'Type' in *Calmet's Dictionary of the Holy Bible*, London, [6]1837, II:768–769.

Coppens, J. 1958: *Le Problème du Sens Plénier des Saintes Écritures*, Louvain, 1958 (reprinted from *ETL* 34:5–20).

Daniélou, J. 1950a: *From Shadows to Reality: Studies in the Biblical Typology of the Fathers*, ET: London, 1960 (French, 1950).

Daube, D. 1963: *The Exodus Pattern in the Bible*, London.

Davidson, A. B. 1903a: *Old Testament Prophecy*, Edinburgh.

Davidson, R. M. 1981: *Typology in Scripture: A study of hermeneutical* typos *structures*, Berrien Springs, Michigan.

Eichrodt, W. 1957a: 'Is Typological Exegesis an Appropriate Method?', ET in *EOTI*: 224–245 (German, 1957).

Ellison, H. L. 1953b: 'Typology', *EQ* 25:158–166.

Fairbairn, P. 1864: *The Typology of Scripture, Viewed in Connection with the Whole Series of The Divine Dispensations*, Edinburgh, [5]1870 ([4]1864; two volumes).

France, R. T. 1970: 'In all the Scriptures – a Study of Jesus' Typology', *The Theological Students' Fellowship Bulletin* 56:13–16.

Fritsch, C. T. 1946/47: 'Biblical Typology', *Bibliotheca Sacra* 103:293–305, 418–430; 104:87–100, 214–222.

—1966: 'TO ANTITYPON' in *Studia Biblica et Semitica: Theodoro Christiano Vriezen dedicata* (ed. W. C. van Unnik & A. S. van der Woude), Wageningen: 100–107.

Goppelt, L. 1939: *Typos: The Typological Interpretation of the Old Testament in the New*, ET: Grand Rapids, Michigan, 1982 (German, 1939).

—1969: '*typos*' in *TDNT* 8:246–259.

Goulder, M. D. 1964: *Type and History in Acts*, London.

Gundry, S. N. 1969: 'Typology as a Means of Interpretation: Past and Present', *Bulletin of the Evangelical Theological Society* 12:233–240.

Hartley, J. E. 1982: 'The Use of Typology Illustrated in a Study of Isaiah 9:1–7' in *Interpreting God's Word for Today* (ed. W. McCown & J. E. Massey, Wesleyan Theological Perspectives 2), Anderson, Indiana: 195–220.

Hebert, A. G. 1947: *The Authority of the Old Testament*, London.

Hooke, S. H. 1961: *Alpha and Omega: A Study in the Pattern of Revelation*, Welwyn.

Hummel, H. D. 1964: 'The Old Testament Basis of Typological Interpretation', *Biblical Research* 9:38–50.

Jewett, P. K. 1954: 'Concerning the Allegorical Interpretation of Scripture', *The Westminster Theological Journal* 17:1–20.

Lambert, J. C. 1918: 'Type' in *Dictionary of the Apostolic Church* II (ed. J. Hastings), Edinburgh: 623–626.

Lampe, G. W. H. 1953: 'Typological Exegesis', *Theology* 56:201–208.

—1957: 'The Reasonableness of Typology' in *Essays on Typology* (G. W. H. Lampe & K. J. Woollcombe), London (SBT 22):9–38.

LaSor, W. S. 1978: 'Prophecy, Inspiration, and *Sensus Plenior*', *TB* 29:49–60.

Lubac, H. de 1947: '"Typologie" et "Allégorisme"', *Recherches de science religieuse* 34:180–226.

—1950: *Histoire et Esprit: L'intelligence de l'Écriture d'après Origène*, Paris (Théologie 16).

Lys, D. 1967: *The Meaning of the Old Testament: An Essay on Hermeneutics*, Nashville/New York: especially 54–75.

Marcus, R. A. 1957: 'Presuppositions of the Typological Approach to Scripture', *CBQ* 158:442–451.

Mickelsen, A. B. 1963: *Interpreting the Bible*, Grand Rapids, Michigan.

Miskotte, H. H. 1966: *Sensus spiritualis: De verhouding tussen het Oude*

Testament en het Nieuwe Testament in de rooms-katholieke hermeneutiek sinds het verschijnen van de encycliek 'Divino afflante Spiritu' in 1943, Nijkerk.

Moorehead, W. G. 1939: 'Type' in *The International Standard Bible Encyclopaedia* (ed. J. Orr *et al.*), Grand Rapids, Michigan, 1939 (revised edition): 3029–3030.

Pannenberg, W. 1953: 'Zur Bedeutung des Analogiegedankens bei Karl Barth: Eine Auseinandersetzung mit Urs von Balthasar', *TZL* 78:17–24.

Payne, J. B. 1962: *The Theology of the Older Testament*, Grand Rapids, Michigan.

Phythian-Adams, W. J. 1944: *The Way of At-one-ment: Studies in Biblical Theology*, London.

Pöhlmann, H. G. 1965: *Analogia entis oder Analogia fidei? Die Frage der Analogie bei Karl Barth*, Göttingen.

Richardson, A. 1947: *Christian Apologetics*, London: 188–193.

Robinson, J. M. 1965: 'Scripture and Theological Method: A Protestant Study in *Sensus Plenior*', *CBQ* 27:6–27.

Rohland, E. 1956: *Die Bedeutung der Erwählungstraditionen Israels für die Eschatologie der alttestamentlichen Propheten*, Munich (inaugural dissertation, Heidelberg).

Röhr, H. 1973: 'Buddhismus und Christentum; Untersuchung zur Typologie zweier Weltreligionen', *Zeitschrift für Religions- und Geistesgeschichte* 25:289–303.

Sailer, J. 1947: 'Über Typen im Neuen Testament', *Zeitschrift für Katholische Theologie* 69:490–496.

Sanders, J. A. 1974: 'Reopening Old Questions About Scripture', *Int* 28:321–330.

Scharleman, M. H. 1972: 'Roman Catholic Biblical Interpretation' in *Festschrift to Honor F. Wilbur Gingrich: Lexicographer, Scholar, Teacher, and Committed Christian Layman* (ed. E. H. Barth & R. E. Cocroft), Leiden: 209–222.

Sharp, J. R. 1986: 'Typology and the Message of Hebrews', *EAJT* 4.2:95–103.

Stek, J. H. 1970: 'Biblical Typology Yesterday and Today', *Calvin Theological Journal* 5:133–162.

Sutcliffe, E. F. 1953: 'The Plenary Sense as a Principle of Interpretation', *Biblica* 34:333–343.

Trench, R. C. 1870: *Notes on the Parables of our Lord*, London, [11]1870.

Vawter, B. 1964: 'The Fuller Sense: Some Considerations', *CBQ* 26:85–96.

Verhoef, P. A. 1962: 'Some Notes on Typological Exegesis' in *New Light on Some Old Testament Problems: Papers read at 5th Meeting of OTWSA*, Pretoria: 58–63.

Wenham, G. J. 1987: *Word Biblical Commentary Volume 1: Genesis 1 – 15*, Waco, Texas.

Wifall, W. 1974: 'David – Prototype of Israel's Future?', *BThB* 4:94–107.

Wolff, H. W. 1956b: 'The Old Testament in Controversy: Interpretive Principles and Illustration', ET in *Int* 12 (1958): 281–291 (German, 1956).

—1960: 'The Understanding of History in the Old Testament Prophets', ET in *EOTI*:336–355 (German, 1960).

Wood, J. E. 1968: 'Isaac Typology in the New Testament', *NTS* 14:583–589.

Woollcombe, K. J. 1957: 'The Biblical Origins and Patristic Development of Typology' in *Essays on Typology* (G. W. H. Lampe & K. J. Woollcombe), London (SBT 22):39–75.

Yewangoe, A. A. 1987: *Theologia Crucis in Asia: Asian Christian Views on Suffering in the Face of Overwhelming Poverty and Multifaceted Religiosity in Asia*, Amsterdam.

8

Promise and fulfilment

8.1 Prediction, prophecy, promise

The terms 'prediction', 'prophecy' and 'promise' are used by different writers in different ways. It is important to understand and correctly distinguish these terms in order to appreciate the significance of 'promise and fulfilment' as one of the key themes which characterize the relationship between the Testaments. We shall look initially at the writings of a variety of theologians before attempting to define the terms.

a. Three British scholars

B. F. Westcott (1889) approached the matter from the perspective of the letter to the Hebrews. He stated that God's purpose for humanity is entry into the divine rest, but this was never completely achieved in the Old Testament:

> Each promise fulfilled brings the sense of a larger promise. The promises connected with the possession of Canaan (for example) quickened a hope of far greater blessings than the actual possession gave ... and ... *there remaineth a Sabbath-rest for the people of God* (Hebr. iv. 9) (p. 482).

> The teaching of the Old Testament as a whole is a perpetual looking forward (p. 485).

The accomplishment of God's purpose required a long preparation by discipline, to foster natural moral growth to maturity and
to right the wrongs caused by the Fall. This is seen in the
intimately related revelations of the two Testaments, preparatory in the Old and final in the New.

Westcott discussed in detail the work of the messianic nation
and that of the personal Messiah as interpreted by Hebrews,
concluding that:

> The Old Testament does not simply contain prophe-
> cies, but is one vast prophecy, in the record of
> national fortunes, in the ordinances of a national
> Law, in the expression of a national hope. Israel . . . is
> a unique enigma . . . of which Christ is the complete
> solution (p. 491).

Finally, Westcott considered the application of the interpretative principles of Hebrews in the Christian church (pp. 492–
495). He showed that the Old Testament is an indispensable
part of the Bible. It still has moral and social lessons to teach, but
above all it records the history of Judaism as a type of God's
action in history. This was fulfilled in Christ, but even in the
Christian era it points to the future:

> Our highest joy is to recognise the divine law that
> each fulfilment opens a vision of something yet
> beyond. The Wilderness, Jordan, Canaan, necessarily
> take a new meaning as the experience of man extends
> . . . as yet we do not see the end (p. 495).

C. H. Dodd[1] concurred with Westcott that the Old Testament
is not final. The prophets believe that God is at work in Israel's
history and is revealing his purpose there, though this purpose
is not completely revealed within the Old Testament. Many
questions are raised in the Old Testament, such as the relationship between nationalism and universalism, righteousness and
grace, and divine justice and the human situation, which are left
unanswered (cf. above: ch. 1.2.d). The Old Testament in Dodd's
view is a process, not a completed whole, and it is pervaded by a
sense of inconclusiveness. This process is set in the context of a
history which moves forward, but whose goal is not seen clearly

---

[1] 1928: 182–183, 195–196, 261; 1938: 24–26; 1951a: 26; 1951b: 158;
1971: 82–84.

within the Old Testament since there are different strands pointing forward in different directions which are not yet resolved. Now that the goal has been reached it is possible to look back and see that the Old Testament was really looking forward to the centre of history, the cross and resurrection of Christ (1951b: 160).

Dodd argued that the New Testament – in contrast to the Old Testament – is final, or at least it inaugurates the finale of history.[2] It announces that the time is fulfilled and the expected event has taken place. The coming, death and resurrection of Christ bring to a conclusion the whole complex drama of judgment and redemption which made up the history of Israel. God has established a new covenant, which does not simply supplement, amend or supersede the old covenant but is its fulfilment. The New Testament writers assert that the climactic event of history anticipated by the prophets and apocalyptists has been realized in Jesus Christ; and this led Dodd to describe the ministry of Jesus, in a phrase that has since become famous, as 'realized eschatology' (1935: 41, 148; 1936: 79–87; see further below: ch. 8.3.d).

Whereas Westcott and Dodd were New Testament scholars and were primarily concerned with New Testament material relating to the problem, H. H. Rowley approached the problem of the relationship between the Testaments from the point of view of the Old Testament. One of the central ideas in his approach was that of 'prophecy and fulfilment'. He pointed out that the unfashionable idea of 'prediction' was in fact a vital element of prophecy, although undoubtedly not only prediction was involved (1946a: 203–206). Some predictions were neither intended nor expected to be fulfilled literally (*e.g.* Is. 40:4), some were not fulfilled because they provoked a change of heart (*e.g.* Jon. 3) and for some the fulfilment was delayed or different from what was expected (*e.g.* Je. 4:23–28; 51:28–29). Nevertheless the essence of prediction is that it expects the fulfilment of what is predicted. According to the New Testament, this fulfilment occurred supremely in Jesus Christ, who applied the term 'Son of man' to himself and accepted the title 'Christ' from his followers, so linking himself directly with Old Testament hopes for the future (1946a: 210; *cf.* ch. 11). Sometimes prophecies which do not refer directly to Jesus, such as the Immanuel

---

[2]1928: 194–211; 1935: 148; 1936: 13, 21, 43, 47, 52–53, 69–70; 1938: 26, 96–101; 1946a: 10, 74–75, 151; 1946b: 129; 1951b: 158; 1952a: 72, 88, 102–103, 129–130.

oracle, are 'taken up and filled with new meaning in Him' (1946a: 207), while others, such as the Servant Songs, 'so deeply influenced our Lord that he entered into their spirit, and so embodied their mission and message in Himself, and became their fulfilment' (1946a:208). Thus, in Jesus Christ 'the hopes of the prophets were not so much realized as transmuted, and given a higher realization than their authors dreamed' (1946a:211).

There is, however, more to be said than that Christ fulfils the predictions and prophecies of the Old Testament. Rowley concluded from his studies that 'the Old Testament constantly points to something beyond itself' (1949: 17), it 'looks forward to something which should follow it' (1953: 94); and the New Testament looks back to the Old Testament, offering the answer to its expectation, the response to its faith and hope, and the fulfilment of its promise (1949: 17, 28; 1953: 106, 117). Thus we find the fulfilment of the Old Testament in the New, even though fulfilment is not complete here but awaits consummation in the more distant future (1953: 109–110). Not only does the New Testament discharge the promises of the Old, but it takes up the mission and message of the former covenant and makes them its own. Israel was called to be a light to the nations, and Jesus Christ as the Suffering Servant takes this task upon himself (Jn. 8:12) and passes it on to his followers (Mt. 5:14; so 1946a: 215; cf. 1939: 89–94).

b. Three German scholars

During the period of the German Church Struggle Emil Brunner persistently maintained that the church stands or falls with the Old Testament, just as it stands or falls with Jesus Christ, since without the Old Testament there is no Jesus Christ (1934: 7). He argued that the Old Testament is a beginning, the New Testament its completion (1930: 263); revelation is promise in the old covenant, fulfilment in the new (1941: 81–118).

In the same decade Walther Eichrodt concluded the first volume of his classic *Theology of the Old Testament* (1933) with a section on 'Prediction and fulfilment' (pp. 501–511). He considered dead the old orthodox view that the messianic prophecies of the Old Testament gave a complete picture of Christ before he came and thus prove the truth of the New Testament gospel. Old Testament predictions arose in and were primarily directed towards specific historical situations, and are not necessarily significant for other periods of history. Nevertheless, Old

Testament eschatological thought does have a concentrated focus on the future of God's sovereignty. The decisive factor in the hope of Israel is not the supplying of material needs nor the attaining of political aims, but the establishment of the kingdom of God. This involves a personal relationship of communion with God, achieved by the elimination of sin as the cause of separation between God and mankind. And it is this essential hope of the realization of God's sovereignty, not the details of individual predictions, which is the key to recognizing the New Testament as the fulfilment of Old Testament prediction. Thus Jesus' saving work is not to be understood mechanically as the working out of Old Testament predictions, as though it were the logical solution to a problem, but organically as '*the unfolding and unveiling of a mystery of Creation subject to the divine omnipotence*, as a sovereign act of re-shaping, which only now fully brings to light the will of God concealed in prophecy, and is related to all prediction as clear knowledge is related to stammering presentiment' (p. 510).

Friedrich Baumgärtel (1952) investigated in detail the subject of promise in the Bible (see also above: ch. 3.3.b) and argued that the Old Testament has its own understanding of promise, which it expresses by terms such as word, mercy, statute, covenant, speak, swear (pp. 16–27). He found three groups of promises in the Old Testament:

- pledges which are affirmed to have been realized in historical facts;
- promises attached by God to the law, whose realization is dependent on keeping the law; and
- prophetic promises, whose realization is tied to the realization of future historical events.

He then distinguished promise from prediction (pp. 28–36; *cf.* Westermann 1955: 128–132). Prediction, he argued, stems from the basic promise, 'I am the Lord your God', and its fulfilment is closely linked with the realization of the promise. It is communicated by the prophets and apocalyptists, though, unlike soothsaying, it is concerned not with detailed knowledge about the future but with the divine completion of the whole event. Baumgärtel defined the essential difference between promise and prediction by a series of contrasts:

Promise	*Prediction*
1. Absolute divine pledge	Conditioned human witness
2. Event	Word
3. Realization of communion with God	Announcement of future event
4. Conditional: received by faith	Unconditional: God acts in spite of man
5. Always open to the eye of faith	Not always open, dependent on prophets
6. To be believed, because authenticated as true	To be established by fulfilment, so that its accuracy may be recognized

In the New Testament prediction is important: it cites Old Testament texts directly with reference to New Testament events and adduces prediction to prove that Jesus is the Christ (pp. 71–86). However Baumgärtel (like Bultmann) considered such procedures to be neither possible nor relevant today. He argued that the New Testament also understands the Old Testament message as a witness of God's promise, which is over the old covenant and has come true in the promise in Christ, and it is this which is relevant for Christian faith. Christian existence is based not on scholarly insight into historical processes (prediction), but on the absolute unbreakable pledge of God. Thus Christian interpretation conceives the Old Testament word as a word of promise and incorporates it into the promise in Christ.[3]

c. The *Biblischer Kommentar* group

We look next at the work of three of the Old Testament scholars involved in the preparation of the *Biblischer Kommentar* (see above: ch. 2.7).

Walther Zimmerli's programmatic essay on 'Promise and

---

[3]Rudolf Bultmann (1949a) discusses the understanding of prophecy as prediction (in the manner of the New Testament) and as history (as proposed by von Hofmann, 1841–44) and rejects both. His proposal to understand it as the promise which arises from the miscarriage of Old Testament history has already been analysed (see ch. 3.1.b) and criticized (ch. 3.2.d) above.

Fulfillment' (1952) points out that this formulation is New Testament language, and he devotes the first part of the essay to a discussion of whether or not it corresponds to genuine Old Testament ideas. After considering evidence in the Pentateuch, prophets and elsewhere he concludes that in the whole Old Testament 'we find ourselves involved in a great history of movement from promise toward fulfillment' (pp. 111–112). The promises are to be understood in their historical context for they are 'bound inseparably to history' (p. 96) and 'anyone who knows of promise and fulfillment is responsible to a yesterday about which he has heard something, and he walks toward a tomorrow' (p. 97). Within the Old Testament fulfilments are always incomplete and continually raise the question of deeper fulfilment in the future, whereas in the New Testament a definitive fulfilment is attested in the person of Christ who is both the end and the consummation of the Old Testament.

Gerhard von Rad takes these ideas further in his *Old Testament Theology* (1957–60) and other writings. He does not dispute the importance of prophecy, nor deny its predictive element, but like Zimmerli he prefers the concept of 'promise' which embraces more readily the historical traditions of the Old Testament as well as the prophetic traditions. The Hexateuch, according to von Rad, is spanned by a 'massive arch leading from promise to fulfilment' (1957: 170); the Deuteronomic history presents a course of history 'determined by a whole pattern of corresponding prophetic promises and divine fulfillments' (1952a: 27; *cf.* 1947: 74–91); the several Old Testament historical works are united in their understanding of history as 'a continuum of events determined by Jahweh's promise, which flows forward to the fulfilment intended by him' (1963: 426–427); and the Old Testament as a whole is to be seen as 'the ceaseless saving movement of promise and fulfilment' (1960: viii). Von Rad shows that this pattern of promise and fulfilment found in the Old Testament is also an aspect of its relationship to the New: the Old Testament is oriented to the future and 'can only be read as a book in which the expectation keeps mounting up to vast proportions' (1960: 321), and the New Testament is concerned not only with the newness of the Christ-event but also with the way in which it fulfilled promises and predictions of the Old (1960: 328–335).

Another member of the *Biblischer Kommentar* group who has written on promise and fulfilment is Claus Westermann. In a critique of the theses of Bultmann and Baumgärtel (1955) he expresses dissatisfaction with their treatment of these concepts, and in a later article (1964) he elaborates his own view. To understand promise and fulfilment, according to Westermann, it is necessary to start by examining the Old Testament words and events themselves in the context of the totality of salvation history. He distinguishes three kinds of promise in the Old Testament:

> ● assurance of salvation, which in the perfect tense 'announces something coming in such a way as to assure that with God it had already happened' (1964: 203–204; *e.g.* Ex. 3:7–8; Is. 43:1);
> ● announcement of salvation, which in the future tense declares that God will intervene in the history of his people (*e.g.* Is. 8: 1–4; 43:2); and
> ● portrayal of salvation, which depicts the contrast between present distress and the transcendent reality of salvation (*e.g.* Is. 11:1–10).

These promises are made in three realms (to the people of God, to individuals, and to the world) and they have a history as they are transmitted in the life and worship of Israel and are a constant source of encouragement to the faithful. There are also the messianic promises (all of which are based on Nathan's promise to David in 2 Sa. 7) and the promises of suffering (*e.g.* Je. 1:18–19; the Servant Songs). The climax of the promises, however, is to be found in the oracles concerning a coming divine event which will bring about the renewal of the covenant (Je. 31:31–34), the revival of the people of God (Ezk. 37), and the offer of salvation to the Gentiles (Is. 45:20–24). So Westermann concludes that the Old Testament presents not one promise but a 'way' of promise, and the coming and work of Christ is a fulfilment of that entire way of promise. The essence of the relationship between the Testaments is thus not in the New Testament quotations of the Old, but in the crucial event reported in the New Testament which fulfils the promises of the Old.

d. Consensus achieved

By the early 1960s the understanding of the Old Testament as 'promise' had become widely accepted in both Protestant and Catholic biblical scholarship, in Europe and in America, and the ideas of 'prediction' and 'prophecy' faded into the background.

A clear statement of this consensus is given by James D. Smart (1961: 80–85, 101–115). He points out that the Old Testament was essential to the early church because it understood the gospel to be the fulfilment of God's purpose as revealed in the

Old Testament. Jesus began his preaching with the announcement that 'The time is fulfilled' (Mk. 1:15; *cf*. Lk. 4:21; Mt. 5:17), and as he died on the cross he prayed in the words of an Old Testament psalm. Virtually all the New Testament writers quote frequently from the Old Testament as the promise of those events which have brought the church into being. Promise-fulfilment is a basic biblical category that expresses God's plan for his people which is worked out in history. 'What God promises he fulfils, and, because the fulfilment is only partial, it contains within it an unfulfilled promise that points forward to a new fulfilment' (p. 102). So the pattern of promise and fulfilment unites the two Testaments into one because of the conviction that the Old Testament promises of salvation and the kingdom, new covenant and new creation, have been fulfilled in Jesus Christ (2 Cor. 1:20).

Many other writers have agreed that promise (and fulfilment) is a key theme in the Old Testament and particularly in its relationship to the New Testament, such as the Dutch Reformed theologian, G. C. Berkouwer (1952: 113–152), the German systematic theologian, Wolfhart Pannenberg (1959), the Swiss Old Testament scholar, Samuel Amsler (1960a: 122–134) and the American Roman Catholic scholar, Roland E. Murphy (1964). Norman W. Porteous, who approves with reservation the approaches to Old Testament theology of both Eichrodt and von Rad, asserts that the Christian believes 'that the Old Testament and the New Testament correspond to each other as promise to fulfilment' (1954: 168); likewise F. F. Bruce states that 'the specifically Christian approach to the Old Testament . . . sees the relation of the Old Testament to the New as that of promise to fulfilment' (1955: 4). For Jürgen Moltmann (1964: 102–112) God's word of promise and the future fulfilment which it implies is a key to understanding Israel's 'religion of expectation' and so the Christian 'theology of hope'. John L. McKenzie devalues salvation history and typology as expressions of the relationship between the Testaments (1974: 28, 324–325) but nevertheless affirms the importance of promise and fulfilment (1964; 1968: 766–767; *cf*. 1974: 139–144); while Walter C. Kaiser structures his whole exposition of Old Testament theology (1978) around the theme of 'promise'.[4]

---

[4]See also Gross (1959); Achtemeier (1962); Larcher (1962: especially pp. 399–488); Sauter (1965: 251–262) and Schniewind (1966).

e. Definitions

It is clear that many writers during the past hundred years have helped us to understand the role of prediction, prophecy and promise in the Old Testament and its relationship to the New, and on the basis of their works we are in a position to define the terms more precisely.

The term *prediction* refers to the foretelling of specific future events. There are predictions in the Old Testament (*cf.* Barr 1966: 118–126) and some of them are referred to in the New Testament as being fulfilled in the coming of Jesus Christ (*cf.* France 1971: 83–163; Jensen 1988). However we should note:

● the Old Testament consists of a great deal more than predictions, and the New Testament often quotes Old Testament passages which are not predictions, for example to establish points of theology and ethics (*cf.* Kaiser 1985);

● not all of the Old Testament predictions are fulfilled in the New Testament, because some were fulfilled in the Old Testament itself, some still await fulfilment after the New Testament and some will never be fulfilled (because they were conditional and the conditions were not met); and

● the Old Testament by no means predicts all of the New Testament (some aspects of the coming of Christ were quite unexpected).

It is therefore clear that although there is an element of 'prediction and fulfilment' in the relationship between the Testaments, this is only a small part of the truth.

The term *prophecy* is much broader than prediction, and is sometimes distinguished from it by describing it as 'forth-telling' rather than 'foretelling'. We may define prophecy as the receiving and passing on of a divine message, and the Old Testament prophets are characterized by their call from God and message for the people. Their messages include predictions and also many other kinds of saying. They address individuals, communities and nations with the words of God to remind them of the past, challenge them about the present and prepare them for the future. In the New Testament Jesus is presented as the one Prophet (Acts 3:22), whose message of salvation is the fulfilment of the hopes and longings of many centuries; but he is also presented as the one Judge (Acts 10:42), Priest (Heb. 4:14–16), King (Rev. 19:16) and in many other ways as fulfilling the Old

Testament. So the New Testament is not only the fulfilment of Old Testament prophecy, but of the whole Old Testament, including the law, history, psalms and wisdom literature.

The term *promise* refers to a (divine) assurance of something to be done or not done in the future, which may be expressed in a formal announcement or agreement, or may be implied in an action or attitude. It includes specific predictions of the future and also more general prophecies which have implications that are only fully worked out in the New Testament. It also includes instructions, commands, assurances, warnings and other sayings which are incomplete or unsatisfying in the Old Testament, but which are taken up and developed in a fuller and more satisfying way in the New Testament. Moreover the concept of 'promise' may also include events which have an implicit forward reference, even if not accompanied by explicit interpretative words (as we speak of a 'person of great promise' or a 'promising beginning'). So there are many promises in the Old Testament – explicit and implicit, specific and general, positive and negative, in words and events – and all of them are aspects of the movement of history according to God's plan towards his intended conclusion ('salvation history').

A more rigorous definition of promise is provided by the sevenfold statement of Moltmann (1964: 102–106):

(a) A promise is a declaration which announces the coming of a reality that does not yet exist.
(b) The promise binds man to the future and gives him a sense for history.
(c) The history which is initiated and determined by promise does not consist in cyclic recurrence, but has a definite trend towards the promised and outstanding fulfilment.
(d) If the word is a word of promise, then that means that this word has not yet found a reality congruous with it, but that on the contrary it stands in contradiction to the reality open to experience now and heretofore.
(e) The word of promise therefore always creates an interval of tension between the uttering and the redeeming of the promise.
(f) If the promise is not regarded abstractly apart from the God who promises, but its fulfilment is entrusted directly to God in his freedom and faithfulness, then ... the fulfilments can very well contain an element of newness and surprise over against the promise as it was received.
(g) The peculiar character of the Old Testament promises

213

can be seen in the fact that the promises were not liquidated by the history of Israel – neither by disappointment nor by fulfilment – but that on the contrary Israel's experience of history gave them a constantly new and wider interpretation.

On the basis of Moltmann's statement, David Clines (1978: 111–118) clarifies further the definition of promise in the Old Testament and in particular we may note one additional point:

(h) Promise is more than hope. Hope is the kernel of human existence, but the divine promise transcends even that as the word of the God who initiates and sustains the history of his people. Whereas hope is 'realistic' and envisages possibilities inherent in the real world as it is presently known, promise envisages possibilities that are only possible to the God of the promise.

To sum up, the concept of 'promise' expresses a major aspect of the Old Testament in its relationship to the New, and is to be preferred as a more comprehensive term than the alternatives 'prediction' and 'prophecy'.[5] We now turn to a closer examination of the nature of the promise in the Old Testament and of its New Testament fulfilment.

8.2 The Old Testament promise

That the Old Testament looks forward to the future was noted in the introductory chapter (ch. 1.2), and some examples of its future expectation were given there. We shall now look in greater detail at the promises of the Old Testament in the light of the theological discussion of promise above (ch. 8.1).[6]

---

[5]A rereading of the writings of Westcott and Eichrodt shows that – although they used the terms 'prophecy' and 'prediction' respectively – they were also expressing the same basic conviction that the whole Old Testament looks forward to the future and finds its fulfilment in the New Testament.

[6]The following study is particularly indebted to the researches of Zimmerli (1952); Clines (1978: 29–60) and van Roo (1986: 55–73). On the promise of the land, see further Davies (1974: 15–48) and Brueggemann (1977); on blessing, see Westermann (1968c); on the promise of the kingdom, see Ladd (1974: 45–101). For a rather different exposition, focusing on four elements of God's purpose – salvation, covenant, knowledge of God, land – see Martens (1981; cf. above: ch. 6.3.g).

a. Terminology

There is no word in the Hebrew Old Testament which corresponds exactly to the English word 'promise'. The concept is certainly there, but it is expressed by such words as *'āmar* ('say') and *dābār* ('word'). A general picture may be obtained by an analysis of the use of the word 'promise' in the RSV Old Testament:

- 37 times concerning God's promise to Abraham, Isaac and Jacob;
- 19 times concerning God's promise to David;
- 12 times concerning other promises of God;
- 16 times concerning God's promise(s) in general; and
- 9 times concerning human promises.

The New Testament takes up this concept of promise and expresses it by the word *epangelia*, which is used both concerning the Old Testament promises and also new promises given in Christ:

- 35 times concerning God's promise to Abraham, Isaac and Jacob;
- 12 times concerning other promises of God in the Old Testament;
- 16 times concerning new promises to those who are 'in Christ';
- 5 times concerning human promises; and
- once figuratively.

Although statistics of word usage do not in themselves prove the importance of concepts in the life and thought of a people, the above figures nevertheless show that when the biblical writers wrote of 'promise' they were very often referring to God's promise to Abraham, Isaac and Jacob. As we shall see in the exposition below, this promise may be considered the basic biblical promise and other promises were often expansions or reinterpretations of this basic promise.

b. The basic promise

The key text for the understanding of promise in the Old Testament is the call of Abraham:

Now the LORD said to Abram, 'Go from your country and your kindred and your father's house to the land that I will show you. And I will make of you a great nation, and I will bless you, and make your name great, so that you will be a blessing. I will bless those who bless you, and him who curses you I will curse; and by you all the families of the earth shall bless themselves' (Gn. 12:1–3).

God's call includes three main elements of promise, which are then repeated, expanded and expounded throughout the whole Pentateuch (*e.g.* Gn. 12:7; 13:14–17; 15; 17):

● a land;
● descendants ('a great nation'); and
● a relationship with God ('blessing').

The major emphasis in the remainder of Genesis is the promise of *descendants*, a promise of something which for Abraham himself was unlikely in the extreme (in human terms, Gn. 11:30; 12:4; 16:1; 17:1; 18:11) and yet was kept (Gn. 21:1–2). One of history's greatest dramas then took place as it seemed God was about to retract the promise and its fulfilment (Gn. 22). Abraham's other wives and concubines bore him many children (Gn. 25:1–18), but only Sarah's son Isaac was counted as child of the promise (vv. 5, 11, 19). The threefold promise is repeated to Isaac (Gn. 26:2–5, 24) and to his son Jacob (Gn. 28:13–15), both of whom have wives who are barren until God's time to fulfil his promise of descendants (Gn. 25:20–21; 29:31; 30:1, 22–24). The barrenness of Sarah, Rebekah and Rachel is significant because it makes clear that the fulfilment of the promise – if it is to be fulfilled at all, which at many stages of the story seems improbable – is in divine not human hands. Many other problems occur which threaten the fulfilment of the promise, such as the three-times repeated endangering of the ancestress (Gn. 12; 20; 26). By the end of Genesis Abraham's descendants have become a family of seventy people (Gn. 46:27) but it is not until the time of the Exodus several hundred years later that they can be described as a great nation (Ex. 1:7, 9, 12, 20).

In the books of Exodus and Leviticus the emphasis shifts to the *relationship*-element of the basic promise, though the promise of the land is never far in the background (Ex. 3:8; 12:25; 33:1–3). The special relationship between Abraham's descendants and God has already been described in general terms in Genesis, with such words as blessing (Gn. 12:3; 22:17), covenant (17) and God's presence with his people (26:3; 28:15; 31:5). The meaning of these words becomes clearer in the two focal events of the books which follow: the Exodus from Egypt and God's revelation at Sinai. In the crisis which preceded the Exodus, Israel is consistently depicted as the people of God (Ex. 3:7, 10; 6:7; 7:4, 16) who are to be freed from Egyptian bondage in order to serve him (Ex. 7:16; 8:1, 20; 10:24–26). And it is pre-eminently in the Exodus itself that God's promise to be with his people is seen to be a reality (Ex. 13:17–18, 21; 14:13–14; 15:1–2). On the basis of this event the divine-human relationship is formalized at Sinai:

> 'You shall be my own possession among all peoples; for all the earth is mine, and you shall be to me a kingdom of priests and a holy nation' (Ex. 19:5b–6a).

The essence of the event which takes place there is the establishment of a covenant relationship between God and Israel, in fulfilment of the basic divine promise (Ex. 20:2–3), and the details of the relationship are set out by God in laws and stipulations to which the people are expected to respond in obedience (Ex. 19:5a, 8; 24:3). Within a short time the continuance of this relationship is seriously threatened (Ex. 32:1–10), and only through Moses' appeal to God's promise (vv. 11–14) and challenge to the people (vv. 15–35) is the relationship saved. Once again the essence of the relationship is seen to be God's presence with his own people (Ex. 33:12–16). The means by which this relationship is to be maintained is elaborated further in the book of Leviticus, and it is here that we find the most succinct statement of the relationship:

> 'I will walk among you, and will be your God, and you shall be my people' (Lv. 26:12; cf. Ex. 29:45–46).

However it cannot be said that the promise of a special divine-human relationship is thereby fulfilled: on the contrary, it is just the beginning. Israel has yet thousands of years of history in which to learn what it means to be the people of God.

The third element of the basic promise, the *land*, comes to the fore in Numbers and Deuteronomy. The journeying recorded in Numbers is clearly toward 'the place of which the LORD said, "I will give it to you"' (Nu. 10:29; cf. 13:2; 14:40; 15:2; 20:24). But although the land is to be God's gift to his people, that does not exempt them from the need to fight for it (Nu. 13:25–30; 33:50–56), and the census taken before setting out from Sinai toward the promised land is of those eligible for military service (Nu. 1), as also is the second census taken before beginning the occupation (Nu. 26). As with the other two elements of the promise, there are frequent setbacks in the fulfilment of the promise of the land. It seems at one point that God is about to destroy his people and give the land to someone else (Nu.

14:1–12), but again Moses saves the situation by appealing to the promise to the patriarchs (vv. 13–19, especially v. 16). Nevertheless the people's sin results in a forty-year delay in the receiving of the promise (Nu. 14:20–35). The last five chapters of Numbers are concerned almost exclusively with matters relating to the land, and the whole of Deuteronomy is concerned to prepare the people to live in the land in accordance with God's promise (Dt. 1:8–11; 4:1, 40; 6:3, 18–19; *etc.*). They are reminded again of the special relationship with God that they are privileged to experience and of the obligation to obedience which it entails (Dt. 26:17–19; 29:13). At the end of the Pentateuch the people of Israel do not yet live in the promised land, but they are standing on its borders and prepared to appropriate God's promise.

Thus we see how in the Pentateuch the basic divine promise to the patriarchs is given, repeated, almost retracted, renewed and partially fulfilled. We also see mixed human reactions to the promise: Abraham responds in obedience (Gn. 12:4; 22:3) and faith (Gn. 15:6) but as often as not his descendants are disobedient and disbelieving. In the end it has become more than clear that it is neither great leadership nor pious membership of the people which has brought about any fulfilment at all of the promise (Dt. 9:4–24; 32:48–52), but only God's love and power (Dt. 10:14 – 11:7).

c. The promise to David

In the historical books it is affirmed initially that 'Not one of all the good promises which the LORD had made to the house of Israel had failed; all came to pass' (Jos. 21:45; *cf.* 23:14). A less positive picture is presented in the book of Judges, but it is explained that the problems are not due to God's failure to keep his promise but are a result of the disobedience of the people (Jdg. 2:1–3). Although not often mentioned explicitly in the historical books, the promise to Abraham, Isaac and Jacob continues to be the basis of Israel's life and faith from the earliest days in Palestine (Jos. 24:2–3) throughout the monarchy (1 Ch. 16:15–18; 27:23; 2 Ch. 20:7; 2 Ki. 13:23) until after the exile (Ne. 9:7–8).

A new element in the historical books is the promise which King David receives through the prophet Nathan (2 Sa. 7:8–16; *cf.* vv. 18–29; 1 Ch. 17; Ps. 89:3–4, 19–37). In many respects this promise is similar to the basic patriarchal promise, with mention of:

● relationship with God (2 Sa. 7:9a, 14–15; *cf.* vv. 23–24);
● the land (v. 10a); and
● descendants (vv. 11b–12).

However, the emphasis in the promise of descendants is not on their number (as with Abraham), but on their role in building the Temple and forming a dynasty to rule Israel (vv. 13, 16). God also promises David a great name (v. 9b) and national security (vv. 10b–11a).

At the dedication of the Temple a generation later, Solomon acknowledges that his accession to the throne and building of the Temple has been a fulfilment of God's promise to his father (1 Ki. 8:15, 20), and he links this with the basic promise in his prayer: 'Blessed be the LORD who has given rest to his people Israel, according to all that he promised; not one word has failed of all his good promise, which he uttered by Moses his servant' (v. 56). Solomon prays that God will continue to keep his promise that David's descendants will rule Israel in the future (vv. 25–26), and God accepts his prayer and confirms that the promise will be kept so long as David's descendants live in a right relationship with God as David had done (9:3–9).

However, only three chapters further on we read that 'the LORD was angry with Solomon, because his heart had turned away from the LORD, the God of Israel' (11:9), and the promise is partially retracted (vv. 11–13). After that things get progressively worse, though the promise to David is not forgotten (2 Ki. 8:19; *cf.* 2 Ch. 21:7) and his dynasty lasts for several hundred years. By the end of the books of Kings and Chronicles it seems that virtually every aspect of the promises to Abraham and David has been retracted: because of their sin the people of Israel have to leave their land, no longer a great nation but a decimated remnant, the Temple destroyed and the Davidic kingdom brought to an end. And in such circumstances does a special relationship with God mean anything at all (*cf.* Ps. 137:1–6; La. 1 – 2)? Many at that time must have echoed the words of the psalmist: 'Are his promises at an end for all time?' (Ps. 77:8b).

d. The prophetic books[7]

The prophets are clearly aware that God's promises to Abraham and David have never been completely fulfilled, albeit largely

---

[7]It is primarily the promises found in the books of the major and minor prophets that are discussed here, as distinct from promises made

through the fault of the people who have repeatedly shown disdain for them by their unbelief and disobedience. They are, indeed, God's instruments to warn his people of the dangers of sin and to announce the effective cancellation of the promises. However, even the most impassioned prophets of judgment retain an element of hope and new promises are given for the future. Beyond judgment there is still the possibility of new life.

The predominant emphasis of the promises in the prophetic books is the renewal of the people of God.[8] The people will be brought back from exile to live again in the promised *land* (Je. 16:14–15; 29:10; 32:42–44; Ezk. 20:42; 36; Am 9:11–15), where they will experience peace and abundance (Je. 31:10–14; Ezk. 34:25–31) and a renewed *relationship with God* (Je. 31:31–34; Ezk. 16:62–63; 37:26–28; Ho. 2:16–23). God will pour out his Spirit on them (Is. 32:15; 59:21; Ezk. 39:29; Hg. 2:4–5) and they will have a new heart and a new spirit (Je. 24:7; Ezk. 36:25–27). The promise of *descendants* is scarcely mentioned in the prophetic books, except that the continuance of the Davidic dynasty is reinterpreted in terms of the coming of the messianic king (Je. 23:5–6; 33:14–26; Ezk. 34:23–24; Mi. 5:2–4) who will bring about a new age of righteousness and justice (*cf.* Is. 32:1; 42:1–3; Ho. 2:19). However, an aspect of the basic promise that seemed not to have been fulfilled in any significant way during Israel's history – that Abraham and his descendants would be a blessing to 'all the families of the earth' – is reasserted by the prophets, and Israel is to be the mediator of salvation for all the nations (Is. 2:2–4; 19:16–25; 66:18–23; *cf.* 45:22–23; Je. 4:2; Zp. 3:9–10; Zc. 8:13, 20–23; *cf.* Jonah).

There are also some quite new elements of promise in the prophetic books. Throughout her history Israel had theoretically recognized God as her king (Ex. 15:18; Dt. 33:5; Is. 43:15), indeed as universal king (2 Ki. 19:15; Ps. 145:11–13; Is. 6:5), and her system of government was ideally a theocracy rather than a monarchy (Jdg. 8:23; 1 Sa. 8:4–7). Nevertheless, the

---

by prophets (which would include some material from the historical books, and even the Pentateuch, such as the promise to David) and prophetic promises (which would exclude promises in the prophetic books that are apocalyptic rather than prophetic in nature).

[8]*Cf.* above: ch. 1.2.b. The texts cited as examples here are mostly different from those in chapter one and are intended to complement those already cited there. The purpose of this section is to indicate the kind of promises found in the prophetic books and their relationship to the promises to Abraham and to David. It is not intended to be an exhaustive survey of prophetic eschatology.

reality did not match the theory, and many of the prophets looked forward to a day when God would decisively establish his kingdom and visibly reign on earth (Is. 24:23; 33:17–22; 52:7; Ob. 21; Zc. 14:9–21). This is also the theme of many of the psalms which celebrate the kingship of *YHWH* (Pss. 46 – 48; 93 – 99) and of his Messiah (Pss. 2; 110; *cf.* 89).

Another new element of promise is found in the poems about the servant of the Lord, who will be a light to the nations and suffer for his people (Is. 42:1–4; 49:1–6; 50:4–9; 52:13 – 53:12). In Zechariah 9:9 the ideas of messianic kingship and humility are combined. Finally, we should mention a number of passages which tend toward an apocalyptic view of the future, where visions are recounted of the consummation of history, the resurrection of the dead and the creation of a new heaven and earth (Dn. 7:9–14; 12:1–3; Is. 65:17–25).

8.3 The fulfilment of promise

What happened to God's promises in the Old Testament? How far have they been fulfilled and how far is such fulfilment to be found in the New Testament in particular? Our concern here will be to attempt an answer to these questions by means of a study of the biblical material, but first of all we may cite the definitions of fulfilment of two scholars from different countries and centuries.

A British scholar of the nineteenth century, A. F. Kirkpatrick (1891: 124–125), argued that fulfilment should not be understood too narrowly as an event which has been recorded in advance by prophecy. Prophecy directs people to the future in many different ways and the fulfilment satisfies their hopes and longings, although not always in the way expected. Fulfilment goes far beyond expectations and yet it is not so complete that it does not point once more to the future, to the final goal of redemption.

More recently a French scholar, Samuel Amsler (1960a: 122–123), stated two ways in which the relationship between the Testaments may be understood in terms of fulfilment:

● God's historical activity in Jesus Christ finishes and goes beyond all his words and acts in the history of Israel; and
● the new covenant confirms the promises and demands of the old covenant to be those of God.

a. Terminology

There are various words in the Hebrew Old Testament which express the idea of fulfilment, in particular *millē'* (piel of *ml'*) and *hēqîm* (hiphil of *qwm*). The former word comes from a very common root meaning 'full, fill' which is used both spacially (*e.g.* Ex. 10:6) and temporally (*e.g.* Gn. 25:24), and is used in the piel form concerning God's fulfilment of his promises (*e.g.* 1 Ki. 2:27; 2 Ch. 36:21) and also in a more general way of the fulfilling of requests (*e.g.* Ps. 20:5). The latter word derives from another common root meaning 'stand up, arise, come about', and one of its uses in the hiphil form is concerning the performance of vows and keeping of promises (*e.g.* Gn. 6:18; Dt. 9:5; 1 Sa. 3:12; 1 Ki. 2:4). The two words are used interchangeably to express the fulfilment of God's promise to David in 1 Kings 8:15, 20, 24. Other words which occasionally express the same idea include *'āśâ* 'do' (*e.g.* Nu. 23:19), *bā'* 'come' (*e.g.* Jos. 23:15) and *lo-nāpal* 'not fail' (*e.g.* Jos. 21:45).

In the New Testament the main word which expresses the idea of 'fulfil' is *plēroō*, and this is the word which most often translates the Hebrew *millē'* in the Septuagint. Like its Hebrew equivalent, it means 'fill, make full' both in the spatial (*e.g.* Mt. 13:48) and temporal (*e.g.* Mk. 1:15) senses, and is often used of the fulfilling of words and promises:

- 15 times concerning Old Testament prophecies (*e.g.* Mt. 1:22);
- 14 times concerning the Old Testament Scriptures, both as a whole (*e.g.* Mt. 5:17; Lk. 24:44) and referring to particular texts (*e.g.* Lk. 4:21);
- twice concerning words of Jesus (*e.g.* Jn. 18:9);
- once concerning words of an angel (Lk. 1:20);
- once concerning the promise to the patriarchs (Acts 13:32–33).

It is also used of fulfilling of demands (*e.g.* Mt. 3:15; Rom. 8:4) and of hopes (Heb. 6:11), and of the completing of an assigned task (*e.g.* Acts 12:25).

The words *teleō* and *teleioō* have a very similar though less frequent usage referring to the fulfilling of the Scriptures (Lk. 22:37; Jn. 19:28) and of prophecy in particular (Lk. 18:31; *cf.* Rev. 10:7); also to the fulfilling of the law (Jas. 2:8) and of a divinely-given task (Jn. 17:4). In Acts 13:27–29 both *plēroō* and *teleō* are used with apparently identical meanings.[9]

---

[9]Moule (1968) in a detailed study attempts to distinguish between the meanings and uses of *millē'*/*plēroō* and other terms such as *hēqîm* and *teleō* but, as he admits himself, there is considerable overlap and the latter terms are often used synonymously with the former. Texts using all of these terms will be used in the exposition below to illustrate the fulfilment of promise.

There are also many other ways in which the New Testament writers express their conviction that aspects of the Old Testament have been fulfilled, such as the expressions 'it is written' (*e.g.* Mt. 11:10; 26:31), 'this is what was spoken by the prophet' (*e.g.* Acts 2:16) and 'in accordance with the scriptures' (*e.g.* 1 Cor. 15:3–4). The concept of fulfilment is by no means limited to those passages where the words *plēroō* and *teleō* appear, on the contrary it is found throughout the New Testament.[10]

b. Fulfilments within the Old Testament

It has already been mentioned above (ch. 8.2) that partial fulfilments of the promises to Abraham and to David took place within the Old Testament period (*cf.* Jos. 21:45; 23:14; 1 Ki. 8:15, 20, 24; Ne. 9:8). It is God's nature to do what he has promised to do (Gn. 26:3; Nu. 23:19; Ps. 138:8; *cf.* Ezk. 21:7), though it should not be forgotten that there are conditions attached to the fulfilment of the promise (Dt. 8:18–19; Jos. 23:15–16; 1 Ki. 2:4; 6:12) and lack of fulfilment may be due to lack of faith and obedience on the part of the recipients of the promise. In the historical books there are many other promises (and threats) which are said to have been fulfilled (*e.g.* 1 Ki. 2:27; 12:15; 2 Ki. 10:10; 15:12; 2 Ch. 36:21; *cf.* La. 2:17; Dn. 4:33).

Zimmerli (1952: 112) claims that 'all Old Testament history, insofar as it is history guided and given by Yahweh's word, receives the character of fulfillment; but in the fulfillment it receives a new character as promise'. Many events raise the question of whether they are the fulfilment of what has been promised or whether something more is still to be expected. This may be seen in the history of the kings of Judah: from one point of view the succession of Davidic kings through four centuries fulfils the promise to David; from another point of view it is a history of failure,[11] to use Bultmann's phrase, and in this failure the promise to David is reinterpreted by the prophets in terms of a coming messianic king (Is. 9:2–7; 11:1–10; Je. 33:14–15). The return of the people of Judah from exile also raises the question of how far it may be understood as the fulfilment of the prophetic promises concerning restoration of

---

[10]See, for example, the listing of 142 New Testament verses which include the words 'scripture/it is written, *etc.*' in *MCNT*: 687–688.

[11]Few of the Davidic kings matched up to the standard he had set for faithfulness to God (*e.g.* 1 Ki. 9:4; 11:4, 6; 15:3, 5; 2 Ki. 14:3; 16:2; 18:3; 21:1–9; 22:2; 24:9, 19), and the kingdom was quickly reduced in size (1 Ki. 11:9–13; 12:16–24) and eventually brought to an end (2 Ki. 24:20 – 25:7).

the promised land. In a sense it is that fulfilment (2 Ch. 36:22–23) though, as Ezra points out in his prayer of national repentance, they did not return as a free and sovereign people (Ne. 9:36–37; *cf.* Ezr. 9:8–9) and in many respects their high hopes must have been disappointed as they began to realize the harsh realities of rebuilding a shattered nation with limited resources and only sporadic enthusiasm (Ezr. 3:12–13; 4:4–5; Ne. 1:3; 5:1–5).

Certainly much was fulfilled within the bounds of the Old Testament, but much more was to come in the future, more than even the greatest prophets could imagine, as is expressed by the author of Hebrews at the end of his history of Old Testament heroes and heroines:

> And all these, though well attested by their faith, did not receive what was promised, since God had forseen something better for us, that apart from us they should not be made perfect (Heb. 11:39–40).

c. Fulfilment in Jesus Christ

Early in the Synoptic Gospels we read Jesus' programmatic words:

> Think not that I have come to abolish the law and the prophets; I have come not to abolish them but to fulfil them (Mt. 5:17).

> The time is fulfilled, and the kingdom of God is at hand (Mk. 1:15).

> Today this scripture has been fulfilled in your hearing (Lk. 4:21).

In the Gospel of John it is Philip who declares:

> We have found him of whom Moses in the law and also the prophets wrote, Jesus of Nazareth, the son of Joseph (Jn. 1:45).[12]

All of the Gospel writers quote words of Jesus to the effect that his passion took place in fulfilment of the Old Testament

---

[12]John gives Jesus' own statement of his fulfilment of the scriptures rather later in his account (Jn. 5:39).

scriptures (*e.g.* Mt. 26:24, 54, 56; Mk. 14:49; Lk. 18:31; Jn. 13:18). Speeches of Peter and Paul in Acts make the same point and mention the resurrection as well (Acts 2:23–32; 3:18; 13:27–33; *cf.* 1 Cor. 15:3–4). Matthew and – to a lesser extent – John also point to other ways in which they believe that Jesus has fulfilled prophecy, for example in his birth (Mt. 1:22–23; 2:5–6, 15, 17–18), place of residence (Mt. 2:23; 4:14–16), healing ministry (Mt. 8:17; 12:15–21), teaching ministry (Mt. 13:35), and the unbelief of the people (Jn. 12:37–38). One of Jesus' last recorded sayings expresses the same conviction that his coming has been a fulfilment of the scriptures:

> These are my words which I spoke to you, while I was still with you, that everything written about me in the law of Moses and the prophets and the psalms must be fulfilled (Lk. 24:44; *cf.* vv. 25–27, 45–47).

And after his ascension Jesus continues to fulfil promises of the Old Testament, in particular by pouring out the Holy Spirit on his disciples (Lk. 24:49; Jn. 15:26; Acts 2:33; *cf.* Is. 32:15; Ezk. 39:29; Joel 2:28–32). As R. T. France (1971: 83–171) has shown in his detailed study of Jesus' application of Old Testament predictions to himself and his mission, 'the earthly life and future glory of Jesus of Nazareth is presented as the fulfilment of the Old Testament hopes of the day of Yahweh ... The coming of Jesus is that decisive act of God to which the Old Testament looked forward, and in his coming all the hopes of the Old Testament are fulfilled; the last days have come' (p. 161).

Outside the Gospels and Acts the words *plēroō* and *teleō* are rarely used with the meaning 'fulfil', but the letters have other ways of expressing the apostolic conviction that Jesus is the supreme fulfilment of the promises of the Old Testament. Paul expresses it most clearly:

> All the promises of God find their Yes in him (2 Cor. 1:20).

Both the promise to Abraham (Rom. 15:8; Gal. 3:14, 16, 22, 29) and the promise to David (Rom. 15:12; *cf.* Acts 13:22–23) find their fulfilment in Jesus Christ. The gospel of Jesus Christ is the gospel of God 'which he promised beforehand through his prophets in the holy scriptures' (Rom. 1:1–4). The death of Christ is 'once for all' (Rom. 6:10), the one perfect sacrifice which replaces all other sacrifices (Heb. 7:27; 9:12–14; 10:11–14).

Christ is the 'end (*telos*) of the law' (Rom. 10:4) and the 'perfecter (*teleiōtēs*) of our faith' (Heb. 12:2; *cf.* 7:28). Indeed 'in him all the fulness (*plērōma*) of God was pleased to dwell' (Col. 1:19; *cf.* 2:9). Wilhelm Vischer has pointed out that the Old Testament defines the meaning of 'Christ' and the New Testament tells us who he is (*cf.* above: ch. 4.2.b). Thus the New Testament takes up the messianic promises of the Old Testament and asserts that Jesus is the Christ who fulfils them all (*cf.* Mk. 8:29; 14:61–62; Lk. 2:11, 26; Jn. 1:41; 20:31; Acts 9:22; 17:2–3). Some of the most significant elements of the messianic promises which are fulfilled by Jesus are as follows:[13]

● the son of David (Mt. 1:1; 21:9, 15; Mk. 10:47; Lk. 1:32, 69; 2:4; Jn. 7:42; Acts 2:29–31; Rom. 1:3; 15:12; 2 Tim. 2:8; Rev. 22:16; *cf.* 2 Sa. 7; Is. 9:7; 11:1, 10);
● the Son of man (Mt. 8:20; 9:6; 12:8; 16:27–28; 25:31–33; Mk. 8:31; 10:45; 14:62; Jn. 3:13–14; 6:27; Acts 7:56; 1 Cor. 15:25, 27; Rev. 1:13; *cf.* Ps. 8:4–6; Dn. 7:13–14);
● the Son of God (Mt. 11:25–27; 14:33; 16:16; 26:63; Mk. 1:1, 11; 9:7; 14:36; 15:39; Lk. 1:30–35; Jn. 1:14, 34, 49; 20:31; Acts 13:33; Rom. 8:32; Heb. 1:2, 5; 1 Jn. 4:15; *cf.* 2 Sa. 7:14; Ps. 2:7; Is. 7:14);
● the servant of the Lord (Mt. 8:17; 12:17–21; Lk. 2:32; Jn. 12:38; Acts 3:13; 8:32–35; Phil. 2:5–8; 1 Pet. 2:22–25; *cf.* Is. 42:1–6; 52:13 – 53:12);
● the Lamb of God (Jn. 1:29, 36; 19:14–16, 36; 1 Cor. 5:7; 1 Pet. 1:19; Rev. 5:6–14; 7:9–17; *cf.* Ex. 12:1–27, 43–46; Is. 53:7; Je. 11:19);
● the good shepherd (Mk. 6:34; Jn. 10:1–18; Heb. 13:20; 1 Pet. 2:25; *cf.* Nu. 27:17; Ps. 23; Je. 23:1–4; Ezk. 34; 37:24; Zc. 10:2; 13:7);
● the wisdom of God (Jn. 1:2–3; 1 Cor. 1:24, 30; Col. 1:15–18; Heb. 1:2–3; Rev. 3:14; *cf.* Pr. 8:22–31);[14]

---

[13]See Bruce (1963); Achtemeier (1973: 88–99) and van Roo (1986: 139–146, 178–180 *et al.*) for further information, and Guthrie (1981: 235–343) for a detailed exposition. Note that not all of the Old Testament passages mentioned here are 'messianic': some simply contain ideas that in other places are interpreted in messianic terms.

[14]Bruce (1963: 49) suggests that the origins of the identification of Jesus with the wisdom of God are to be found in Jesus' own teaching, in particular the 'comfortable words' of Mt. 11:28–30 which echo the words of wisdom in Ecclus. 51:23–26.

● the Lord (Jn. 13:13; Acts 2:34–36; Rom. 10:9–13; 1 Cor. 8:6; 12:3; 16:22; Phil. 2:9–11; *cf.* Ps. 110:1; Is. 45:22–23; Joel 2:32).

There are also many other titles given to Jesus which declare him to be the fulfilment of Old Testament promises, such as Immanuel (Mt. 1:23; *cf.* Is. 7:14), the humble king (Mt. 21:5; *cf.* Zc. 9:9), the Word (Jn. 1:1–18; Rev. 19:13),[15] the stone rejected by the builders (Mk. 12:10; Acts 4:11; 1 Pet. 2:7; *cf.* Ps. 118:22), the prophet like Moses (Jn. 6:14; Acts 3:22–26; *cf.* Dt. 18:15), and the priest after the order of Melchizedek (Heb. 5:5 – 7:28; *cf.* Gn. 14:18–20; Ps. 110:4).

It is abundantly clear that the New Testament understands Jesus to be the supreme fulfilment of the promises of the Old Testament, both in what he did and who he was. Just as many Old Testament events, persons and institutions may be understood as types of Christ (see above: ch. 7), so many Old Testament words are fulfilled in the coming of Jesus (*cf.* Amsler 1960a: 135–147). Amsler points out that the New Testament often applies a text which originally referred to God, David, Israel, a prophet, *etc.* to Jesus Christ or the church; and in this he notes a striking agreement between the New Testament authors in their interpretation of such Old Testament passages, for example in the Christological use of individual psalms of lament by the Synoptics, Acts and Hebrews. He suggests that these transpositions are based on the belief that the text of Scripture finds its real meaning only with reference to Christ and the church. This does not mean that Old Testament texts are pure prediction (not referring to anything within the old covenant), but that every word has its own significance in salvation history and also witnesses to its fulfilment in Christ. It is not just specific texts but the old covenant as a whole, the entire history of the promises, which is fulfilled in Jesus Christ.

d. Fulfilment without consummation

We have seen that the New Testament writers believe and assert that the 'day of the Lord', anticipated by the prophets and apocalyptists of the Old Testament, has dawned in the coming

---

[15]*Cf.* the importance of the word of God throughout the Old Testament, especially in creation (Gn. 1), the giving of the law (*e.g.* Ex. 20:1), and in the messages of the prophets (*cf.* Is. 55:10–11; Je. 23:16–32).

of Jesus Christ. As Phillips Brooks' hymn 'O little town of Bethlehem' expresses it, 'the hopes and fears of all the years are met in thee tonight'. What was for so long a possibility has become a reality.

To describe this, C. H. Dodd coined the expression 'realized eschatology' (1935: 41, 148; 1936: 79–87; cf. Wolfzorn 1962), by which he meant that in the ministry of Jesus the eschatology of the Old Testament has found its goal and fulfilment. In using this expression he distinguished his understanding of the New Testament from that of Schweitzer and others who had proposed a 'consistent eschatology', in other words that Jesus' message is exclusively eschatological and looks to the future for the fulfilment of the promises and the coming of the kingdom.[16] Schweitzer interpreted the essence of Jesus' message as 'not yet', whereas Dodd interpreted it as 'already'. Like Schweitzer, Dodd overstated his case and in response to criticism he later admitted that the expression 'realized eschatology' was 'not altogether felicitous' (1953: 447). Nevertheless, in his later works Dodd continued to maintain his basic thesis that in Christ's coming the crucial event of history expected by the prophets had taken place (cf. 1951a: 25–32; 1971: 115–116).

A different view was propounded by W. G. Kümmel (1945) and Oscar Cullmann (1946; 1965). They rejected interpretations of Jesus' eschatology as exclusively futuristic (Schweitzer) or present (Dodd), and insisted that 'the basic feature characterizing Jesus' eschatology was that the Kingdom of God was proclaimed to be at once present and future' (Cullmann 1965: 37). Cullmann (1946:84) used an analogy from the Second World War which has been often quoted since, that Christ's death and resurrection may be compared to the decisive battle ('D-Day') but it is not yet the final victory ('Victory Day'). Christians live within the interval between that decisive battle and the conclusion of the war (Jesus' second coming), and thus experience a tension between what has already been fulfilled and what has not yet been completed (1965: 166–185; cf. Hoekema 1979: 68–75).

Various terms have been suggested to express this view of eschatology as both present and future, such as *sich realisierende Eschatologie* ('eschatology that is the process of realization',

---

[16]For surveys of the debate over eschatology from Schweitzer to the 1960s, see Perrin (1963) and Ladd (1974: 4–42); and for the continuing debate to the late 1970s, see Travis (1980).

Haenchen/Jeremias[17]) and 'inaugurated eschatology' (Florovsky 1951: 179–180). Perhaps partly because Haenchen's German alternative cannot be succinctly translated into English, the term 'inaugurated eschatology' has been more readily accepted in English-speaking scholarship (*e.g.* J. A. T. Robinson 1957: 101; France 1971: 162). The same idea is expressed by the term 'fulfilment without consummation' (Ladd 1974: 105–121). Jesus' first coming has inaugurated the *eschaton* ('last days'); his second coming will consummate it. To take up the words used above of Schweitzer's and Dodd's interpretations, it is 'already *and* not yet' (*cf.* Gutiérrez 1971: 160–168). Jesus announces that the kingdom has come and will come: it has both present and future aspects.

How does this relate to the theme of promise and fulfilment in the relationship between the Testaments? In the preceding section we have seen how the New Testament presents Jesus Christ as the supreme fulfilment of Old Testament promises. We shall now look at the same matter from a different point of view, and ask how far the Old Testament promises have already been fulfilled in Jesus Christ and how far they still await completion in the future.

The promise of *descendants* as reinterpreted messianically by the prophets was fulfilled in the coming of Jesus as the Christ (*cf.* above: section c), and the original sense of the promise concerning the formation of a people found renewed fulfilment in the emergence of the Christian community as the true inheritors by faith of the promise to Abraham (Rom. 4:13–25; see further below: ch. 9.3).

The promise of *relationship* has been fulfilled in a new way in the new covenant (Lk. 22:20; 1 Cor. 11:25; Heb. 8 – 9) and new life (Jn. 3; Rom. 5 – 6) made possible by the coming of Jesus. Through him the believer has direct access to God (Heb. 10:19–22) and God's promise to be with his people is renewed (Heb. 13:5b; *cf.* Mt. 28:20b; Jn. 10:27–29). The promised Holy Spirit has come (Acts 2; Eph. 1:13), and in the power of that Spirit Jesus' disciples are to take his message of salvation to all nations (Mt. 28:18–20; Acts 1:8).

The promise of *land*, however, does not have any obvious fulfilment in the coming of Jesus. Very little is said specifically in the New Testament about the question of land, even though the fact that the promised land was under enemy occupation must

---

[17]A term suggested by E. Haenchen and taken up by J. Jeremias (1962: 230; first edition 1947).

have been a major theological problem. Jesus himself apparently owned no land ('the Son of man has nowhere to lay his head', Lk. 9:58) and he was unwilling to get involved in family disputes over land (Lk. 12:13–14). Indeed he pointed out the dangers of covetousness in relation to land-ownership (vv. 15–21). Jesus assured the meek that they would inherit the earth (Mt. 5:5; *cf*. Ps. 37:11), though his intention was presumably not to promise his followers worldly prosperity but to assure them that in the broader perspective of eternity they could rely on their needs being abundantly supplied (*cf*. Jn. 10:10b; 1 Cor. 3:21–23; 2 Cor. 6:10). Only in the letter to the Hebrews does the land have a prominent place, and there it is clearly a promise as yet unfulfilled (Heb. 11:8–16; *cf*. the promise of 'rest' in Heb. 3 – 4).[18]

Some of the promises in the *prophetic books* have been clearly fulfilled in the coming of Jesus, for instance the image of the suffering servant which finds its supreme fulfilment in the Cross. Others have been partially fulfilled but still await consummation in the future, such as the promise of the Kingdom of God which Jesus announces to be 'at hand' (Mk. 1:15; *etc*.; see Kümmel 1945; Ladd 1974). And the promises that relate to the consummation of history remain unfulfilled, though Christians are encouraged to hope for their fulfilment in the near future (*cf*. Heb. 12:26), such as the resurrection of the dead (Jn. 6:39–40; 1 Cor. 15:12–57; 1 Thes. 4:13–18) and the creation of a new heaven and new earth (2 Pet. 3:11–13; Rev. 21 – 22).

There are also *new promises* in the New Testament, given to those who believe in Christ. Perhaps the greatest of all is the promise of eternal life, which was part of God's eternal plan (Tit. 1:2; *cf*. Kelly 1963) but only revealed in and through the work of Christ (Jn. 3:16; Rom. 16:25–26; 2 Tim. 1:1; 1 Jn. 2:25).[19] Several promises of Jesus concern the preaching of the Good News and the formation of the international church (Mt. 4:19; 16:18; 24:14; 28:18–20), and this is explicitly linked with the basic promise to the patriarchs (Mt. 8:10–11; *cf*. Eph. 3:6).

---

[18]For a much fuller discussion of the land in the New Testament, differing in some respects from the summary view given here, see Davies (1974; *cf*. Brueggemann 1977: 167–183). On 'rest', see von Rad (1933).

[19]'Everlasting life' is mentioned briefly in Dn. 12:2, and there are occasional hints of the possibility of life after death in the Old Testament, but these glimpses of eternal life are at the fringe of Old Testament faith and I have not included them among the major promises of the Old Testament.

Finally Jesus' promise to come again should be mentioned, although it is not entirely new if it may be understood as a reaffirmation of the promise of the eschatological coming of the Lord in Malachi 3:1–2 (*cf.* Rev. 6:16–17). This Old Testament promise is filled with new content and related to other promises concerning the consummation of history throughout the New Testament (*e.g.* Mt. 24 – 25; Jn. 14:3, 28; 1 Cor. 1:7–8; 11:26; 1 Thes. 2:19; 5:23; 2 Thes. 2:1–8; 2 Pet. 3:3–10; Rev. 19).

So it is clear that the fulfilment of promise which the New Testament announces is an open-ended fulfilment. Many promises have been fulfilled, but others still await fulfilment in the future. Moreover, there are new promises made in Christ which will also be fulfilled. Jesus came and announced the presence of the kingdom of God, yet the church continues to pray 'Thy kingdom come' (Mt. 6:10) and 'Come, Lord Jesus!' (Rev. 22:20; *cf.* 1 Cor. 16:22). As Christians wait and prepare for Jesus' return at the end of time and the consummation of history, there are continuing opportunities for faith and hope in the promises of God (*cf.* 2 Cor. 7:1; Phil. 3:12–14; Heb. 6:11–12; 10:36).

e. A relationship of interdependence

The exposition above shows beyond doubt that a major theme in both Old and New Testaments is that of promise and fulfilment. It is not simply a matter of the verification of predictions nor of the fulfilling of prophecies, though both of those have their place in the Bible. Rather, we have seen that the promise given by God to the patriarchs forms the basis for the very existence of the people of God throughout the Old and New Testaments. The basic promise received by Abraham was reaffirmed, partially fulfilled, restated, partially fulfilled, reinterpreted, partially fulfilled and renewed to become further promise. There were many stages in the process: Abraham, Isaac and Jacob; Moses and Joshua; David and Solomon; the prophets; supremely in the person of Jesus Christ; the apostles. By the end of the New Testament a great deal has been achieved in fulfilment of the promises, but new possibilities and hopes for the future consummation of the kingdom of God and the re-creation of the universe leave no room for complacency as though Christians were those who have already arrived at their destination. To quote Jesus' words, 'the end is not yet' (Mk. 13:7).

The theme of promise and fulfilment points to a complementary relationship between the Old Testament and the New Testament, a relationship of mutual dependence. Neither stands alone nor can be understood fully without the other. The *Old Testament* without the New Testament would be a disappointment, a promising beginning with outstanding ethical ideals and wonderful pictures of the future but no conclusion. More than two thousand years since it was written it would now surely be no more than a monument to great ideas and lofty visions. To be realistic we would have to relegate the Old Testament to the museum. On the other hand, the *New Testament* without the Old Testament would be a tree with no roots, a child with no parents, an ending without a beginning. 'What are you?' we should ask it, and 'Where do you come from?' What reason would there be to believe that the events recounted in the New Testament were promised ages beforehand, if no record of those promises were preserved? And what significance would those events have if they were purely incidental and not the fulfilment of a divine plan?

In fact the Old Testament and New Testament belong together, they are interrelated and interdependent. Thus we may conclude that another aspect of the theological relationship between the Testaments is interdependence: they cannot be rightly understood except in relationship to each other.

Bibliography (8)

Achtemeier, P. & E. 1962: *The Old Testament Roots of Our Faith*, London, 1964 (USA, 1962).

Berkouwer, G. C. 1952: *Studies in Dogmatics: The Person of Christ*, ET: Grand Rapids, Michigan, 1954 (Dutch, 1952): 113–152.

Bruce, F. F. 1955: *The Christian Approach to the Old Testament*, London.

—1963: 'Promise and Fulfilment in Paul's Presentation of Jesus' in *Promise and Fulfilment: Essays Presented to Professor S. H. Hooke* (ed. F. F. Bruce), Edinburgh: 36–50.

Clines, D. J. A. 1978: *The Theme of the Pentateuch*, Sheffield (JSOT Supplement Series 10).

Davies, W. D. 1974: *The Gospel and the Land: Early Christianity and Jewish Territorial Doctrine*, Berkeley.

Dodd, C. H. 1936: *The Apostolic Preaching and its Developments: Three Lectures with an appendix on Eschatology and History*, London. Cited here from 1944 printing (reset).

—1953: *The Interpretation of the Fourth Gospel*, Cambridge.

Gross, H. 1959: 'Zum Problem Verheissung und Erfüllung', *Biblische Zeitschrift* 3:3–17.

Hoekema, A. A. 1979: *The Bible and the Future*, Grand Rapids, Michigan.

Jensen, J. 1988: 'Prediction-Fulfilment in Bible and Liturgy', *CBQ* 50:646–662.

Jeremias, J. 1962: *The Parables of Jesus*, revised ET: London, 1963 (German, 1947, [6]1962).

Kaiser, W. C. 1978: *Toward an Old Testament Theology*, Grand Rapids, Michigan.

Kelly, J. N. D. 1963: *A Commentary on the Pastoral Epistles*, London.

Kümmel, W. G. 1945: *Promise and Fulfilment: The Eschatological Message of Jesus*, ET: London, 1957 (SBT 23; German, 1945, ³1956).

Larcher, C. 1962: *L'actualité chrétienne de l'Ancien Testament, d'après le Nouveau Testament*, Paris (Lectio Divina 34).

McCurley, F. R. 1970: 'The Christian and the Old Testament Promise', *The Lutheran Quarterly* 22:401–410.

McKenzie, J. L. 1968: 'Aspects of Old Testament Thought', *JBC* II:736–767.

—1974: *A Theology of the Old Testament*, London.

Moule, C. F. D. 1968: 'Fulfilment-Words in the New Testament: Use and Abuse', *NTS* 14:293–320.

Ohler, A. 1972–73: *Studying the Old Testament from Tradition to Canon*, ET: Edinburgh, 1985 (German, two volumes 1972, 1973): 311–367.

Perrin, N. 1963: *The Kingdom of God in the Teaching of Jesus*, London.

Porteous, N. W. 1954: 'The Old Testament and Some Theological Thought-Forms', *SJT* 7:153–169.

Premsagar, P. V. 1974: 'Theology of Promise in the Patriarchal Narratives', *The Indian Journal of Theology* 23:112–122.

Rad, G. von 1933: 'There still remains a rest for the people of God: An Investigation of a Biblical Conception', ET in von Rad (1966): 94–102 (German, 1933).

—1947: *Studies in Deuteronomy*, ET: London, 1953 (SBT 9; German, 1947, ²1948).

Robinson, J. A. T. 1957: *Jesus and his Coming: The Emergence of a Doctrine*, London.

Roo, W. A. van 1986: *Telling about God: I. Promise and Fulfillment*, Rome (Analecta Gregoriana 242).

Rowley, H. H. 1939: *Israel's Mission to the World*, London.

Schniewind, J. 1966: 'Die Beziehung des Neuen Testaments zum Alten Testament', *Die Zeichen der Zeit* 20:3–10.

Travis, S. H. 1980: *Christian hope and the future of man*, Leicester.

Westermann, C. 1968c: *Blessing: In the Bible and the Life of the Church*, ET: Philadelphia, 1978 (German, 1968).

Wolfzorn, E. E. 1962: 'Realized Eschatology: An Exposition of Charles H. Dodd's Thesis', *ETL* 38:44–70.

9

Continuity and discontinuity

A sermon by A. F. Kirkpatrick from 1903 may serve to introduce our third key theme. He discusses successively the unity
and the distinction between the two parts of the Christian Bible.
First, the two Testaments are linked by the fact that in both God
is revealing his character and purposes by words and deeds: 'the
whole Bible is the history of redemption' and 'without the New
Testament the Old Testament would be a magnificent failure;
without the Old Testament the New Testament would be an
inexplicable phenomenon' (pp. 7–9). Secondly, the important
distinction between the Testaments is that the Old records an
incomplete, progressive revelation, but the New a complete and
final one (pp. 9–12). Thus the relationship between the Testaments involves elements of continuity and discontinuity, of unity
and diversity.

We shall consider first of all the continuity and discontinuity
in biblical history and secondly the unity and diversity of biblical
theology. Finally, we shall look briefly at one of the crucial
theological issues arising from the study, namely the relationship between Israel and the church.[1]

---

[1]There are many other issues which arise from the continuity and
discontinuity between the Old and New Testaments, particularly in the
area of ethics, for example the question of the continuing relevance of
Old Testament law for the Christian (see Wright 1983: 148–173; *cf.*
Boulton 1982; N. Anderson 1988; Westerholm 1988; Martin 1989).

9.1 Continuity and discontinuity

a. A continuous history

The Old Testament has a double value for the church, according to J. E. McFadyen (1903: 345–364). In an absolute sense, it shows God's purpose in history and its prophets and psalmists can speak directly to the modern age. Apart from this, however, it has a relative value with reference to the New Testament:

> It prepared the way for the Testament by which it was transcended, though not superseded, and for Him whose coming marks a new departure, and yet was no less truly conditioned and directed by all that had gone before (p. 352).

Thus the Old Testament is essential for the New, both historically and religiously, and in spite of obvious differences between the two the continuity is more important than the distinction.

C. H. Dodd[2] has clarified the matter further: the unity of the Bible is based on the common origin of every part of the Bible in a 'community conscious of a continuous history' (1946a: 3). This history, recorded in the Bible as the inner core of world history, may be called 'sacred history' (*Heilsgeschichte*) since it understands history as a process of redemption and revelation. It culminates in the death and resurrection of Christ, though it does not end at that point but is reconstituted in the history of the church. Since God is the creator and sovereign of all people, the meaning of this sacred history is also the ultimate meaning of all history. All history is therefore ultimately sacred, as is shown by the way the Bible puts sacred history into the context of a world history with a real beginning and end. Thus Dodd has shown that there is an essential unity within the Bible, a unity which stems from the history of one community in which God has revealed himself.

So the Old Testament and the New Testament together, and only together, constitute the Christian Bible. The Old Testament records the history of the people of God ('salvation history') and this same history is continued in the New Testament. Jesus was a member of that people of God, indeed he was the

---

Such questions are beyond the scope of the present work, which only sets out to discuss the *theological* relationship between the Testaments.

[2]1928: 10; 1938: 114–125; 1946a: 2–3; 1946b: 129; 1951b: 161–162.

most important figure to appear in the course of its history. Thus the Old Testament can be fully understood only in the light of its continuation and fulfilment in the New; equally the New Testament has its historical background in the Old Testament and is liable to be interpreted in a distorted manner if isolated from that background.

b. The inter-testamental period

There is of course a historical gap between the Old and New Testaments in the sense that Old Testament history is recounted only until about 400 BC, and for information about what happened between that time and the beginning of the New Testament we have to look to extra-biblical sources.[3] But there is also a gap of several hundred years between the arrival and departure of the people of Israel in Egypt in the second millennium BC, with hardly any information in the biblical history; likewise a gap of almost twenty years between the New Testament account of Jesus' childhood visit to the Temple and the beginning of his ministry. These gaps do not imply any historical discontinuity, but simply that the biblical writers did not consider the events of those periods to be of particular significance in the recounting of salvation history. Likewise, we should not draw the conclusion from the historical gap between the Old and New Testament documents that there is a gap in salvation history. Neither Old nor New Testaments offer comprehensive accounts of the history of their times: on the contrary, both are ruthlessly selective in order to achieve their particular aims. Thus the gap in the inter-testamental period by no means alters the conclusion that there is a fundamental historical continuity between the two Testaments.

c. Judaism and Christianity

Closely related to the question of the historical continuity between the Testaments is the question of the continuity between Judaism and Christianity.

The Jewish scholar, Samuel Sandmel (1978), argues that there is an essential historical continuity between Judaism and early Christianity (*cf.* Grant 1960; Vermes 1973). 'Christianity', he

---

[3]On the inter-testamental period, see Förster (1959); Russell (1960); Tcherikover (1966); Ellison (1976) and Gowan (1976).

says, 'was a Judaism both in its origin and in its basic contours' (p. 4). Furthermore, he states that 'not only was Jesus a Jew, but a figure such as he could not have arisen in any other tradition or culture but Judaism. He is to be approached and understood historically only in a Jewish context' (p. 305). Sandmel is not, of course, claiming that Christianity and Judaism are identical, though he does emphasize the similarities more than many other Jewish or Christian writers, but simply pointing out that *historically* speaking there is an unbroken continuum from Judaism to Christianity. Within that continuum Christianity did four things (pp. 305, 418–423):

- perpetuated some aspects of Judaism unchanged;
- carried over some aspects but altered them;
- rejected some aspects of its legacy; and
- created its own new materials.

In due course Christians recognized other writings than those of the Hebrew Bible as Scripture and distinguished the two collections as 'New Testament' and 'Old Testament'. Thus 'in the Christian view, the Old Testament and the New are a single, continuous Bible' (p. 419).

Alan Segal (1976) puts it rather differently. He rejects the idea that Judaism began in the distant past with Abraham, Moses or Ezra, as though it were older than Christianity. On the contrary, he argues, the rabbinic Judaism which was contemporary with early Christianity and became the basis of future Jewish religion was radically different from the religion of the Old Testament (*cf.* Jocz 1961: 166–168). 'The religions we know today as Judaism and Christianity were born at the same time and nurtured in the same environment' (Segal 1976: 1). Likewise, John Bright (1960: 463–464) points out that there are two possible destinations of the history of Israel: Judaism and Christianity. On the one hand, the history of Israel continued in the history of the Jewish people, whose faith was a development of Pharisaism and expressed normatively in the Mishnah and Talmud. For them the hope of the Old Testament is still unfulfilled. On the other hand, Christians believe that 'the destination of Old Testament history and theology is Christ and his gospel' (p. 464). Their faith finds its normative expression in the New Testament. The choice between these two alternatives depends entirely on one's answer to Jesus' question, 'Who do you say that I am?' (Mk. 8:29), but in answering that question one moves beyond the realm of history into that of faith.

The consequence for understanding the relationship between

the Testaments is essentially the same as in Sandmel's exposition: the existence of a fundamental historical continuity between the Old Testament and the New. Christianity did not set out to become a new and separate religion. However, as Segal (1976: 2) points out, there were historical and social forces which forced every variety of Jewish community at the time to 'rebuild its ancient national culture into something almost unprecedented, a religion of personal and communal piety'. Moreover, it soon became clear that the difference between recognizing Jesus of Nazareth as the Messiah and rejecting him as a blasphemer was so great that Christianity and Judaism could not coexist for long without becoming separate religions (cf. Noth 1950: 428–432). Indeed, it was precisely because Christians were convinced that Jesus was the Messiah, and that it was those who believed in him rather than those who rejected him who were in genuine historical continuity with the Old Testament, that the split with Judaism became inevitable.[4]

d. Historical discontinuities

The continuity of biblical history does not mean that there are no differences between the Old and New Testaments. C. H. Dodd[5] has pointed out that while there is indeed a continuity in the sequence of events from the early nomads, through the monarchy and dispersion, to the church, the biblical narrative depicts a series of crises rather than a smooth development[6] and the conclusion is radically different from the beginning. The New Testament writers are aware of being in continuity with the older traditions, but their experience is revolutionary and their interpretation of those traditions original and creative, following the example of Jesus himself. The church is simultaneously the 'Israel of God' (Gal. 6:16) and a 'new creation' (2 Cor. 5:17); it perpetuates the old and inaugurates the new. Moreover, Dodd argues that there is a difference between the Testaments in that the subject in the Old is a community, Israel, whereas in the New

---

[4]There are many other studies of the relationship between early Judaism and early Christianity, e.g. W. D. Davies (1948); Jocz (1949); E. P. Sanders (1977; 1985); Riches (1980); McNamara (1983); Rowland (1985) and Neusner (1989).

[5]1928: 194–196, 227–248; 1938: 96–98; 1946a: 3–4; 1951b: 157; 1952a: 109–110.

[6]Cf. Brueggemann's exposition of the crisis of discontinuity in the Exile (1977: 130–132). See also Ackroyd (1977).

it is a person, Jesus Christ (1946a: 73; *cf.* above: ch. 3.2.e). Thus Dodd's understanding of the relationship between the Testaments is summarized by the statement, 'the writers of the New Testament and of early Christianity in general are clearly aware both of continuity and of newness' (1928: 244).

Likewise, Bernhard W. Anderson (1964) concludes from his study of the relationship between the new covenant and the old in the prophecy of Jeremiah 31:31–34 that it is characterized by both continuity and discontinuity. It is clear that the one God is author of both covenants, which are continuous in that they are based on one Torah, directed toward the establishment of a relationship between God and the people, and made with 'the house of Israel' (pp. 236–238). Nevertheless, the new covenant will be 'not like' the old, in that it will bring about a radically inward relationship to the Lord, mark the end of all tradition and be based on divine forgiveness (pp. 232–236). The New Testament declares that the new covenant has been realized in Jesus Christ, though this is a fulfilment beyond all prophetic expectation. 'Yet manifest within this deepest discontinuity is the continuity of the same almighty grace which had called Israel into existence and had directed her toward the future' (p. 242).

In sum, it may be concluded that within the basic historical continuity between the Testaments there are also elements of discontinuity. The early Christians affirmed their continuity with Abraham and Moses, a continuity grounded in the one God, but at the same time they asserted that Jesus was superior to both (Baird 1988; Hay 1990). Paradoxically therefore, the greatest discontinuity is in the coming of Jesus, for from one perspective he fulfilled the promises and hopes of the Old Testament, and yet from another he so much surpassed all expectation that his coming inaugurated a new and final stage in the history of salvation (*cf.* Heb. 1:1–2; 7:23–28; 8:6, 13). Through his coming a new international people of God was brought into being (Mt. 16:18; 28:18–20); and by the power of his Spirit new life and new hope was offered to all who have faith in him (Jn. 3; Acts 2). In him 'the time is fulfilled' (Mk. 1:15), the 'last days' have arrived (Acts 2:16–17), the day of salvation has dawned (2 Cor. 6:2). Many prophets had proclaimed the word of the Lord, but only one could declare, 'You have heard that it was said to the men of old . . . But I say to you . . .' (Mt. 5:21–48). In no way does the New Testament contradict the Old; but it tells of so many new things that it is rightly called the *New* Testament and without doubt the coming of Jesus represents the most important event in the entire unfolding of God's plan. While the continuity between the Testaments is not to be disputed, and indeed is the foundation of Christian faith, there are also discontinuities which must be taken into account.[7]

9.2 Unity in diversity

a. Theological unity

The essential theological unity of the Old and New Testaments, according to H. H. Rowley,[8] is found in their common divine origin, common teaching about God and mankind, common patterns, and common ethical and liturgical principles. In a similar way, Th. C. Vriezen (1966) considers that both Testaments have certain common perspectives, among which the concepts of communion, prophecy and kingdom are particularly important. The certainty of immediate communion between God and human beings he takes to be 'the underlying idea of the whole of the Biblical testimony' (p. 157; cf. 150–152, 204–205; cf. Harrington 1973: 73). In contrast to von Rad (1952a: 25), for whom the Old Testament is a 'history book', Vriezen asserts that prophecy is the basis of the witness of the Old Testament: only the vision and testimony of the prophets can account for Israel's awareness of God's activity in history.[9] Moreover the prophetic message is continued in the New Testament, which preaches the same God, expects the same kingdom and demands the same life of faith as the Old Testament (1966: 104–109; cf. Goldingay 1981: 16). In particular, the eschatological prospect of the kingdom of God is for Vriezen not only 'the most profound leading motif in the Old Testament' (p. 114), but also the 'true heart' of the message of both Testaments (p. 123; cf. 114–115).

John Bright (1967) affirms that the Bible is a theological book and therefore the unity of the Bible depends on there being unity in biblical theology. The Old Testament records real history, in conjunction with a theological interpretation of that

---

[7]Liberation theology has tended to emphasize the continuity between the Testaments, though not denying that there are new elements in the New Testament (Segundo 1976: 490; Hanks 1983: 43–60; cf. Kirk 1979: 153–156).

[8]1949: 18–25; 1953:10–13, 62–89, 96–97, 118, 121, 139–140, 166.

[9]1966: 51, 101–103, 113–114; cf. J. A. Sanders (1972: 55). But in spite of its obvious importance, it is an exaggeration to make prophecy as central to the Old Testament as Vriezen does. Clements (1970: 136) points out that from a historical and theological point of view the Law has priority over the Prophets in the Old Testament canon.

history, which is understood to be moving toward a destination but which does not reach it. It follows that the Old Testament is theologically incomplete, describing a salvation history in which salvation is not yet achieved (pp. 136–138). Fulfilment and completion occur only outside the limits of the Old Testament, that is, in the New Testament. At the centre of the New Testament message stands one central fact: Jesus Christ has come, God has acted decisively in human history to fulfil his promises and achieve salvation (pp. 138–140). Thus Bright concludes that the 'overarching structure of theology, which in one way or another informs each of its texts, constitutes the essential and normative element in the Old Testament, and the one that binds it irrevocably to the New Testament within the canon of Scripture' (p. 143).

It is, therefore, clear that not only is there historical continuity between Old and New Testaments but there is also a basic theological unity. This does not mean that the theologies of the two Testaments are identical, but that they agree in their fundamental understandings of God, humanity, the world, and the relationships between them. The theology of the Old Testament is assumed as the basis of the theology of the New Testament. It follows that, on the one hand, the Old Testament says more than the New, because a good deal that is already clear in the former is not repeated in the latter but taken for granted as true (*e.g.* the uniqueness of God, creation, human sin, divine providence, the possibility of change). On the other hand, the New Testament says more than the Old, because it assumes the validity of Old Testament theology and goes on to tell of new things which supplement the Old without contradicting it (*e.g.* the fatherhood of God, the cross and resurrection of Christ, the work of the Holy Spirit, the future consummation of history). So we may conclude that from a theological point of view the Old and New Testaments form one Bible, an essentially consistent record of the theology of God's people.

b. Theological diversity

H. H. Rowley points out that the theological unity of the Bible is a dynamic unity (1956: 14), the unity of development, process and growth (1953: 7, 27, 63), and therefore it is manifested not in uniformity but in diversity (1946b: 358; 1953: 1–29). For instance, Rowley argues that certain aspects of the Old Testament such as primitive ideas, sacrifice and much of the old law are superseded in the New Testament (1953: 14–16, 102–108, 129–130), although this does not mean that the Old Testament as a whole is superseded (1953: 2). The Old Testament is an integral part of the Christian Bible, even though in itself it is not a Christian book but an early stage of growth towards the whole (1946a: 9–10; 1956: 14). Indeed, the very differences between the Testaments are an aspect of their unity: 'The most significant bond between the two Testaments . . . is to be found . . . in the fundamental differences between the Testaments' (1953: 89). Prophecy and fulfilment are two quite different things, yet they are intimately linked. From one point of view, both old and new revelations are real and valid in their own right (1953: 98); from another point of view, the two Testaments are complementary and belong together so that neither can be fully understood without the other (1949: 17; 1953: 94, 112; 1956: 45). Thus Rowley expresses the relationship between the Testaments in terms of both unity and diversity.[10]

Such theological diversity is not only true of the relationship between the Testaments but is also found within the Old and New Testaments themselves. Franz Leenhardt (1962) distinguishes the Abrahamic and Mosaic traditions of spirituality which coexist in the Old (and New) Testament. Paul Hanson (1982) finds two major polarities within the Old Testament: between form and reform (kings and prophets), and between visionary and pragmatic approaches to life. John Goldingay (1987) examines three major kinds of diversity in the Old Testament: in meaning (of concepts, themes and institutions), in message (of different Old Testament books and traditions), and in significance (different interpretations of the same event or motif). James Dunn (1977) investigates the major strands and layers within the New Testament material, and discovers there a broad diversity in the understanding of the gospel, organization of the community, patterns of worship and spiritual experience. He then identifies four major currents in early Christianity – Jewish Christianity, hellenistic Christianity, apocalyptic Christianity and early Catholicism – and shows that all have roots within the New Testament, though none can claim to be the normative form of Christianity in the first century. The

---

[10]Smart (1961: 90) asserts that Rowley does not take the discontinuity seriously enough, but this must be rejected in view of Rowley's clear statement that the differences between the Testaments provide their most important link (see above), his warning of the danger of equating the two Testaments (1953: 90), and his reply to Smart which reaffirms that he recognizes fully both continuity and discontinuity between the Testaments (1949: 20n.; *cf.* 1941: ch. 4; 1947: 15; 1950c: 35).

unifying focus for all Christians was the person of Jesus Christ, and there was general agreement concerning the unity and continuity between Jesus of Nazareth and the exalted Christ; but within this essential unity there was a great deal of scope for diversity in belief and practice.[11]

There is a tendency to ignore or harmonize the diversities within the Bible in the attempt to maintain the traditional beliefs of a particular stream of Christianity. Catholics and Lutherans, Puritans and Pentecostals, conservatives and liberals, all have their favourite parts of the Bible ('canon within the canon'), and often attempt to interpret the rest of the Bible in the light of what they consider to be the heart of the matter.[12] However, a more genuinely 'biblical' approach is to recognize the value of the diversity in the Bible and to refuse to force that diversity into the mould of an artificial unity (*cf.* Cullmann 1986: 13–33; Bruce 1988: 270–275). We should not be afraid of diversity: it does not stand in contradiction to the unity of the Bible but is complementary to it. To put it another way, the basic theological unity of the Bible is expressed in and through diverse words and forms.

c. A relationship of tension

We may conclude, therefore, that there is continuity and also discontinuity between the Old and New Testaments, unity and also diversity.

The tension between continuity and discontinuity is the essence of the view of the relationship between the Testaments presented by Th. C. Vriezen (1966). As was mentioned above, he recognizes that the Old and New Testaments have a good deal in common; but he points out that there is also a decisive discontinuity, namely, that Jesus' disciples were convinced that he was the Messiah (pp. 106, 109). In the thought of Jesus (pp. 11–13) and Paul (pp. 93–95) there is a tension between acceptance of the Old Testament as the word of God and reinterpretation in the conviction that it is superseded with the coming of Christ. This tension has continued through the history of the church and remains unresolved today (pp. 95–99). On the one

---

[11]For a critique of Dunn's work, see Carson (1983).

[12]*Cf.* the debates in the sixties and seventies about the 'centre of the Old Testament' and the 'centre of the New Testament' (see Baker 1976: 377–386; Hasel 1978: 140–170; 1985: 37–40). On the 'canon within the canon', see Goldingay (1987: 122–127); Bruce (1988: 270–275).

hand, there are various attempts to overcome the tension: some (*e.g.* Vischer, von Rad) have attempted to reconcile unity and diversity in the Bible, while others (*e.g.* van Ruler) have replied to the threat to the authority of the Old Testament by affirming its independent theological significance. On the other hand, some (*e.g.* Bultmann) have stressed the tension so strongly that the Old Testament is understood to be a non-Christian book. None of these attempts have provided a satisfactory solution, according to Vriezen, who argues that the tension is not to be overcome, but to be recognized as central to the understanding of the relationship between the Testaments.

It follows that for Vriezen there is a double relationship between the Testaments: organic spiritual unity, and historical difference and distance (1966: 100, 120–121). A balanced solution to the problem must take account of both the fundamental theological agreement between the two Testaments and the radical inward renovation of Israel's religion accomplished by Jesus Christ (pp. 89, 110). In this the person of Jesus has a double role: not only is he the decisive difference between the Testaments, but also – paradoxically – the essential unity of the Bible becomes evident in him. 'Jesus Christ is the end of God's self-disclosure to Israel and at the same time He is the man through whom God made the world share in his redeeming work in Israel' (p. 28; *cf.* 122–124).

Likewise John Bright (1967: 184–197) is dissatisfied with the various modern schemata for understanding the relationship between the Testaments, and argues that the only way to a satisfactory solution to the problem is to recognize that the relationship is a complex one. He attempts to sum up his solution in one sentence: 'The Old Testament is the history of our own heritage of faith – but before Christ; it is the record of the dealings of our God – but before Christ' (p. 201). This formulation makes clear the dual nature of the relationship, which includes both continuity and discontinuity:

> The continuity lies in the obvious fact that Christianity is historically a development out of Judaism; the discontinuity in the equally obvious fact that Christianity is not a continuation, or even a radical reform, of Judaism, but an entirely separate religion. The continuity lies in the fact that the theological structure of the two Testaments is fundamentally the same, with the major themes of the theology of the Old carried over and resumed in the New; the discontinuity lies in the fact that these themes receive

244

radical reinterpretation in the light of what Christ has done. Above all, continuity lies in the New Testament's affirmation that Jesus is the Christ (Messiah), who has fulfilled the law and the prophets; the discontinuity lies in the fact that this fulfillment, though foreshadowed in the Old Testament, is not necessarily deducible from the plain sense of the Old and was in fact so surprising that the majority of Israelites could not see it as fulfillment. The New Testament, while unbreakably linked with the Old, announces the intrusion of something New and, therewith, the end of the Old. It affirms the fulfillment of Israel's hope – and pronounces radical judgement on that hope as generally held. It announces the fulfillment of the law – and the abrogation of the way of the law. In a word, the two Testaments are continuous within the unity of God's redemptive purpose; but their discontinuity is the discontinuity of two aeons (p. 201).

More recently, Morna Hooker in her Sanderson Lectures (1986) has discussed the tension between continuity and discontinuity in early Christianity's relationship to its Jewish setting. She uses Jesus' analogy of new wine and old wineskins to point to the ambivalent attitude to what is old which runs through much of the New Testament (pp. 21–25). There is a tension between the beliefs and ideas inherited from the past and the new events and insights of the gospel. Christianity was not simply a reform movement within Judaism, but neither was it an entirely separate movement. If in time Christians came to see the old and new as incompatible and diametrically opposed to each other, that was largely because Jews had rejected Jesus as the Messiah and effectively forced Christians to choose between doing the same or leaving Judaism. However, it should not be forgotten that Jesus grew up in Judaism and there is an essentially Jewish element in his teaching. An example of the tension between old and new is the contrast in Matthew 5 between 'the revelation of God's will given in the past and the new understanding of that will which had come through Jesus' (p. 31). It is not a question of contrast between two laws (of Moses and of Jesus); rather there is one will of God which is partially understood through the Old Testament law and understood more fully through the teaching of Jesus. Likewise Paul, the apostle to the Gentiles, contrasted the old and the new, but never forgot that God had been at work in the past, and saw both continuity and discontinuity between his past beliefs and present faith (p. 38).

So we see in the relationship between the Old Testament and the New Testament there is a tension between continuity and discontinuity, unity and diversity. This tension should not be ignored or suppressed but recognized and welcomed. On the one hand, the sixty-six books of the Christian canon form one Bible, a unique and continuous account of salvation history which presents a unified and consistent picture of the nature of God and of his plan for the world he created. On the other hand, it should not be forgotten that the one Bible consists of two Testaments, and that between and within those two Testaments there are many discontinuities and a good deal of diversity. We will understand the Bible properly only if we grasp these two truths simultaneously and refuse to emphasize either at the expense of the other. The motto of Indonesia, a nation of several hundred racial and linguistic groups united by their common principles and purposes, could also be applied to the Bible: unity in diversity.

9.3 Israel and the church

One of the major theological issues raised by the question of continuity and discontinuity between the Testaments is that of the relationship between Israel and the church. A thorough study of the problem is beyond the scope of this book, and the following discussion will not do more than indicate some of the views that have been and are held, and give some pointers to an understanding of the relationship between Israel and the church which is consistent with the view of the relationship between the Testaments advocated above.[13]

a. The new Israel

C. H. Dodd[14] states clearly the implications of his view of the continuity and discontinuity between the Testaments. Jesus is the Messiah of Israel and thus his mission is primarily to Israel,

---

[13]A great deal has been written on this subject. Bibliographies are given by Küng (1967: 116, 132–133, 141); Harrington (1980: 119–121) and Reventlow (1983: 64–144).

[14]1928: 260; 1938: 90–96; 1946a: 4–5, 70, 76; 1951b: 158; 1952a: 88, 111–123; 1971: 91–92, 99–103.

246

he claims to be the answer to their hopes of a coming king and it is in Jerusalem that his career comes to its climax. However, Jesus' claim to be their Messiah is rejected by Israel, so he institutes a new people of God to fulfil the mission which had been entrusted to Israel. He founds this new community with the twelve apostles, symbolizing the twelve tribes, and it is confirmed as the 'Israel of God' by the gift of the Spirit. Jesus and the New Testament authors apply Old Testament texts concerning Israel to the church, thus forming the basis for use of the Old Testament in Christian life and worship. In short, the church is the new Israel.

Roderick Campbell (1954) expounds this at length and emphasizes the newness of the new age which Christ has brought into being. This does not mean, however, that the Old and the New are completely discontinuous. On the contrary, it was the faithful remnant of the Jewish people who recognized Jesus as their Messiah and became the nucleus of the new theocracy, the 'Israel of God' (Gal. 6:16) and 'commonwealth of Israel' (Eph. 2:12). With such words 'Paul recognizes the continuity of the Remnant with the Christian church, together with its claim to be the rightful heir to all the ancient covenant privileges and promises' (1954: 121). Likewise, many other scholars have argued that the church is the new Israel, the Israel of God, the 'remnant chosen by grace' (*e.g.* Wiesemann 1965; Huffmon 1969; LaRondelle 1983). Peter Richardson (1969), however, claims that the identification of the church with the new Israel was later than the New Testament, and first stated explicitly by Justin (*c.* AD 160).

A similar view is expressed by Hans Küng (1967: 107–125). He points out that the idea of the people of God was at the heart of biblical faith (Ex. 6:6–7; 19:5–6; Lv. 26:9–12). The disciples of Jesus were convinced that he was the fulfilment of the promises of the Old Testament and, since the majority of the people of Israel at that time rejected the Christian message, it was inevitable that the disciples should begin to describe their own community as the true people of God. Thus Christians saw themselves as the new Israel, and the ways of the new Israel and the old progressively diverged. Although the early Christian community had close links with the Jewish people, it developed distinctive forms from the beginning, such as the sacraments and prayer, leadership and fellowship. Gentile Christianity developed without obedience to the Jewish laws, and the destruction of Jerusalem resulted in the end of Temple worship. After AD 70 Jewish Christianity was of little importance, and the church (founded less than half a century earlier as a church of

Jews) became substantially a church of Gentiles. Nevertheless, there is a typological relationship between the old Israel and the new, which is made particularly clear in the letter to the Hebrews, so that the church should never forget its Old Testament roots (*cf*. E. Achtemeier 1973: 116–123).[15]

b. One people of God

The concept of the new Israel tends to emphasize the discontinuity between the Old Testament and the New Testament, and a number of scholars have attempted to redress the balance by insisting on the continuity of the one people of God.

Jakób Jocz (1958: 102–155) argues that there is only one Israel, that it cannot possibly be plural, and that the people of God is continuous from the time of Abraham to the church of Christ. The 'Israel of God' is thus the Christian church which consists of both Jews and Gentiles, the 'Israel who is inspired by the spirit of the Master' (p. 126). There is an indissoluble bond between the church and the Jewish people (*cf*. Clark 1972; Harrington 1980). The difference between the Gentile and the Jew is that the former has to renounce his religious past to become a member of the Israel of God, whereas the latter has only to reaffirm it.

Howard Taylor (1985) points out that 'New Israel' is not a biblical term, and considers it to imply that the church has taken the place of Israel. He shows the continuity of the people of God in the Old and New Testaments and concludes:

> The Christian Church is the People of God through its spiritual union with Jesus Christ as it bears conscious witness to Him. Israel retains its status as the

---

[15]Van Ruler (1955: 28–33/30–36; *cf*. 89–92/95–98) argues that the church is a repetition of Israel 'in the Spirit' and that the church is Israel, although this does not mean that Israel is the church. For van Ruler, Israel is theologically more important than the church since the church is dependent on Israel for its self-understanding. This is perhaps a strange conclusion for a Christian writer, but it is a natural corollary of van Ruler's view that the Old Testament is the essential Bible (see above: ch. 5). He sees a typical relationship between Israel and a Christian nation (*Christenvolk*), and considers that Israel as a nation still has a place in God's plan alongside the church, though he does not make clear precisely what that place is. He also allows for the possibility that God may eventually restore his people Israel.

people of God in its physical union with Christ and unconsciously bears testimony to Christ in its history.

Miskotte (1963: 315–318, 308; *cf.* 1932) also affirms that in the church Gentiles are 'grafted into the ancient tree of the Covenant people' (Rom. 11: 12–18) and that it is Israel's election which is the root of the salvation of Christendom. However, he believes that neither Jews nor Christians alone are Israel, but rather the church and synagogue together form one congregation of God.[16] The present breach is therefore not to be removed by missions to Jews, but by a call to brothers and sisters to realize their unity with each other. Miskotte takes up the words of Franz Rosenzweig, 'What Christ and his church mean in the world, on that we are agreed: no one comes to the Father but by him ... but it is different if a person no longer needs to come to the Father, because he is *already* with him' (1963: 77–78, *cf.* 421). Thus Miskotte concludes that Christians must face realistically the fact that the Old Testament has two sequels: the New Testament and the Talmud.[17] Failure to do this leads to oversimplification and misunderstanding, as in Bultmann's idea of miscarriage.

It is, of course, true that Judaism and Christianity came from the same root and worship the same God. The two faiths have a great deal in common, and should be able to learn from each other and with each other and live in love and peace together. Nevertheless, there is a fundamental difference which cannot be ignored, namely, the Christian claim that Jesus of Nazareth was the promised Messiah and the Jewish rejection of this claim. Jesus' words 'no one comes to the Father, but by me' (Jn. 14:6) were addressed to Jews, and Paul (the missionary to the Gentiles) made a point of preaching salvation to the Jews first (Acts 13:5, 14, 46; *etc.*). As Davies (1968a; *cf.* 1968b) has shown, the centrality of the Torah to Judaism, and of Christology to Christianity, means an irreconcilable dogmatic difference between the two faiths. It would make nonsense of both Judaism and Christianity to pretend that they are really much the same thing.

---

[16]*Cf.* Berkhof (1969). Markus Barth (1983) agrees, and also includes 'the State of Israel, as well as all secularised Jews' (p. 71) in the people of God.

[17]Miskotte (1963: 165–167); *cf.* Horst (1932: 172); Childs (1964: 444–449); Schofield (1964: 118–120); Vriezen (1966: 121).

c. Palestine, the Jews and Judaism

It is clear that there is historical and theological continuity between Israel (the people of God in the Old Testament) and the Christian church (the people of God in the New Testament). There are also discontinuities, for example, the fact that the former was a nation ruled by judges and kings living in a land with geographical boundaries, whereas the latter is an international spiritual community living throughout the world (and even beyond it, if the 'communion of saints' is taken to include the departed). The descendants of Abraham are not limited to those who can trace their physical ancestry to him, but consist of all those who share the faith of Abraham in the God who gives life to the dead (Rom. 4:11–25).

The major problem for Christians concerns their attitude to those who believe in the same God but disagree about the identity of his Messiah. Are the promises of the Old Testament fulfilled to Christians or Jews or both? Does the establishment of the state of Israel fulfil Old Testament promises concerning the land, or is it irrelevant to Christian faith? What is the relationship of the Jewish people to the church and to the Old Testament people of God? Are Christianity and Judaism equally valid sequels to the Old Testament, or is one right and the other wrong? Should the church be evangelizing the Jews, or reminding them of their spiritual heritage, or learning from them as elder brothers and sisters in the one faith? These questions remain the subject of intensive study and prolonged debate by both Christian and Jewish scholars (cf. LWF 1982). Without a lengthy discussion of the issues our answers can only be very tentative indeed.

Concerning the land of Palestine, some Christians and many Jews see the establishment of 'Israel' as a state in its own homeland ('*ereṣ yiśrā'ēl*') to be a fulfilment of the Old Testament promises of land. However, the New Testament view is of the true Israel as a spiritual reality rather than a political one, and the promises of land are no longer tied to the boundaries of Palestine.[18] The Jews and Arabs both have historical claims to Palestine, and both need territory which they can call their own, but this is a matter to be settled on the basis of justice and compassion rather than theology.

---

[18]LaRondelle (1983: 135–146); cf. Brueggemann (1977: 190–191); van Buren (1983: 184–209).

Concerning the Jewish people, one of the greatest enigmas of history is expressed in the jingle:

How odd of God to choose the Jews,
but not so odd as those who chose
the Jewish God then slew the Jews.

During the first few centuries of the Christian era the Jews were largely ignored by Christians, though the Gentile hostility to the Jews which had existed before Christianity surfaced from time to time (Küng 1967: 132–138). However, the formation of the imperial church under Constantine led to Gentile hostility to Jews becoming *Christian* hostility to Jews. While it would be an exaggeration to suggest that Christians and Jews have always been in conflict with one another, and many have lived and worked together in peace and harmony, the fact cannot be denied that some who have called themselves Christians have persecuted Jews, particularly in the Middle Ages and in the twentieth century. There is hardly a greater disgrace in the history of Christendom than the pogroms and the holocaust. Nevertheless, emotion and guilt should not lead us to confuse the issue: the sufferings of the Jews highlight the appalling behaviour of some who named the name of Christ, but they do not make those who suffered the chosen people. The Jews continue to have a special place in God's plan of salvation (Rom. 3:1–4; 9:3–5), but that does not alter the Christian conviction that salvation is granted to those and only those who acknowledge Jesus as the Messiah of Israel and Saviour of the world (Rom. 9:6–8; 10:1–13; *cf.* Acts 4:12).

Finally, concerning Judaism as a religion, the question arises of the church's 'mission to the Jews' (Küng 1967: 142, 149; *cf.* van Buren 1983: 320–352). Should Christians preach the Gospel to Jews in the same way as to Muslims and Hindus, atheists and humanists? Or are the Jews already 'saved' and simply to be accepted as brothers and sisters in the same faith, with certain matters on which we agree to differ? I suggest that both these extreme views are to be rejected. Christianity and Judaism acknowledge the same God as Creator of the world and Saviour of his people. Both acknowledge Abraham and Moses as the founding fathers of the people of God, and both accept the Law, Prophets and Writings as a definitive statement of the perfection of creation and of human sin, of God's gracious way of salvation and of the proper human response to divine grace in obedience and love. Nevertheless it would be dishonest to gloss over the fundamental difference which exists between the answers of the two religions to Jesus' question, 'Who do you say that I am?' (Mk. 8:29). Perhaps 'mission to the Jews' is an inappropriate term, implying a patronizing Christian attitude to those who knew the God of Israel centuries before they did; nevertheless those who have been privileged late in time to know the God of Israel as the Father of their Lord Jesus Christ are divinely commissioned to be witnesses of that knowledge to all who do not yet have it, including the Jews (Acts 1:8; 9:15). The gospel of Jesus Christ is addressed to both Jews and Gentiles, for 'God so loved the world that he gave his only Son, that *whoever* believes in him should not perish but have eternal life' (Jn. 3:16).

Bibliography (9)

Ackroyd, P. 1977: 'Continuity and Discontinuity: Rehabilitation and Authentication' in Knight (1977): 215–234.

Anderson, N. 1988: *Freedom Under Law*, Eastbourne.

Baird, W. 1988: 'Abraham in the New Testament: Tradition and the New Identity', *Int* 42:367–379.

Barth, M. 1983: *The People of God*, Sheffield (JSNT Supplement Series, 5).

Berkhof, H. 1969: 'Israel as a theological problem in the Christian church', *JES* 6:329–347.

Boulton, W. G. 1982: *Is Legalism a Heresy?*, New York/Ramsey.

Buren, P. M. van 1980–: *A Theology of the Jewish-Christian Reality*, San Francisco (three volumes published so far):
1980 *Part I: Discerning the Way.*
1983 *Part II: A Christian Theology of the People of Israel.*
1988 *Part III: Christ in Context.*

Caird, G. B. 1965: *Jesus and the Jewish Nation*, London.

Campbell, R. 1954: *Israel and the New Covenant*, Philadelphia.

Carson, D. A. 1983: 'Unity and Diversity in the New Testament' in *Scripture and Truth* (ed. D. A. Carson & J. D. Woodbridge), Grand Rapids, Michigan: 65–95.

Clark, K. W. 1972: 'The Israel of God' in *Studies in New Testament and Early Christian Literature – Essays in Honor of Allan P. Wikgren*, Leiden (SNovT 33):161–169.

Cullmann, O. 1986: *Unity through Diversity*, ET: Philadelphia, 1988 (German, 1986).

Davies, W. D. 1948: *Paul and Rabbinic Judaism: Some Rabbinic Elements in Pauline Theology*, London, 1948 (^{2}1955).

—1968a: 'Torah and Dogma: A Comment', *HTR* 61:87–105.

—1968b: 'Reflections on Judaism and Christianity' in *L'Évangile, hier et aujourd'hui: Mélanges offerts au Professeur Franz-J. Leenhardt*, Geneva: 39–54.

Dunn, J. D. G. 1977: *Unity and Diversity in the New Testament: An Enquiry into the Character of Earliest Christianity*, London.

Ellison, H. L. 1976: *From Babylon to Bethlehem: The People of God Between the Testaments*, Exeter.

Förster, W. 1959: *Palestinian Judaism in New Testament Times*, ET: Edinburgh, 1964 (German, [3]1959).

Gowan, D. E. 1976: *Bridge between the Testaments: A Reappraisal of Judaism from the Exile to the Birth of Christianity*, Pittsburgh, Pennsylvania.

Grant, F. C. 1960: *Ancient Judaism and the New Testament*, Edinburgh, [2]1960 (New York, [1]1959).

Hanson, P. D. 1982: *The Diversity of Scripture: A Theological Interpretation*, Philadelphia (Overtures to Biblical Theology 11).

Harrington, D. J. 1980: *God's People in Christ: New Testament Perspectives on the Church and Judaism*, Philadelphia.

Hay, D. M. 1990: 'Moses Through New Testament Spectacles', *Int* 44:240–252.

Hooker, M. D. 1986: *Continuity and Discontinuity: Early Christianity in its Jewish Setting*, London.

Horst, F. 1932: 'Das Alte Testament als Heilige Schrift und als Kanon', *ThBl* 11:161–173.

Huffmon, H. B. 1969: 'The Israel of God', *Int* 23:66–77.

Jocz, J. 1949: *The Jewish People and Jesus Christ*, London.

—1958: *A Theology of Election: Israel and the Church*, London.

—1961: *The Spiritual History of Israel*, London.

—1972: 'God's "Poor" People', *Judaica* 28:7–29.

Kirkpatrick, A. F. 1903: 'How to read the Old Testament' in *Critical Questions* (A. F. Kirkpatrick *et al.*), London: 3–25.

Knight, G. A. F. 1958: 'Israel – A Theological Problem', *RefTR* 17:33–43.

Küng, H. 1967: *The Church*, ET: London, 1968 (German, 1967): 107–150.

Ladd, G. E. 1964: 'Israel and the Church', *EQ* 36:206–213.

Larondelle, H. K. 1983: *The Israel of God in Prophecy: Principles of Prophetic Interpretation*, Berrien Springs, Michigan.

Leenhardt, F. J. 1962: *Two Biblical Faiths: Protestant and Catholic*, ET: London, 1964 (French, 1962).

LWF 1982: *The Significance of Judaism for the Life and Mission of the Church: Report of a Consultation, August 1982*, Geneva, 1983 (Lutheran World Federation).

Martin, B. L. 1989: *Christ and the Law in Paul*, Leiden (SNovT 62).

McNamara, M. 1983: *Palestinian Judaism and the New Testament*, Wilmington, Delaware.

Miskotte, K. H. 1932: *Het Wezen der Joodsche Religie*, Amsterdam: 448–556.

Motyer, S. 1989: *Israel in the plan of God: Light on today's debate*, Leicester. An interpretation of Romans 9–11.

Neusner, J. 1989: 'The Absoluteness of Christianity and the Uniqueness of Judaism: Why Salvation Is Not of the Jews', *Int* 43:18–31.

Riches, J. 1980: *Jesus and the Transformation of Judaism*, London.

Rowland, C. 1985: *Christian Origins: An Account of the Setting and*

Character of the most Important Messianic Sect of Judaism, London.
Rowley, H. H. 1946: 'The Unity of the Old Testament', *Bulletin of the John Rylands Library* 29:326–358.
—1956: *The Faith of Israel*, London.
Russell, D. S. 1960: *Between the Testaments*, London.
Sanders, E. P. 1977: *Paul and Palestinian Judaism: A Comparison of Patterns of Religion*, London.
—1985: *Jesus and Judaism*, London.
Sanders, J. A. 1972: *Torah and Canon*, Philadelphia.
Sandmel, S. 1978: *Judaism and Christian Beginnings*, New York.
Schelkle, K. H. 1985: *Israel im Neuen Testament*, Darmstadt.
Schofield, J. N. 1964: *Introducing Old Testament Theology*, London.
Segal, A. F. 1986: *Rebecca's Children: Judaism and Christianity in the Roman World*, Cambridge, Massachusetts/London.
Tanenbaum, M. H. *et al.* (ed.) 1978: *Evangelicals and Jews in Conversation on Scripture, Theology and History*, Grand Rapids, Michigan.
Taylor, H. 1985: 'The Continuity of the People of God in Old and New Testaments', *The Scottish Bulletin of Evangelical Theology* 3.2:13–26.
Tcherikover, V. 1966: *Hellenistic Civilization and the Jews*, Philadelphia/Jerusalem.
Vermes, G. 1973: *Jesus the Jew: A historian's reading of the Gospels*, London.
Westerholm, S. 1988: *Israel's Law and the Church's Faith: Paul and His Recent Interpreters*, Grand Rapids, Michigan.
Wiesemann, H. 1965: *Das Heil für Israel: Was sagt darüber das Neue Testament?*, Stuttgart.
Wright, C. J. H. 1983: *Living as the People of God: The relevance of Old Testament ethics*, Leicester.

Part 4

Conclusion

——10——

The theological relationship between the Testaments

10.1 Summary of the problem

a. Biblical and historical survey

The starting-point for understanding the theological problem of the relationship between the Testaments is in the Bible itself (chapter one above).

Future expectation is an important factor in the Old Testament, as is clear from a survey of hopes for the future found in the early strata, along with the prophetic eschatology of much of the Old Testament and finally the apocalyptic elements of the later Old Testament writings. Much of this expectation remains unfulfilled at the end of the Old Testament period, and there are also fundamental tensions in the Old Testament which are unresolved at its conclusion. The Old Testament is therefore an incomplete book.

The New Testament, on the other hand, affirms the fulfilment of Old Testament hopes and promises. This affirmation does not imply that the Old Testament is obsolete, but rather it points to the fact that the New Testament is substantially dependent on Old Testament categories for the understanding and expression of the events which it records. The evidence suggests that this positive attitude to the Old Testament is not an innovation of the early church, but derives from Jesus himself.

Throughout the succeeding history of biblical interpretation there has been a variety of views of the relationship between the

Old Testament and the New Testament (chapter two). Marcion is remembered for his rejection of the Old Testament; others affirmed its vital importance for the church. Most were convinced that the two Testaments belong together as one Bible, though some emphasized the similarities between them and others the differences. Many considered Christ to be the key to understanding the Bible and the link between its constituent parts.

Allegorical interpretation was often popular, though other interpreters preferred to stress the literal meaning. By the nineteenth century it became almost universally recognized that a satisfactory interpretation of the Bible must be based on a literal understanding of the texts in their historical contexts. However, at the same time the importance of theological understanding (which had been central in other periods) was all but forgotten.

At the turn of the twentieth century biblical studies were dominated by the developmental approach, which understood the relationship between the Testaments in terms of 'progressive revelation'. Dissatisfaction with this approach provoked new consideration of the matter, particularly during the nineteen-thirties and nineteen-fifties. Aside from the radical depreciation of the Old Testament in neo-Marcionism and the perpetuation of the developmental approach in certain other circles, the general trend in the twentieth century has been towards a more distinctively theological approach to the problem. The many attempts at a solution fall into four major categories, and the most significant works in each category have been analysed and criticized above (chapters three to six).

b. 'New Testament' solutions

The solutions of Bultmann, Baumgärtel and others discussed in chapter three agree in recognizing both an existential similarity and a theological contrast between the Testaments. In other words, the understanding of existence in the Old Testament is essentially the same as that in the New Testament, though there are differences in detail; but the theology of the Old Testament, with its national and legal concern, stands in clear contrast to the New Testament theology of 'grace' or 'promise in Christ'. For Bultmann the Old Testament is the presupposition of the New Testament, recording a miscarriage of history which in its very failure becomes a promise. For Baumgärtel the Old Testament stems from one basic promise ('I am the Lord your God') which is also at the root of the New Testament promise in Christ. For both of them, however, the Old Testament is a non-Christian book; and the New Testament, at least from the Christian point of view, is the essential Bible. It is only when understood in the light of the New Testament that the Old Testament has meaning for Christians.

The heart of the matter is that for these scholars it is the New Testament which is important, and the Old Testament is only of secondary value in relation to the New. The argument of Bultmann, and to a lesser extent the other scholars mentioned, is presented with considerable force and contains much truth, so that it is possible to overlook its serious inadequacy. Several areas of disagreement have been discussed in the critique above and, although a good deal may be learnt from these 'New Testament' solutions, in the end they must be rejected.

c. 'Old Testament' solutions

The views of the relationship between the Testaments considered in chapter five have in common that they regard the Old Testament as having a certain theological priority and independence with respect to the New Testament. Van Ruler's view may be summarized as follows: the Old Testament is the essential (real, intrinsic, true) Bible and the New Testament is its [Christian] interpretative glossary. Miskotte and Barr also reject the idea that the Old Testament should be interpreted in the light of the New, because they consider such a procedure to be based on the false presupposition that Christ is the known and the Old Testament is the unknown. They argue that the reverse is the case, that Christian faith must have the Old Testament as its basis from the beginning. Miskotte carries the argument further by pointing to the surplus which the Old Testament has over the New, and by urging that the Old Testament must be allowed to speak for itself. Some Christian sects do much the same thing but tend to apply the principle in a very literal manner, often to trivial rather than essential parts of the Old Testament.

In contrast to the Jewish view in which the Old Testament is the Bible and the New Testament its false Christian supplement, these scholars do not depreciate the New Testament in itself. They ascribe theological priority to the Old Testament, but acknowledge the New Testament as its true and necessary Christian supplement without which the Bible would be incomplete. The works of van Ruler and Miskotte in particular are valuable for their powerful expression of certain central issues, such as the importance of God's creation and kingdom, as well as for their penetrating insights into many aspects of biblical interpretation. However a fundamental criticism of these 'Old Testament' solutions is that they take inadequate account of the radical newness of the event which occurred in Jesus Christ. Like the 'New Testament' solutions mentioned above, these 'Old Testament' solutions are unsatisfactory, and must also be reluctantly rejected.

d. The need for a 'biblical' solution

A recurring feature in the Old and New Testament solutions is the isolation of supposed incongruities between the two Testaments. Creation/salvation, theocracy/soteriology, earthly/spiritual, law/gospel, community/individual, wrath/love, glory/suffering, human Messiah/divine Messiah and other contrasts are adduced as evidence of incongruity between the Old Testament and the New. However, some of these contrasts have been drawn too sharply, and others represent genuine biblical categories which are important throughout the Bible as contrasts, and not to be divided so that one half characterizes Old Testament thought and the other half that of the New Testament. The existence of contrasts and paradoxes in the Bible is not to be denied, but they are subordinate to its essential theological unity. That unity centres on Jesus Christ, who is not merely the difference between the New Testament and the Old, but in his person brings together the two Testaments into one Bible.

Both 'Old Testament' and 'New Testament' solutions have their attractions. It makes things simpler, apart from anything else, to have a smaller book as the standard expression of one's faith and then understand other books in the light of that standard. Contrasts such as 'law and gospel' and 'creation and salvation' are appealing in their clear formulation of categories for understanding the two Testaments and their relationship to each other. For some, the Old Testament is attractive in its down-to-earth approach to life, and they prefer this to the [supposedly] sophisticated spirituality of the New Testament. For others, the Gospel has been declared in all its fullness in the New Testament so that the Old Testament fades into relative insignificance in comparison with the wonder of the New.

These solutions have both the advantages and disadvantages of oversimplification. However, the fact remains that the canon of the Christian Bible contains two Testaments, and a satisfactory solution to the problem of their relationship must take that fact seriously. It is too late to create a new canon, whether with more or less books than the present one. The vast majority of

Christians throughout the Christian era have recognized the inspiration and authority of the books of both Old and New Testaments. Of course, the fact that this is the majority view does not of itself make it the correct one, nevertheless it is the present author's conviction that it is a well-founded view.[1] The two Testaments form one Bible, and to properly understand either one of the Testaments it is necessary to do so in relation to the other. Like Siamese twins, they are so closely linked together that separation is impossible without damage to both.

What is needed therefore is neither an 'Old Testament' nor a 'New Testament' solution, but a 'biblical' solution to the problem of the relationship between the Testaments.

10.2 Towards a 'biblical' solution

We shall now review five concepts which point towards a 'biblical' understanding of the theological relationship between the Testaments.[2]

a. Christology

The first point to be made is that the Old Testament and the New Testament are equally Christian Scripture (chapter four). No doubt there are many differences between the two Testaments in content, but in terms of theology and revelation they are one. Vischer has argued this point especially clearly, and the main features of his approach are that Jesus is the Christ of the Old Testament; the New Testament is to be taken seriously in interpreting the Old Testament, leading to Christological interpretation of the latter; and salvation is essentially the same in both Testaments. It may be summed up in words from the title of Vischer's major work: the Old Testament is a witness to

---

[1]In the earliest years of the church's existence there was probably no official listing of books, but the books which were used and valued in practice were essentially the same as those which were later formally recognized as 'canon'. The only major dispute since the early years has been over the role of the apocryphal /deuterocanonical books. On the canon, see von Campenhausen (1968); Kline (1972); Barr (1983); Beckwith (1985); Childs (1985); J. A. Sanders (1987); Bruce (1988). *Cf.* above: ch. 4.3.d.

[2]No claim is made to completeness: other concepts such as covenant (see Eichrodt 1933–39; Hillers 1969; Dumbrell 1984), kingdom (see above: ch. 5.2.e), and wisdom (Goldsworthy 1987) are also important.

Christ. Barth follows Vischer closely; Jacob, Knight and Childs accept in principle that the Old and New Testaments are equally Christian Scripture, though in practice their Old Testament interpretations are less influenced by the New Testament than those of Vischer.

Vischer's work provoked a considerable amount of disagreement, but this was partly because of misunderstanding of his aims and methods. His main point, at least, is fundamental for a Christian approach to the Old Testament. Christ is the centre of the Christian faith and if the Old Testament is to remain in the Christian Bible – and virtually every Christian agrees that it should, in theory if not always in practice – it can only be as Christian Scripture, and thus in some sense as a witness to Christ. The two Testaments are united in their theology: the New Testament bases itself explicitly on the Old Testament and claims that the God of Israel, who gave the law to Moses and spoke to the prophets, has sent his Son to be Christ and Lord. It would be a mistake to ignore the substantial differences between the Old and New Testaments, or to let either dominate the interpretation of the other. However, Vischer and the other scholars mentioned in chapter four are concerned to let each Testament speak for itself, though never in isolation from the other, and generally avoid allegorical or fanciful interpretations. It is not necessary to surrender the historical-critical approach to the Bible to recognize the central truth that the Bible revolves around the person of Jesus Christ, and therefore the relationship between the Testaments inevitably involves the concept of Christology.

b. Salvation history

Perhaps the most popular modern solution is that which centres on the idea of 'salvation history' (chapter six). It takes different forms, but all essentially express the same conviction that the two Testaments are bound together by divine revelation which occurs in the history of the people of God. Cullmann and Wright have shown that the Bible tells of a God who reveals himself by his acts in history to save his people and that it presents the coming of Jesus Christ as the climax of that history of salvation. Von Rad makes use of the tradition-historical method and the ideas of typology and 'promise and fulfilment' to interpret the relationship between the Testaments in terms of 'actualization'. Thus for him the relationship is a progressive one, in the sense that the events of salvation history are continually actualized or re-presented in the Old Testament and above all in the New Testament. Amsler also affirms the centrality of salvation history to the relationship between the Testaments, but he is aware of the unsatisfactory separation between salvation 'history' and reality in von Rad's thought, and attempts to find a solution which does justice to both. According to Pannenberg and Moltmann revelation takes place in real history, though it is apocalyptic eschatology rather than salvation history which is central to their thought. Gese and Weber emphasize tradition history as the key to understanding the relationship between the Testaments.

It is true, as van Ruler has pointed out, that it is creation rather than salvation which is the ultimate goal of God's activity according to the Bible. We were not created to be saved, but are saved in order to become what we were originally intended to be. Everyone who believes in Christ becomes a 'new creation', and the final act of biblical history is the creation of a new heaven and a new earth. Moreover, Martens shows that God's purpose in history does not merely concern salvation in the sense of deliverance, but also the positive benefits of a relationship with God, membership of the covenant community and life in the land.

Nevertheless, the 'salvation history' solution is basically consistent with the character of the biblical documents and expresses clearly many of the central issues. The majority of the biblical record is concerned with recounting the events in which God was at work to make possible salvation for his people Israel and for all who believe in his Son, Jesus Christ. To say that salvation is the dominant theme of the Bible is not to say that it is of greater ultimate importance than creation, but simply that it is the immediate problem which confronts mankind and which is dealt with at length in the Bible. Moreover, the problem is not dealt with in an abstract or mystical way, but by words which are spoken and events which happen in the history of the people of God. Thus we may justifiably claim that the Bible presents a history of salvation.

c. Typology

In the second half of the twentieth century there has been a revival of interest in biblical typology (chapter seven). Typology has often been rejected as a fanciful kind of interpretation, along with allegory and other over-imaginative kinds of biblical study, but there is now a good deal of scholarly agreement that typology has a historical basis and is to be taken seriously. Beyond this basic agreement, however, the concept still needs clarification, and so a new approach to typology has been developed here by means of a reconsideration of the meaning of *typos* in biblical Greek and 'type' in modern English. As a result of this, two fundamental principles for interpretation of types in the Bible have been established, namely, that they must be historical in nature and that a real correspondence between events, persons or institutions is implied, not simply a superficial resemblance or coincidence of detail. A 'type' is thus defined as an example or pattern, and 'typology' as the study of historical and theological correspondences between types on the basis of God's consistent activity in history.

The implication of typology for the problem of the relationship between the Testaments, hinted at by Wolff in his essay on Old Testament hermeneutics, is that there is a relationship of analogy between the two. There are, for example, analogies between the people of God, salvation and God's gifts in the Old and New Testaments. In contrast to ancient near Eastern and Rabbinic literature, which illuminate the Old Testament but are essentially different from it, the New Testament is fundamentally analogous as a witness to God's covenant. In the present book this idea has been developed further, in conjunction with the idea of typology as the study of examples and patterns within God's consistent activity in history. Thus the aspect of analogy, as expressed in the typical approach to the relationship between the Testaments, may be set alongside that of theological identity expressed in the Christological approach to the problem.

d. Promise and fulfilment

The formula 'promise and fulfilment' uses biblical terminology to express the relationship between the Testaments (chapter eight). It is more comprehensive than the old formulae 'prediction and fulfilment' and 'prophecy and fulfilment', though these are still used by a few authors, sometimes with much the same meaning as 'promise and fulfilment'.

The basic biblical promise is that given to Abraham and the fathers, the promise of descendants, land and a special relationship with God. This promise was partially fulfilled in the early history of Israel, but never completely fulfilled within the Old Testament. Another promise was given to David, which repeated and reinterpreted the essence of the basic promise and added some new elements. The prophets took up again the earlier promises and added many new ones. Most of them remained unfulfilled or only partially fulfilled by the end of the Old Testament period.

The New Testament announces that the promises have been fulfilled, above all in the coming of Jesus as the promised Messiah. All the hopes of the Old Testament find their supreme fulfilment in the one who is both Son of God and Son of man; who is Judge, Priest, King, Prophet and Teacher; who is the Lamb of God and the good shepherd; who is the servant of the Lord and the wisdom of God. Those who have faith in him become descendants of Abraham and enjoy a renewed relationship with God. More clearly than ever before, the offer of salvation is made to the Gentiles, and so the promise that through Abraham all the nations of the world will be blessed becomes a reality. Nevertheless this fulfilment is still incomplete: the perfection of God's relationship with mankind and the final establishment of God's universal kingdom will only take place at the consummation of history.

Thus we may accept 'promise and fulfilment' as a key aspect of the relationship between the Testaments, without forgetting that there is more to the Old Testament than promise, and that the New Testament's fulfilment goes far beyond the expectations of the Old.

e. Continuity and discontinuity

The final aspect of a 'biblical' solution that we have considered here is the continuity and discontinuity between the Testaments (chapter nine). To put it another way, the Bible is characterized by both unity and diversity. One of the best expressions of this is in the first part of Vriezen's Old Testament theology. He finds a tension between recognition of the Old Testament as Scripture and critical reinterpretation in the light of Jesus Christ, who might be thought to have made the Old Testament obsolete. This approach to the relationship between the Testaments has been particularly popular among British and American scholars such as H. H. Rowley, C. H. Dodd and John Bright. They show the importance of recognizing the existence of both continuity and discontinuity in biblical history; and that there is theological diversity in both Old and New Testaments, as well as a fundamental theological unity which binds together the two Testaments into one Bible.

Thus a 'biblical' solution to the problem must recognize the tension between continuity and discontinuity, unity and diversity. On the one hand, the two Testaments have a number of common perspectives and patterns:

● they are concerned with the same fundamental issues (particularly the relationship between God and mankind, the people of God, the kingdom of God); and
● they are essentially continuous in their history and united in their theology.

On the other hand, there are not a few differences between the Testaments:

● many Old Testament ideas and practices are superseded by those of the New Testament;
● the Old Testament is characterized by promise and is thus a preparatory revelation, in contrast to the final revelation of the New Testament which is characterized by fulfilment; and
● the new covenant is marked by a more personal relationship with God than was experienced by most who lived under the old covenant.

Paradoxically, however, the most radical discontinuity lies in the New Testament's claim that Jesus is the Christ, for it presents him not only as the Christ of the Old Testament but also as a Christ who surpasses expectations, completely renews the religion of Israel and inaugurates the new aeon. Thus in the person of Jesus Christ, who stands at the centre of Christian faith as both God and man, the two Testaments are both distinguished and brought together.

10.3 Implications for theology and church

These conclusions about the relationship between the Old Testament and the New Testament have important consequences for theology and the church. They raise questions such as the authority of the Old Testament for Christian doctrine and ethics, and the related issue of the canon; the way in which the Old and New Testaments should be understood by the church today; and the possibility of a 'biblical theology'. It is beyond the scope of this book to deal with such issues in detail, and I simply give a few pointers to the implications of the understanding of the relationship between the Testaments proposed here for dealing with them. A number of more detailed studies are mentioned in footnotes for those who wish to read further on these matters.

a. The authority of the Old Testament

Is the Old Testament God's word for Christians? If it is, does it have the same authority as the New Testament or a lesser degree of authority? These are fundamental questions which will be answered differently depending on one's view of the relationship between the Testaments. Marcion's answer is simple: the Old Testament is no longer God's word for those who live within the new covenant. Van Ruler, at the other extreme, considers the Old Testament to be *the* Bible, and its authority to be prior to and in a sense more fundamental than that of the New. I would reject both of these views. The implication of the understanding of the relationship between the Testaments proposed here is rather that the Old Testament has authority for Christians as part of the Christian Bible.

The authority of the Old Testament is not to be measured, in the sense of being more or less than that of the New Testament, but to be understood in terms of function. Its function is not the same as that of the New Testament, any more than the function of the Gospels is the same as that of Paul's letters, or the function of the Pentateuch the same as that of the wisdom literature. Not all of the Old Testament applies directly to the Christian, but then neither does all of the New Testament. All the books of the Bible have their specific historical and cultural settings and were written originally to people other than us. But if Christians want to know where they have come from, spiritually-speaking, they will want to read the history of their salvation, and that begins in the Old Testament with Abraham. Some elements of the history are of the nature of promise, others of fulfilment, but all have their place in giving meaning to the whole. Within that history there is a great deal that is typical of the sort of thing that happens to believers (and unbelievers), and which is therefore of relevance to our lives. To those who have become followers of Jesus Christ, the texts which tell about him may be considered to be of greatest value, though that does not make other texts valueless.

Since the earliest days of the church, Christians have believed and affirmed that the books of both Old and New Testaments are the foundation documents of their faith and through them God has spoken and continues to speak to his people.[3] The

---

[3]On the canon, see above: note 1. On the inspiration of Scripture, see P. J. Achtemeier (1980); Abraham (1981); Marshall (1982); Gnuse (1985); Trembath (1987).

authority of the Old Testament, like that of the New, is based on the conviction that it is a definitive human expression of the Word of God.[4] Thus both Old and New Testaments are fundamental for the Christian theologian in the establishment of church doctrine[5] and for the Christian believer in providing guidance for living.[6]

b. Old and New Testament interpretation

A number of misunderstandings about biblical interpretation may be cleared up by a correct understanding of the relationship between the Testaments.

Often Old Testament interpretation is considered to be a problem. However, the interpretation of the Old Testament is no more problematical than the interpretation of the New Testament or of any other ancient or modern text. On the basis of the understanding of the relationship between the Testaments presented here, there is nothing *essentially* different about interpreting the first part of the Christian Bible as compared with interpreting the second part. Of course, the world of the Old Testament is farther removed from us than that of the New Testament, and the problems of interpretation are correspondingly more numerous and more difficult. But the aim of interpretation in both cases is to understand the text in its original context, in order to be in a better position to consider its relevance in the modern world; and the method of interpretation in both cases is to use the tools of modern scholarship as effectively as possible in order to achieve that aim.

It is sometimes thought that the key to interpreting the Old Testament is in the New Testament's use of the Old (*cf.* above: ch. 1.3.c). However, we live in a different world from the authors of the New Testament, and our task is not to imitate the way they interpreted the Old Testament but to develop our own way. Their methods of interpretation were ideally suited to the needs of the first century, but cannot be simply repeated at the

---

[4]On the authority of the Old Testament, see further Bright (1967); Barr (1971); McKim (1983); Goldingay (1987); Edwards & Stott (1988: 41–106, 241–243, 260–264).

[5]On the use of the Bible in theology, see Kelsey (1975); Clements (1978: 179–200); Brown (1985); Johnston (1985).

[6]On the use of the Bible in ethics, see Marshall (1978); Goldingay (1981: 38–65); Ogletree (1983); Swartley (1983); Wright (1984); Cahill (1986); Birch (1988); Wilson (1988); Green (1990).

end of the twentieth century. We can learn a great deal from the way the early Christians read and understood the Old Testament; but in order that we may truly understand and respond to the Word of God today it is necessary to use the methods of modern hermeneutics.

Another misunderstanding is the idea that the Old Testament is to be interpreted in the light of Christ or through the eyes of the New Testament. Although there is an element of truth in this, it would be more accurate to say that Old Testament texts, as also New Testament texts, should be interpreted in the context of the whole Bible.

How then should we interpret texts from the two Testaments of the one Christian Bible? Although interpreters vary in the details of their methods, there are four main stages in the interpretation of any biblical text: textual criticism and translation (defining exactly what the text is); historical and literary criticism (determining the historical setting and literary form of the text); explanation (clarifying the intention of the author and the meaning of the text for its original readers); and theological reflection (relating the text to its context in the whole Bible and suggesting possible meanings of the text for today). There may be differences in detail because of the different languages and cultural settings involved, nevertheless the same basic principles apply to the interpretation of both Old Testament and New Testament texts. So the problem is not how to interpret the Old Testament in particular, but how best to interpret texts from both Old and New Testaments, taking account of the contexts in which they were originally written and their present context in the whole Bible, and explaining them in such a way that people who live at the end of the twentieth century may understand them and be in a position to respond appropriately to them.[7]

c. Biblical theology

The majority of theological approaches to the Bible offer theologies of the Old Testament or of the New Testament, or of smaller sections such as theologies of the Psalms or of Paul. Few have written biblical theologies in the sense of attempting to

---

[7]On biblical interpretation, see further Smart (1961; 1965); Bright (1967: chs. 4–5); E. Achtemeier (1973); Marshall (1977); B. W. Anderson (1979); Baker (1980); Gowan (1980); Thiselton (1980); Goldingay (1981); Goldsworthy (1981); Fee & Stuart (1982); Barton (1984a); Ferguson (1986); Longenecker (1987).

write a theology of the whole Bible.[8] On the basis of the conclusions of this book, however, there is no reason in principle why one should not write a theology of the Bible as a whole. Indeed, in view of the enormous number of theologies of parts of the Bible, it may be argued that the most urgent need in this area is now for a theology of the whole Bible.

This is not the place to document the rise and fall of the so-called 'Biblical Theology Movement', nor to propose a better way of doing biblical theology.[9] Whatever the merits or otherwise of particular approaches to biblical theology, it can scarcely be disputed that the Bible contains a great deal of theology, at least in the general sense of assumptions, thoughts and teachings about God. This theology is of interest to both biblical scholars and systematic theologians, and a study of it may serve to form a bridge between their respective disciplines.

If the view of the relationship between the Testaments presented here is correct, such a theology of the whole Bible would take account of both the unity and the diversity of the biblical witnesses. It would consider the function of typology and of promise and fulfilment in the recounting of salvation history. Above all, it would recognize the centrality of Jesus, the Christ of the Old Testament and of the New Testament, descendant of Abraham and David and firstborn of a new creation, who in his person and coming unites the two Testaments into one Bible.

---

[8]The works of Burrows (1946) and Vos (1948) were thorough, but neither became widely accepted and used, and neither interacts a great deal with modern scholarship. Minear (1946) intended only to provide a preface for a biblical theology. During the next thirty years hardly any book was published which covered the theology of the whole Bible, although a number of works dealt with particular themes in their biblical context (e.g. Bright 1953; Rowley 1953; Bruce 1968a; Ellul 1970; Gese 1977). At the end of the nineteen-seventies Brueggemann and Donahue launched a series of monographs with the deliberately low-key title 'Overtures to Biblical Theology' (e.g. Brueggemann 1977; Bailey 1979) and several similar works were published independently (e.g. Simundson 1980; Dyrness 1983; Dumbrell 1985). More comprehensive works have been written by Terrien (1978), Cronk (1982), Seebass (1982), McCurley & Reumann (1986) and Weber (1989). However, as yet there is no major work of biblical theology to compare with Old Testament theologies such as those of Eichrodt (1933–39) and von Rad (1957–60), or New Testament theologies such as those of Bultmann (1948–53), and Goppelt (1975–76).

[9]On biblical theology, see further Childs (1970); Kraus (1970); Harrington (1973); Haacker (1977); Westermann (1978: 230–232); Smart (1979); Barton (1983); Reventlow (1983); Baker (1988); Barr (1988); Scobie (1991).

Bibliography (10)

Abraham, W. J. 1981: *The Divine Inspiration of Holy Scripture*, Oxford.

Achtemeier, P. J. 1980: *The Inspiration of Scripture: Problems and Proposals*, Philadelphia.

Anderson, B. W. 1979: *The Living Word of the Bible*, London.

Bailey, L. R. 1979: *Biblical Perspectives on Death*, Philadelphia.

Baker, D. L. 1980: 'Interpreting texts in the context of the whole Bible', *Themelios* 5.2:21–25.

—1988: 'Biblical Theology' in *New Dictionary of Theology* (ed. S. B. Ferguson & D. F. Wright), Leicester/Downers Grove, Illinois: 96–99.

Barr, J. 1971: 'The Old Testament and the New Crisis of Biblical Authority', *Int* 25:24–40.

—1988: 'The Theological Case against Biblical Theology' in Childs Fs: 3–19.

Barton, J. 1983: 'Old Testament Theology' in *Beginning Old Testament Study* (ed. J. Rogerson), London: 90–112.

Beckwith, R. 1985: *The Old Testament Canon of the New Testament Church and its Background in Early Judaism*, London.

Birch, B. C. 1988: 'Old Testament Narrative and Moral Address' in Childs Fs: 75–91.

Brown, R. E. 1985: *Biblical Exegesis and Church Doctrine*, London, 1986 (USA, 1985).

Burrows, M. 1946: *An Outline of Biblical Theology*, Philadelphia.

Cahill, L. S. 1986: 'Canon, Authority, Norms? Recent Studies in Biblical Ethics', *Int* 40:414–417.

Cronk, G. 1982: *The Message of the Bible: An Orthodox Christian Perspective*, New York.

Dumbrell, W. J. 1985: *The End of the Beginning: Revelation 21 – 22 and the Old Testament*, Homebush West, NSW.

Dyrness, W.A. 1983: *Let the Earth Rejoice! A Biblical Theology of Holistic Mission*, Westchester, Illinois.

Edwards, D. L. & Stott, J. 1988: *Essentials: A liberal-evangelical dialogue*, London.

Fee, G. D. & Stuart, D. 1982: *How to Read the Bible for All Its Worth: A Guide to Understanding the Bible*, Grand Rapids, Michigan.

Ferguson, D. S. 1986: *Biblical Hermeneutics: An Introduction*, Atlanta (John Knox).

Gnuse, R. 1985: *The Authority of the Bible: Theories of Inspiration, Revelation and the Canon of Scripture*, New York.

Gowan, D. E. 1980: *Reclaiming the Old Testament for the Christian Pulpit*, Atlanta.

Green, G. L. 1990: 'The Use of the Old Testament for Christian Ethics in 1 Peter', *TB* 41:276–289.

Haacker, K. *et al.* 1977: *Biblische Theologie heute: Einführung – Beispiele – Kontroversen*, Neukirchen-Vluyn.

Johnston, R. K. (ed.) 1985: *The Use of the Bible in Theology: Evangelical Options*, Atlanta.

271

Kline, M. G. 1972: *The Structure of Biblical Authority*, Grand Rapids, Michigan.

Longenecker, R. N. 1987: '"Who is the prophet talking about?" Some reflections on the New Testament's use of the Old', *Themelios* 13:4–8.

Marshall, I. H. (ed.) 1977: *New Testament Interpretation: Essays on Principles and Methods*, Exeter.

—1978: 'Using the Bible in Ethics' in *Essays in Evangelical Social Ethics* (ed. D. F. Wright), Exeter: 39–55.

—1982: *Biblical Inspiration*, London.

McCurley, F. R. & Reumann, J. 1986: *Witness of the Word: A Biblical Theology of the Gospel*, Philadelphia.

McKim, D. K. (ed.) 1983: *The Authoritative Word: Essays on the Nature of Scripture*, Grand Rapids, Michigan.

Minear, P. S. 1946: *Eyes of Faith: A Study in the Biblical Point of View*, Philadelphia.

Ogletree, T. W. 1983: *The Use of the Bible in Christian Ethics: A Constructive Essay*, Philadelphia.

Sanders, J. A. 1987: *From Sacred Story to Sacred Text: Canon as Paradigm*, Philadelphia. Includes essays written from 1975 onwards.

Scobie, C. H. H. 1991: 'The Challenge of Biblical Theology' (Part 1), *TB* 42: 31–61.

Seebass, H. 1982: *Der Gott der ganzen Bibel: Biblische Theologie zur Orientierung im Glauben*, Freiburg/Basel/Vienna.

Simundson, D. J. 1980: *Faith under Fire: Biblical Interpretations of Suffering*, Minneapolis.

Smart, J. D. 1965: *The Old Testament in Dialogue with Modern Man*, London.

—1979: *The Past, Present and Future of Biblical Theology*, Philadelphia.

Swartley, W. M. 1983: *Slavery, Sabbath, War and Women: Case Issues in Biblical Interpretation*, Scottdale, Pennsylvania.

Terrien, S. 1978: *The Elusive Presence: Towards a New Biblical Theology* (ed. Ruth Anshen), San Francisco.

Trembath, K. R. 1987: *Evangelical Theories of Biblical Inspiration: A Review and Proposal*, New York/Oxford.

Vos, G. 1948: *Biblical Theology: Old and New Testaments*, Grand Rapids, Michigan.

Wilson, R. R. 1988: 'Approaches to Old Testament Ethics' in Childs Fs: 62–74.

General bibliography

A. Serials, reference works, symposia

Anderson (1964)   See below: *OTCF*.
BGBH   Beiträge zur Geschichte der biblischen Hermeneutik
BK   Biblischer Kommentar Altes Testament
Boisset (1955)   *Le Problème Biblique dans le Protestantisme* (ed. J. Boisset), Paris (Les Problèmes de la Pensée Chrétienne 7).
Branson & Padilla   *Conflict and Context: Hermeneutics in the Americas*,
(1983)   Grand Rapids, Michigan, 1986 (report of 1983 conference, ed. M. L. Branson & C. R. Padilla).
BThB   *Biblical Theology Bulletin*
CBQ   *The Catholic Biblical Quarterly*
Childs Fs   *Canon, Theology, and Old Testament Interpretation: Essays in Honor of Brevard S. Childs* (ed. G. M. Tucker, D. L. Petersen, and R. R. Wilson), Philadelphia.
Cullmann Fs   *Oikonomia: Heilsgeschichte als Thema der Theologie* (ed. F. Christ, Oscar Cullmann zum 65.Geburtstag gewidmet), Hamburg-Bergstedt, 1967.
EAJT   *The East Asia Journal of Theology*
EOTI   *Essays on Old Testament Interpretation* (ed. C. Westermann), ET: London, 1963 (German, 1960; a collection of essays originally published 1949–60).
EQ   *The Evangelical Quarterly*
ETL   *Ephemerides Theologicae Lovanienses*

ETR	*Études théologiques et religieuses*
EvTh	*Evangelische Theologie*
ExpT	*The Expository Times*
Gottwald (1983)	*The Bible and Liberation: Political and Social Hermeneutics* (ed. N. K. Gottwald), Maryknoll, New York.
HTR	*Harvard Theological Review*
IDB	*The Interpreter's Dictionary of the Bible* (ed. G. A. Buttrick *et al.*), New York/Nashville, 1962 (four volumes) and 1976 (supplementary volume).
ITC	International Theological Commentary
Int	*Interpretation: A Journal of Bible and Theology*
JB	The Jerusalem Bible (1966)
JBC	*The Jerome Biblical Commentary* (ed. R. E. Brown *et al.*), London, 1968.
JCBRF	*The Journal of the Christian Brethren Research Fellowship*
JES	*Journal of Ecumenical Studies*
JR	*The Journal of Religion*
JSNT	*Journal for the Study of the New Testament*
JSOT	*Journal for the Study of the Old Testament*
JTC	*Journal for Theology and the Church*
KJV	The King James Version (Authorized Version, 1611)
Knight (1977)	*Tradition and Theology in the Old Testament* (ed. D. A. Knight), Philadelphia.
Laurin (1970)	*Contemporary Old Testament Theologians* (ed. R. B. Laurin), London.
May Fs	*Translating & Understanding the Old Testament: Essays in Honor of Herbert Gordon May* (ed. H. T. Frank & W. L. Reed), Nashville, 1970.
MCNT	*Modern Concordance to the New Testament* (ed. M. Darton), London, 1976.
Mulder (1988)	*Mikra* (ed. M. J. Mulder), Assen/Philadelphia (Compendia Rerum Iudaicarum ad Novum Testamentum II.1).
NEB	The New English Bible (1970)
NIV	New International Version (1978)
NTS	*New Testament Studies*
OTCF	*The Old Testament and Christian Faith: Essays by Rudolf Bultmann and others* (ed. B. W. Anderson), London, 1964.
OTWSA	[Papers read at Meetings of] *Die Ou Testamentiese Werkgemeenskap in Suid-Afrika*
von Rad Fs	*Probleme biblischer Theologie* (ed. H. W. Wolff), Munich, 1971.
RB	*Revue Biblique*
RefTR	*The Reformed Theological Review*

RHPR	*Revue d'histoire et de philosophie religieuses*
Richardson & Schweitzer (1951)	*Biblical Authority for Today: A World Council of Churches Symposium* (ed. A. Richardson & W. Schweitzer), London.
Rogerson (1988)	*The Study and Use of the Bible* (ed. John Rogerson *et al.*), Basingstoke (The History of Christian Theology, ed. P. Avis, volume 2).
RSV	Revised Standard Version (Old Testament: 1952; New Testament: 1946, ²1971)
RThPh	*Revue de théologie et de philosophie*
SBL	Society of Biblical Literature
SBT	Studies in Biblical Theology
SJT	*Scottish Journal of Theology*
SNovT	Supplements to *Novum Testamentum*
SNTS Mon	Society for New Testament Studies Monograph Series
TB	*Tyndale Bulletin*
TDNT	*Theological Dictionary of the New Testament* (ten volumes, ed. G. Kittel & G. Friedrich), ET: Grand Rapids, Michigan, 1964–76 (German, 1933–73).
ThBl	*Theologische Blätter*
ThSt	Theologische Studien
ThZ	*Theologische Zeitschrift*
TLZ	*Theologische Literaturzeitung*
Vischer Fs	*maqqél shâqédh, La branche d'amandier: Hommage à Wilhelm Vischer* (ed. D. Lys), Montpellier, 1960.
VT	*Vetus Testamentum*
Westermann (1963)	See above: *EOTI*.
ZAW	*Zeitschrift für die alttestamentliche Wissenschaft*
ZTK	*Zeitschrift für Theologie und Kirche*

B. Books, articles, dissertations

Works cited in or relevant to more than one chapter of this book are listed below. Others are listed in the bibliographies for each chapter. As explained in the preface, these bibliographies aim to be practical rather than comprehensive. Twenty-four of the most important works listed below are marked by double asterisks (**) and form a basic reading list for the use of students.

Achtemeier, E. 1973: *The Old Testament and the Proclamation of the Gospel*, Philadelphia.

Amsler, S. 1952: 'Où en est la typologie de l'Ancien Testament?', *ETR* 27:75–81.

—1953: 'Prophétie et typologie', *RThPh* 3:139–148.

—1960a: *L'Ancien Testament dans l'Église*, Neuchâtel.**

Anderson, B. W. 1962: 'Exodus Typology in Second Isaiah' in *Israel's Prophetic Heritage: Essays in honor of James Muilenburg* (ed. B. W.

Anderson & W. Harrelson), London: 177–195.
—1964: 'Introduction: The Old Testament as a Christian Problem' in *OTCF*:1–7 and 'The New Covenant and the Old' in *OTCF*:225–242.
Baker, D. L. 1976: *Two Testaments, One Bible: A study of some modern solutions to the theological problem of the relationship between the Old and New Testaments*, Leicester (first edition, with fuller bibliographies than the present edition, though only up to 1975).
Barr, J. 1966: *Old and New in Interpretation: A Study of the Two Testaments*, London.**
—1983: *Holy Scripture: Canon, Authority, Criticism*, Oxford.
Barth, K. 1935: 'Gospel and Law', ET in *God, Grace and Gospel*, Edinburgh/London, 1959 (*SJT* Occasional Papers 8; German, 1935, ²1956):1–27.
Barton, J. 1984a: *Reading the Old Testament: Method in Biblical Study*, London.
Baumgärtel, F. 1952: *Verheissung: Zur Frage des evangelischen Verständnisses des Alten Testaments*, Gütersloh.**
—1954a: 'The Hermeneutical Problem of the Old Testament', ET in *EOTI*:134–159 (German, 1954).
—1954b: 'Der Dissensus im Verständnis des Alten Testaments', *EvTh* 14:298–313.
Boff, L. & C. 1986: *Liberation Theology: From Dialogue to Confrontation*, ET: San Francisco 1986 (expanded translation from Portuguese, 1985).
Boyd, R. H. S. 1975: *An Introduction to Indian Christian Theology*, Madras ¹1969, ²1975.
Bright, J. 1953: *The Kingdom of God: The Biblical Concept and Its Meaning For the Church*, New York/Nashville.
—1960: *A History of Israel*, Philadelphia, ³1981 (London, ¹1960).
—1967: *The Authority of the Old Testament*, London.**
Bruce, F. F. 1968a: *This is That: The New Testament Development of Some Old Testament Themes*, Exeter.
—1969: *New Testament History*, London.
—1978: *The Time is Fulfilled: Five Aspects of the Fulfilment of the Old Testament in the New*, Exeter.
—1988: *The Canon of Scripture*, Glasgow.
Brueggemann, W. 1977: *The Land: Place as Gift, Promise and Challenge in Biblical Faith*, Philadelphia (London, 1978).
Brunner, E. 1930: 'The Significance of the Old Testament for Our Faith', ET in *OTCF*:243–264 (German, 1930).
—1934: *Die Unentbehrlichkeit des Alten Testamentes für die missionierende Kirche: Vortrag am Basler Missionsfest 1934*, Stuttgart/Basle (Basler Missionsstudien N.F. 12).
—1941: *Revelation and Reason: The Christian Doctrine of Faith and Knowledge*, ET: London, 1947 (German, 1941).
Bultmann, R. 1933a: 'The Significance of the Old Testament for the Christian Faith, ET in *OTCF*:8–35 (German, 1933).**
—1948a: *Theology of the New Testament* I, ET: London, 1952 (German, 1948).

—1949a: 'Prophecy and Fulfillment', ET in *EOTI*:50–75 (German, 1949).**
—1949b: *Primitive Christianity in its Contemporary Setting*, ET: London/ New York, 1956 (German, 1949, [2]1954).
—1953: *Theology of the New Testament* II, ET: London, 1955 (German, 1953).
Campenhausen, H. von 1968: *The Formation of the Christian Bible*, ET: London, 1972 (German, 1968).
Cate, R. L. 1982: *Old Testament Roots for New Testament Faith*, Nashville.
Childs, B. S. 1958: 'Prophecy and Fulfillment: A Study in Contemporary Hermeneutics', *Int* 12:259–271.
—1970: *Biblical Theology in Crisis*, Philadelphia.**
—1979: *Introduction to the Old Testament as Scripture*, Philadelphia/ London.
—1985: *Old Testament Theology in a Canonical Context*, London.
Clements, R. E. 1975: *Prophecy and Tradition*, Oxford.
—1978: *Old Testament Theology: A Fresh Approach*, London.
Coppens, J. 1948: *Les harmonies des deux Testaments: Essais sur les divers sens des Ecritures et sur l'unité de la Révélation*, Tournai-Paris, [2]1949 ([1]1949; Cahiers de la Nouvelle revue théologique 6).
Cullmann, O. 1946: *Christ and Time: The Primitive Christian Conception of Time and History*, ET: London, [2]1962 ([1]1951; German, 1946, [3]1962).
—1964: 'The Connection of Primal Events and End Events with the New Testament Redemptive History' in *OTCF*:115–123.
—1965: *Salvation in History*, ET: London, 1967 (German, 1965).
Dodd, C. H. 1928: *The Authority of the Bible*, London, [3]1960 (reset with corrections; [1]1928).
—1935: *The Parables of the Kingdom*, London, 1961 (revised and reset; [1]1935).
—1938: *History and the Gospel*, London, 1964 (revised and reset; [1]1938).
—1946a: *The Bible To-day*, Cambridge.
—1946b: 'Natural Law in the New Testament', reprinted in his *New Testament Studies*, Manchester, 1953: 129–142 (originally 1946).
—1951a: *Gospel and Law: The Relation of Faith and Ethics in Early Christianity*, Cambridge.
—1951b: 'The Relevance of the Bible' in Richardson and Schweitzer (1951): 157–162.
—1952a: *According to the Scriptures: The Substructure of New Testament Theology*, London, 1965 (reset; [1]1952).
—1971: *The Founder of Christianity*, London.
Dumbrell, W. J. 1984: *Covenant and Creation: An Old Testament Covenantal Theology*, Exeter.
Eichrodt, W. 1933: *Theology of the Old Testament* I, ET: London, 1961 (German, 1933, [6]1959).
—1935–39: *Theology of the Old Testament* II, ET: London, 1967 (German, 1935–39, [5]1964).
Ellul, J. 1970: *The Meaning of the City*, ET: Grand Rapids, Michigan, 1970 (French, n.d.).
Englezakis, B. 1982: *New and Old in God's Revelation: Studies in Relations*

Between Spirit and Tradition in the Bible, Cambridge/Crestwood, New York.

Fierro, A. 1977: 'Exodus Event and Interpretation in Political Theologies', reprinted in Gottwald (1983): 473–481.

Filson, F. V. 1951: 'The Unity of the Old and the New Testaments: A Bibliographical Survey', *Int* 5:134–152.

Florovsky, G. 1951: 'Revelation and Interpretation' in Richardson and Schweitzer (1951): 163–180.

Foulkes, F. 1958: *The Acts of God: A Study of the Basis of Typology in the Old Testament*, London (Tyndale Old Testament Lecture 1955).

France, R. T. 1971: *Jesus and the Old Testament: His Application of Old Testament Passages to Himself and His Mission*, London.**

Gese, H. 1977b: *Essays on Biblical Theology*, ET: Minneapolis, 1981 (German, 1977).

Goldingay, J. 1981: *Approaches to Old Testament Interpretation*, Leicester.**
—1987: *Theological Diversity and the Authority of the Old Testament*, Grand Rapids, Michigan.

Goldsworthy, G. 1981: *Gospel and Kingdom: A Christian Interpretation of the Old Testament*, Exeter.
—1987: *Gospel and Wisdom: Israel's wisdom literature in the Christian life*, Exeter.

Goppelt, L. 1975: *Theology of the New Testament*, ET: Grand Rapids, Michigan, 1981 (German, 1975).
—1976: *Theology of the New Testament*, ET: Grand Rapids, Michigan, 1982 (German, 1976).

Grant, R. M. 1963/84: *A Short History of the Interpretation of the Bible*, London. The second edition, 1984, is revised and supplemented with three further chapters by D. Tracy.

Gunneweg, A. H. J. 1977: *Understanding the Old Testament*, ET: London, 1978 (German, 1977).**

Guthrie, D. 1981: *New Testament Theology*, Leicester.

Gutiérrez, G. 1971: *A Theology of Liberation: History, Politics and Salvation*, ET: Maryknoll, New York, 1973 (Spanish, 1971).

Hanks, T. D. 1983: *God So Loved the Third World: The Biblical Vocabulary of Oppression*, ET: Maryknoll, New York (revised and translated from Spanish, 1982).

Hanson, A. T. 1965: *Jesus Christ in the Old Testament*, London.

Hanson, P. D. 1978: *Dynamic Transcendence*, Philadelphia.

Harrington, W. J. 1973: *The Path of Biblical Theology*, Dublin.**

Hasel, G. F. 1972a: *Old Testament Theology: Basic Issues in the Current Debate*, Grand Rapids, Michigan.
—1978: *New Testament Theology: Basic Issues in the Current Debate*, Grand Rapids, Michigan.
—1985: 'Major Recent Issues in Old Testament Theology 1978–1983', *JSOT* 31:31–53.

Hayes, J. H. & Prussner, F. C. 1985: *Old Testament Theology: Its History and Development*, London.

Herbert, A. G. 1941: *The Throne of David: A Study of the Fulfilment of the Old Testament in Jesus Christ and His Church*, London.

Hesse, F. 1958: 'Die Erforschung der Geschichte Israels als theologische Aufgabe', *Kerygma und Dogma* 4:1–19.
—1960a: 'Kerygma oder geschichtliche Wirklichkeit? Kritische Fragen zu Gerhard von Rads "Theologie des Alten Testaments, I.Teil"', *ZTK* 57:17–26.
—1969: 'Bewährt sich eine "Theologie der Heilstatsachen" am Alten Testament? Zum Verhältnis von Faktum und Deutung', *ZAW* 81:1–18.
—1971: *Abschied von der Heilsgeschichte*, Zürich (ThSt 108).
Hillers, D. R. 1969: *Covenant: The History of a Biblical Idea*, Baltimore.
Hofmann, J. Chr. K. von 1841–44: *Weissagung und Erfüllung im alten und im neuen Testamente: Ein theologischer Versuch*, Nördlingen (two volumes).
Jacob, E. 1955a: *Theology of the Old Testament*, ET: London, 1958 (French, 1955).
—1965: *Grundfragen Alttestamentlicher Theologie: Franz Delitzsch – Vorlesungen 1965*, Stuttgart, 1970.
—1966a: 'Possibilités et limites d'une Théologie biblique', *RHPR* 46:116–130.
Jeremias, J. 1971: *New Testament Theology, I: The Proclamation of Jesus*, ET: London, 1971 (German, n.d.).
Kaiser, W. C. 1985: *The Uses of the Old Testament in the New*, Chicago.
Kelsey, D. H. 1975: *The Uses of Scripture in Recent Theology*, Philadelphia.
Kirk, J. A. 1979: *Liberation Theology: An Evangelical View from the Third World*, London/Atlanta.**
Kirkpatrick, A. F. 1891: *The Divine Library of the Old Testament: Its Origin, Preservation, Inspiration and Permanent Value*, London (five lectures, the last of which is on 'The Use of the Old Testament in the Christian Church', pp. 112–143).
Knight, G. A. F. 1962: *Law and Grace: Must a Christian Keep the Law of Moses?*, London.
Koch, K. 1970: *The Rediscovery of Apocalyptic: A polemical work on a neglected area of biblical studies and its damaging effects on theology and philosophy*, ET: London, 1972 (SBT II.22; German, 1970).
Köhler, L. 1953: 'Christus im Alten und im Neuen Testament', *ThZ* 9:241–259.
Kraeling, E. G. 1955: *The Old Testament Since the Reformation*, London.
Kraus, H.-J. 1952: 'Gespräch mit Martin Buber: Zur jüdischen und christlichen Auslegung des Alten Testaments', *EvTh* 12:59–77.
—1970: *Die Biblische Theologie: Ihre Geschichte und Problematik*, Neukirchen-Vluyn.
Ladd, G. E. 1974: *The Presence of the Future: The Eschatology of Biblical Realism*, Grand Rapids, Michigan (revised edition of *Jesus and the Kingdom*, London, 1966).
Loccum report 1977: 'The Significance of the Old Testament in its Relation to the New' (report of the Faith and Order Commission of the World Council of Churches, Loccum [Germany]) in *The Bible: Its Authority and Interpretation in the Ecumenical Movement* (ed. E. F. -van Leer), Geneva, 1980: 58–76.

Martens, E. A. 1981: *Plot and purpose in the Old Testament*, Leicester.

McFadyen, J. E. 1903: *Old Testament Criticism and the Christian Church*, London.

McKenzie, J. L. 1964: 'The Significance of the Old Testament for Christian Faith in Roman Catholicism' in *OTCF*:102–114.

Michalson, C. 1964: 'Bultmann against Marcion' in *OTCF*:49–63.

Mildenberger, F. 1964: *Gottes Tat im Wort: Erwägungen zur alttestamentlichen Hermeneutik als Frage nach der Einheit der Testamente*, Gütersloh.

Miskotte, K. H. 1963: *When the Gods are Silent*, ET: London, 1967 (Dutch, 1956; revised German edition, 1963).**

Moltmann, J. 1964: *Theology of Hope: On the Ground and the Implications of a Christian Eschatology*, ET: London, 1967 (German, 1964, ⁵1965).**

—1973: *The Crucified God: The Cross of Christ as the Foundation and Criticism of Christian Theology*, ET: London, 1974 (German, ²1973).

Murphy, R. E. 1964: 'The Relationship between the Testaments', *CBQ* 26:349–359.

Nixon, R. E. 1963: *The Exodus in the New Testament*, London (Tyndale New Testament Lecture 1962).

Noth, M. 1950: *The History of Israel*, ET: London, ²1960 (¹1958; German, 1950, ²1954).

—1952: 'The "Re-presentation" of the Old Testament in Proclamation', ET in *Int* 15 (1961): 50–60 and *EOTI*:76–88 (German, 1952).

Pannenberg, W. 1959: 'Redemptive Event and History', ET in *EOTI*:314–335 (first part only) and *Basic Questions in Theology* I, London, 1970: 15–80 (German, 1959).

Porteous, N. W. 1951: 'Old Testament Theology' in *The Old Testament and Modern Study: A Generation of Discovery and Research* (ed. H. H. Rowley), Oxford: 311–345.

Preuss, H. D. 1984: *Das Alte Testament in christlicher Predigt*, Stuttgart.

Rad, G. von 1937: 'Gesetz und Evangelium im Alten Testament. Gedanken zu dem Buch von E. Hirsch: Das Alte Testament und die Predigt des Evangeliums', *ThBl* 16:41–47.

—1952a: 'Typological Interpretation of the Old Testament', ET in *Int* 15 (1961): 174–192 and *EOTI*:17–39 (German, 1952).**

—1953b: 'Verheissung: Zum gleichnamigen Buch Fr. Baumgärtels', *EvTh* 13:406–413.

—1957: *Old Testament Theology, Volume I: The Theology of Israel's Historical Traditions*, ET: Edinburgh, 1962 (German, 1957).

—1960: *Old Testament Theology, Volume II: The Theology of Israel's Prophetic Traditions*, ET: Edinburgh, 1965 (German, 1960).**

—1963: 'Offene Fragen im Umkreis einer Theologie des Alten Testaments', *TLZ* 88:401–416. A slightly abridged ET is printed as a postscript to the ET of 1960: 410–429.

—1966: *The Problem of the Hexateuch and other essays*, ET: Edinburgh/London, 1966 (collection of essays originally published in German, 1931–64).

Reventlow, H. G. 1983: *Problems of Biblical Theology in the Twentieth Century*, ET: London, 1986 (German, 1983).

Richardson, A. 1964b: *History Sacred and Profane*, London (Bampton Lectures 1962).

Richardson P. 1969: *Israel in the Apostolic Church*, Cambridge (SNTS Mon 10).

Robinson, J. M. 1964: 'The Historicality of Biblical Language' in *OTCF*:124–158. This is essentially the same as an essay in German published in *EvTh* 22 (1962): 113–141.

Rottenberg, I. C. 1964: *Redemption and Historical Reality*, Philadelphia.

Rowley, H. H. 1946a: *The Re-Discovery of the Old Testament*, London.

—1949: 'The Authority of the Bible', reprinted in revised form in *From Moses to Qumran*, London 1963: 3–31 (originally as Joseph Smith Memorial Lecture, Birmingham, 1949).

—1953: *The Unity of the Bible*, London.**

Ruler, A. A. van 1955: *The Christian Church and the Old Testament*, ET: Grand Rapids, Michigan, 1966 & 1971 (two identical editions; German, 1955). Page numbers are cited here from both the German and English editions thus: German/English.**

Sabourin, L. 1980: *The Bible and Christ: The unity of the two Testaments*, New York.

Sauter, G. 1965: *Zukunft und Verheissung: Das Problem der Zukunft in der gegenwärtigen theologischen und philosophischen Diskussion*, Zürich.

Schmidt, L. 1975: 'Die Einheit zwischen Altem und Neuem Testament im Streit zwischen Friedrich Baumgärtel und Gerhard von Rad', *EvTh* 35:119–139.

Schwarzwäller, K. 1969: 'Das Verhältnis Alte Testament – Neue Testament im Lichte der gegenwärtigen Bestimmungen', *EvTh* 29:281–307.

Segundo, J. L. 1976: 'Faith and Ideologies in Biblical Revelation', reprinted in Gottwald (1983): 482–496.

Shih, D. P. 1971: 'The Unity of the Testaments as a Hermeneutical Problem', Boston University dissertation.

Smart, J. D. 1961: *The Interpretation of Scripture*, London.**

Stamm, J. J. 1956: 'Jesus Christ and the Old Testament: A Review of A. A. van Ruler's book: *Die christliche Kirche und das Alte Testament*', ET in *EOTI*:200–210 (German, 1956).

Thielicke, H. 1948: 'Law and Gospel as Constant Partners', abridged ET in *Theological Ethics* I, London, 1968: ch. 7 (German, 1948).

Thiselton, A. C. 1980: *The Two Horizons: New Testament Hermeneutics and Philosophical Description with Special Reference to Heidegger, Bultmann, Gadamer, and Wittgenstein*, Exeter.

Verhoef, P. A. 1970a: 'The Relationship between the Old and the New Testaments' in *New Perspectives on the Old Testament* (ed. J. B. Payne), Waco, Texas/London: 280–303.

Vischer, W. 1934: *The Witness of the Old Testament to Christ I: The Pentateuch*, ET: London, 1949 (German, 1934, [7]1946).**

—1942: *Das Christuszeugnis des Alten Testamentes II.1: Die früheren Propheten*, Zollikon-Zurich, [2]1946 ([1]1942).

—1960: 'La méthode de l'exégèse biblique', *RThPh* 10:109–123.

—1964a: 'Everywhere the Scripture Is about Christ alone', *OTCF*:90–101.**

Vriezen, Th. C. 1956: 'Theocracy and Soteriology: Comments on A. A. van Ruler's book: *Die christliche Kirche und das Alte Testament'*, ET in *EOTI*:211–223 (German, 1956).

—1966: *An outline of Old Testament theology*, ET: Oxford, [2]1970 (Dutch, [3]1966, revised and enlarged from [1]1949, [2]1954/ET: [1]1958).**

Weber, H.-R. 1989: *Power: Focus for a Biblical Theology*, Geneva.

Wellhausen, J. 1878: *Prolegomena to the History of Israel*, ET: Edinburgh, 1885 (German, 1883; originally 1878 under title *History of Israel volume 1*).

Westcott, B. F. 1889: *The Epistle to the Hebrews: The Greek Text with Notes and Essays*, London, [2]1892 ([1]1889). One of the notes is 'On the Use of the Old Testament in the Epistle', pp. 469–495.

Westermann, C. 1955: 'The Interpretation of the Old Testament – A Historical Introduction' and 'Remarks on the Theses of Bultmann and Baumgärtel', ET in *EOTI*:40–49, 123–133 (abridged from German, 1955).

—1964: 'The Way of the Promise through the Old Testament' in *OTCF*:200–224.

—1968a: *The Old Testament and Jesus Christ*, ET: Minneapolis, 1970 (German, 1968).

—1978: *Elements of Old Testament Theology*, ET: Atlanta, 1982 (German, 1978).

Wolff, H. W. 1952: 'Der grosse Jesreeltag (Hosea 2,1–3): Methodologische Erwägungen zur Auslegung einer alttestamentlichen Perikope', *EvTh* 12:78–104.

—1956a: 'The Hermeneutics of the Old Testament', ET in *Int* 15 (1961): 439–472 and *EOTI*:160–199 (German, 1956).

Wright, C. J. H. 1984: 'The Use of the Bible in Social Ethics: Paradigms, Types and Eschatology', *Transformation* 1.1:11–20.

Wright, G. E. 1952: *God Who Acts: Biblical Theology as Recital*, London (SBT 8).**

—1964: 'History and Reality: The Importance of Israel's "Historical" Symbols for the Christian Faith' in *OTCF*:176–199.

—1969: *The Old Testament and Theology*, New York.

Zimmerli, W. 1952: 'Promise and Fulfillment', ET in *Int* 15 (1961):310–338 and *EOTI*:89–122 (German, 1952).**

—1975: *Old Testament Theology in Outline*, ET: Edinburgh, 1978 (German, [1]1972, [2]1975).

Indexes

A. Authors

B. Subjects

C. Biblical references

See also names of biblical books in the subject index above.